DELVILLE WOOD

The 17th (Northern) Division on the Somme, 1 to 14 August 1916

Wayne Osborne

Salient Books

British Library Cataloguing In Publication Data

A Record of this Publication is available from the British Library

ISBN 978-0-9574459-0-1

First Published 2012 by

Salient Books,
21, Collington Street, Beeston, Nottingham, NG9 1FJ

info@salientbooks.co.uk

www.salientbooks.co.uk

Dedication

Stretcher Bearers, 52nd Field Ambulance,
Private H.E. James, 72851, Private J. Dunkerley, 76938,
Private W. Askew, 41504 and Private C.S. Gluckstein, M.M, 41542.

Buried in their dugout on the night of 5/6 August 1916.

Contents

List of Maps and Tables 8
Acknowledgements 9
Introduction 15
Foreword 17
THE BACKGROUND 19
The 17th (Northern) Division 21
The High Command 27
Orders and Plans 33
THE STORY 35
Prelude 37
Chapter One: 1 August 43
Chapter Two: 2 August 63
Chapter Three: 3 August 83
Chapter Four: 4 August 107
Chapter Five: 5 August 127
Chapter Six: 6 August 147
Chapter Seven: 7 August 162
Chapter Eight: 8 August 179
Chapter Nine: 9 August 195
Chapter Ten: 10 August 207
Chapter Eleven: 11 August 219
Chapter Twelve: 12 August 229
Chapter Thirteen: 13 August 239
Chapter Fourteen: 14 August 245
Appendix 1: Postscript for Lieutenant-Colonel Cardew 249
Appendix 2: Roll of Honour 253
Appendix 3: The attack on the German Second Line. Cavalry Action, 14 July 1916 291
Bibliography and Documents 293
Index 299

List of Maps and Tables

1 The Chain of Command and the (simplified) infantry make-up of the 17th (Northern) Division. 10

2 Delville Wood, August 1916 11

3 High Wood, 1916 12

4 Front Line at Longueval, August 1916 13

Acknowledgements

This book has been a long time in the making but not nearly as long as her sister, *Quadrangles.*

I would like to thank the following for all of their kind help in the research and production of this work. Helen Osborne, Warren Osborne, Keith Case, Bill Williams, John Bourne, Peter Simkins, David Edwards, Steve Erskine, John Dandy, Lyn Case, Ivy Bould, Morris Eddison, Abigail Osborne, the Staff at the Imperial War Museum and the Staff at The National Archive.

Cover image: detail from a photograph in the author's collection.

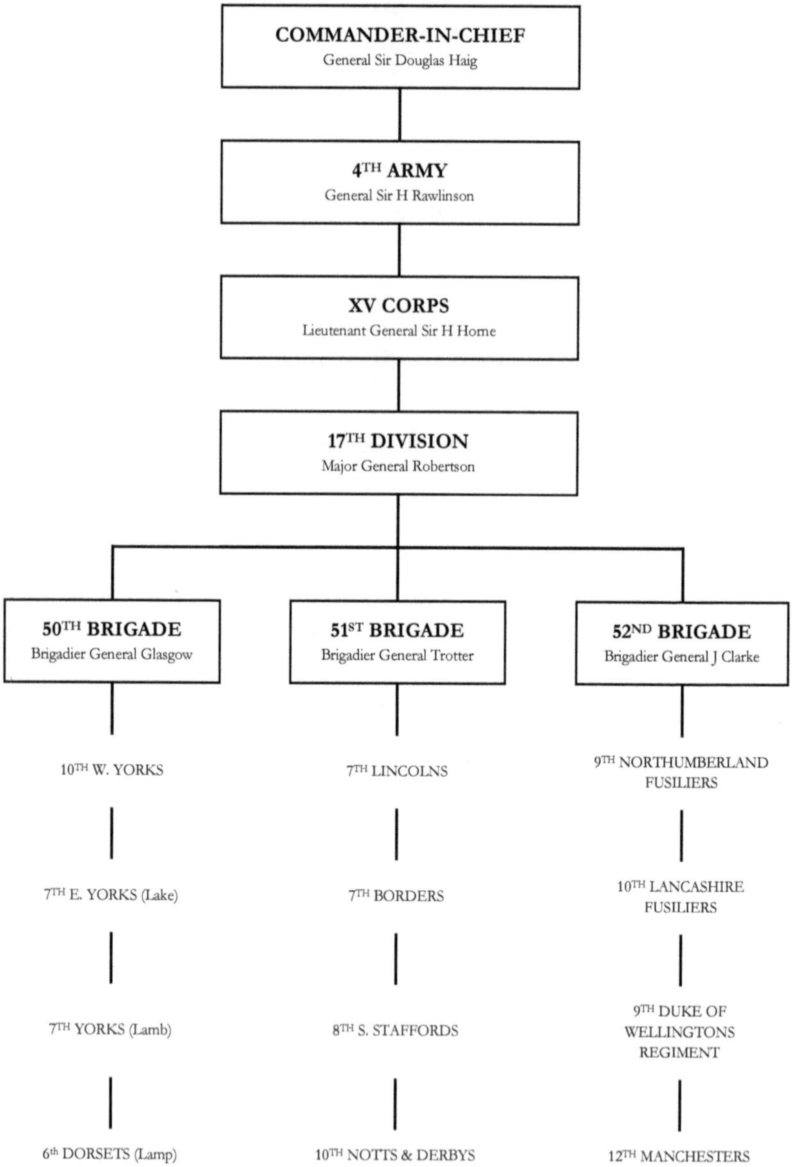

1 The Chain of Command and the (simplified) infantry make-up of the 17th (Northern) Division.

Omitted are Artillery, Signals, Engineers, Medical Staff, The Yorks & Lancs Pioneers, Machine gun companies, the Divisional Troop, Supply Troops, Veterinary personnel, Sanitary personnel and Staff personnel

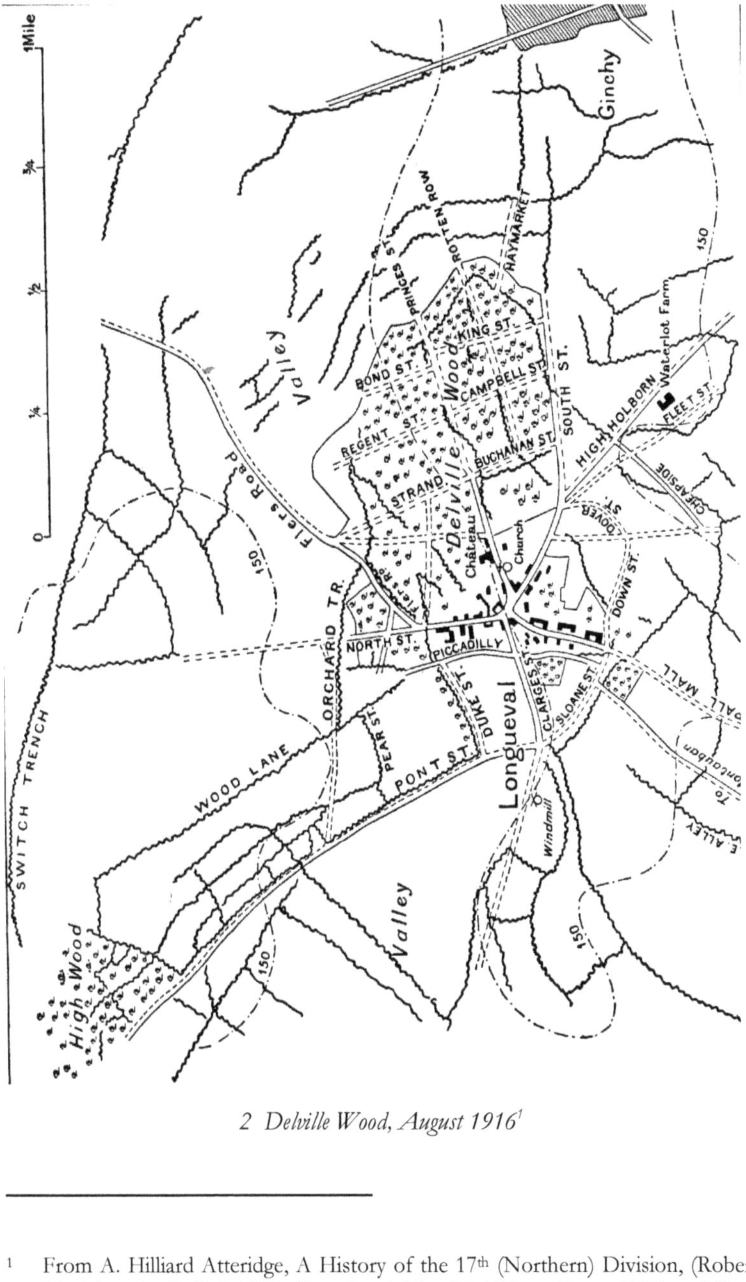

2 Delville Wood, August 1916[1]

1 From A. Hilliard Atteridge, A History of the 17th (Northern) Division, (Robert Maclehose & Co Ltd, 1929. Re-printed, Naval & Military Press, 2003), p. 148

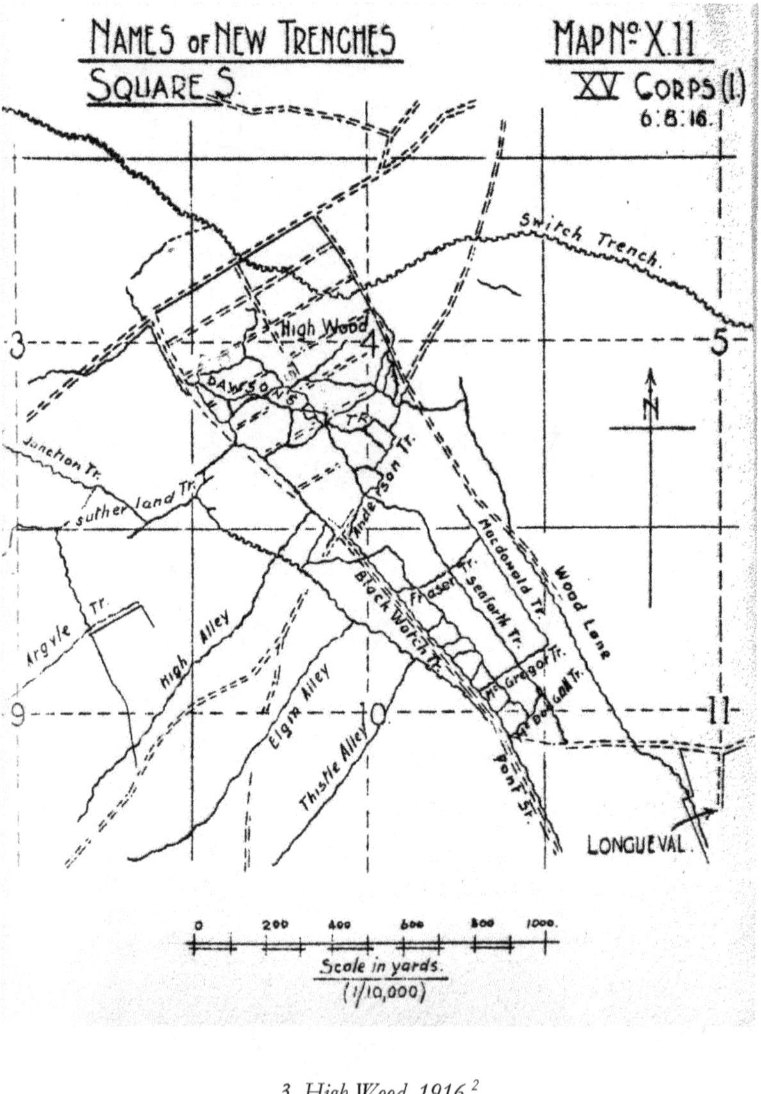

3 High Wood, 1916 [2]

---

2 TNA: PRO WO 157/469. War Diary of XV Corps Intelligence Summaries

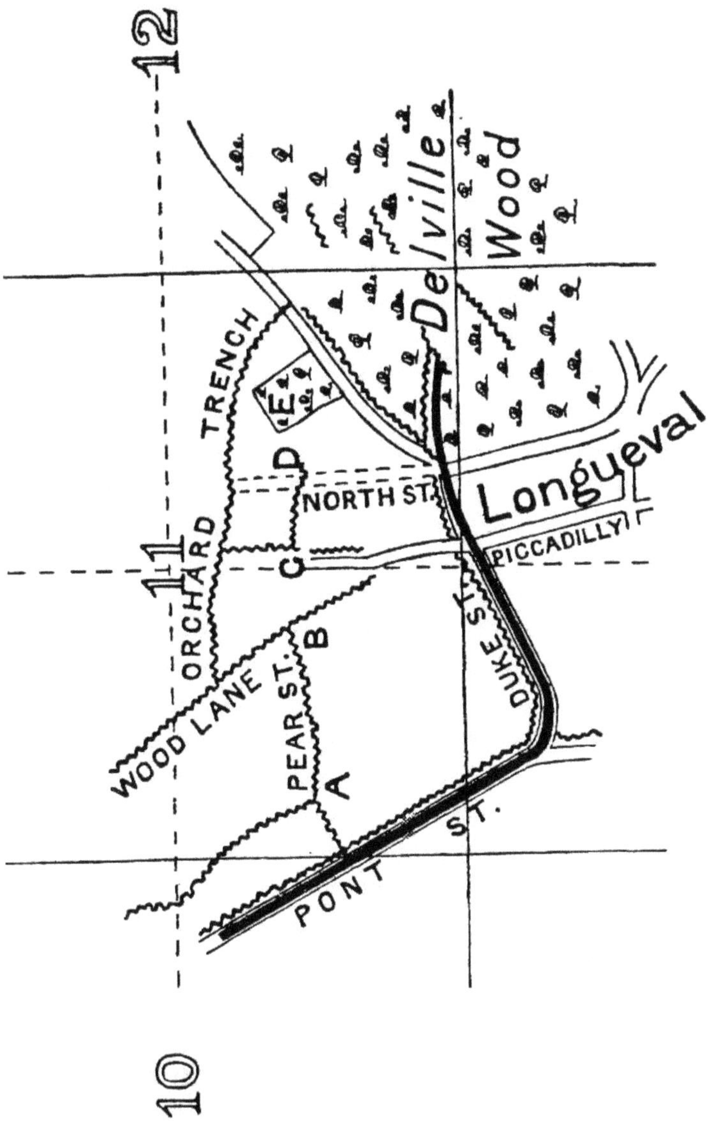

4 Front Line at Longueval, August 1916 [3]

[3] Detail from Hilliard Atteridge, *A History of the 17th (Northern) Division*, p. 151

Introduction

This book, the companion volume to *Quadrangles*, published in 2007 and re-printed in 2010, has taken a good deal longer to get into print that I originally intended. Numerous other projects have turned up since the main text was completed in 2008. Work on my books about the 10th Nott & Derbys, my PhD, my collaboration with Keith Case on the fascinating Colonel Weston Jarvis books and being heavily involved in John Bourne and Bob Bushaway's *Joffrey's War* project have taken up my time. On top of all of that, I am a father and husband and trying to navigate the family through an awful financial depression has not been easy. Sometimes there has not been time to return to one of my favourite topics, the 17th (Northern) Division in the Great War. Personally, I believe that the division was far better than it has been remembered and I hope that my work will one day prove just how good it was in the Great War. It is my intention to write a third book about the division to complete the history of its service on the Somme in 1916. Still, there are other projects to work on so, we shall see!

Quadrangles came about because I went hunting for one dead soldier in documents and in the fields of the old Somme battlefield. *Delville Wood* came about because after looking at so many graves on the Western Front, I was left with an overwhelming sense of so many stories left untold. I hope that in a way I have managed to tell some of those untold tales by giving some of the dead and those who survived and never spoke about the war, a voice.

Wayne Osborne,
Nottingham,
2012

Foreword

This is the second of Wayne Osborne's contributions to the history of the 17th (Northern) Division during the Great War. The first, *Quadrangles*, published in 2007 and 2010, dealt with the Division's first tour of duty in the Somme campaign, operating against a muddy section of the German line between Mametz Wood and Contalmaison, dominated by the Quadrangle Trench and Quadrangle Support Trench. The war on the Western Front was characterised by long periods of trench holding, often in unpleasant and dangerous conditions, time spent 'in reserve' allegedly resting and training, and short intense periods of 'high tempo' warfare, typically lasting only a few days, but during which casualties suffered and inflicted were at their highest. 17th Division's next major involvement, after its Somme debut, was during the first two weeks of August, at Delville Wood. The demanding nature of the Division's first assault had earned it no favours from high command. At Delville Wood, despite being subjected to fierce artillery bombardment, the Division was required to attack well-defended enemy positions with green troops sent as reinforcements after the July battles. Although the opening day of the Somme campaign, 1 July 1916, has attracted most criticism from posterity, in many respects the conduct of the August battles, characterised by poorly planned and unsupported attacks on narrow fronts, were even more costly and less successful. This period represents the nadir of British generalship on the Western Front.

17th Division went into battle in August with a new general in command. Major-General Philip Rynd Robertson (1866-1936) replaced Major-General T.D. Pilcher on 13 July 1916. Robertson was to command the Division until the end of the war, by which time he was the seventh longest serving divisional commander in the BEF. Robertson began the war as CO of the 1st Battalion The Cameronians (October 1913-June 1915), before being promoted to command 19 Brigade. He was 50 years old when he took command of 17th Division, twelve years younger than the Division's first GOC, the 'dugout' Major-General W.R. Kenyon-Slaney, and six years younger than its second, Major-General Pilcher. The tendency, from 1916 onwards, for divisional commanders to get younger, while at the same time be more experienced in command and combat than their predecessors, is apparent in the case of Robertson, without being exceptional. The change in command at 17th Division was welcomed by its recently appointed AA&QMG, W.N. Nicholson, who later wrote a perceptive account of the Division under Robertson's command. Robertson was a devoted family man who hated war. He treated 17th Division like a big battalion. He imposed pre-war Regular Army standards of discipline, which was ill-designed to make him popular among New Army soldiers, but popularity was not on Robertson's agenda. He went round the trenches four mornings a week. He did not demand from his troops more than was humanly possible and was willing to stand up to higher authority, something he had already shown as a brigade commander and which he was to show again at Arras in the spring of 1917. The result was that his troops trusted him and he deserves Nicholson's judgement that he was 'in every respect a most excellent divisional commander'.

Wayne Osborne has again used the divisional war diary as the core of his account. The National Archives' collection of war diaries has been heavily used by military and family historians and many are now in a bad way. It is only a matter of time before all have been digitised in order to preserve them. It is doubly good to see them preserved, too, by publication. But this is more than a facsimile of the war diary. The account is supplemented and reinforced by the war diaries of the Division's subordinate units and by unpublished personal accounts held by the Imperial War Museum. The result is a compelling study of two weeks intensive fighting at a low point of the war that received scant recognition at the time and not much more since. Wayne Osborne has finally set the record straight. I have a feeling that General Robertson would be pleased.

Dr J.M. Bourne
Birmingham
August 2012

THE BACKGROUND

The 17th (Northern) Division

The Division was formed on 11 September 1914, at Wareham in Dorset, under the command of Major-General Kenyon-Slaney. Training began immediately, even though the men lacked absolutely everything that they needed for military life. Rising star and acquaintance of Lord Kitchener's, Major-General Thomas David Pilcher arrived in January 1915 and took over, as a storm battered the south of England and the men huddled in threadbare tents.[4] Major-General Thomas David, 'Von Pilch'[5] and 'the Sardine', Pilcher, C.B., had seen considerable service in West Africa, South Africa and India, where he had got to know Lord Kitchener. He managed to court controversy in India for being too enthusiastic about training and fell out with his immediate boss, General Sir Garrett O'Moore Creagh,[6] about the subject. He had visited Germany during the Autumn Manoeuvres and was considered an expert on German military literature. He was promoted to Major-General in 1907 and was recalled from India in 1914 by Kitchener specifically to command a New Army division. On his return to Britain, before he took up his post, Kitchener sent him to the Western Front on a fact-finding mission. His report apparently contained some useful points, particularly about machine gun barrages.[7]

As time went on equipment, weapons, uniforms and even army huts arrived and the Division took shape. On 15/16 July 1915 the entire 17th Division crossed to France. It learned the art of trench warfare

---

4 The weather in the south in December 1914 and January 1915 was very bad and brought training in the 17th Division to a complete halt. The men's old tents were incapable of keeping them dry and warm. Because there was a shortage of huts, in many cases troops had to be billeted in people's homes.

5 The latter nickname appears to have been given to him in his early days in charge of the division. Captain B. C. Mozley, 6th Dorsets, refers to him as 'Von Pilch' in his unpublished memoir held at the Imperial War Museum, IWM. 01/45/1. As does Brigadier-General H. C. C. Uniacke in a post war letter to Brigadier-General J. E. Edmonds, TNA: PRO. CAB 45/117.

6 It would appear that Sir Garrett was not keen on his generals involving themselves in training…

7 Hilliard Atteridge, *A History of the 17th*, p. 16 -18. & J. Bourne *Lions Led by Donkeys Project*, University of Birmingham.

in the Ypres Salient and in February 1916 it fought and lost its first battle at 'The Bluff'. The rest of the year was spent in training for the forthcoming Somme Offensive. In action early in the Somme Campaign, as part of XV Corps, the Division was involved in the very heavy fighting at Fricourt and for Quadrangle Support Trench situated between Contalmaison and Mametz Wood. Its 50th Brigade suffered very heavy casualties, notably the 10th West Yorks lost their Colonel and most of their fighting strength at Fricourt on 1 July. Withdrawn from the line after the successful, if hollow, victory at Quadrangle Support Trench the 17th Division was sent to the 'Cavillon Area' to the west of Amiens to rest and recuperate.

When he succeeded Field Marshal French, General Sir Douglas Haig was suspicious of Major-General Pilcher's ability, and when Pilcher's 17th Division lost 'The Bluff' in the Ypres Salient in February 1916 his 'card was marked'.[8] Even so, no move was made to remove him from command of the 17th Division at that point. In fact, Haig had held certain views about senior officers for some time. The previous year, on 8 July, while G.O.C of the First Army and aged fifty-four, he entertained Mr. Asquith at lunch and discussed the subject of senior officers with the then Prime Minister. Later that day, demonstrating a forward thinking view that is at odds with the common perception of the commander in chief at the head of a bunch of aging generals, Haig wrote in his diary

> *... for promoting young officers to high command. To make room some of the old ones must be removed. We went through the lists of Major-Generals etc. in the Army List. I said it was important to go low down on the List and get young, capable officers. He [Asquith] agreed.*[9]

Time in post was running out for fifty-eight year old Major-General Pilcher. He came under a good deal of pressure from his Corps Commander during July 1916 and removed his senior brigadier-general on 6 July, possibly as a demonstration of his 'push' and determination. Haig believed that Pilcher had been dismissed from

---

8 G. Sheffield & J. Bourne, (Eds), *Douglas Haig War Diaries and Letters 1914 – 1918,* (BCA, 2005), p. 181

9 Haig from his Diary in J. Terraine, *The Smoke and the Fire,* (Sidgwick and Jackson Ltd, 1980), p. 115

his command on 9 July but that was erroneous.[10] It may well be that moves were made to remove him but in fact Pilcher was removed from his post, for showing too little 'push', by the Corps Commander, Lieutenant-General Sir Henry Sinclair Horne, on 11 July. If the mistakes made at Quadrangle Support were Pilcher's fault or Horne's is a moot point and one wonders how much Kitchener's demise in June 1916 left Pilcher without patronage and open to dismissal.

Pilcher's replacement, fifty-year-old Major-General Robertson, arrived to take over on 13 July. He looked older than his years and when Lieutenant-Colonel Fife of the 7th Yorks (Green Howards) met him for the first time at divisional H.Q on 14 July Fife thought that the man was about sixty. Fife also noted that Robertson wore no war medal ribbons but in conversation he did discover that they had both attended Roscoe's Private School in Harrogate.[11] This new man, Scotsman, Major-General Philip Rynd, 'Blobs', Robertson C.B., C.M.G., had been the Lieutenant-Colonel of the 1st Camerons in 1914 and commanded them in the early stages of the war. He was promoted to Brigadier-General in June 1915 and given the 19th Brigade. He became a capable divisional commander and was known for having no fear of superior officers, speaking his mind when he felt it necessary, often to protect the men under his command. Notably, during the Battle of Arras in 1917, he took on Generals Allenby and Haldane in separate arguments, the former in concert with other divisional generals and the latter alone; he won both contests. He was to remain in command of the 17th Division for the rest of the war and was still defending his Division's reputation in 1934.[12]

During the time that the 17th Division had been having a brief rest, the Fourth Army had moved forward. On the southern side of the Albert - Bapaume Road, in the attack upon the German second line, bitter fighting had taken the British front line to the edge of High Wood and Bazentin-le-Petit and Bazentin-le-Grand had been captured. Most of Delville Wood, the scene of much sacrifice and

---

10 Sheffield & Bourne, *Douglas Haig War Diaries and Letters 1914 – 1918,* p. 201

11 The Personal diary of Lieutenant-Colonel Ronald D'Arcy Fife, C.M.G., D.S.O.

12 Letter from Major-General Sir Philip Robertson to Brigadier-General Edmonds, 15 April 1934. CAB 45/137.

hard fighting by the 9th Division, whose South African Brigade had been ordered to capture the wood, had been taken. Trones Wood had fallen on 14 July.

The gaps in the ranks had been filled and the 17th Division had been reinforced while it was out of the line in the Cavillon Area around Amiens. The old camaraderie of the battalions, built up by the volunteers of 1914 and 1915, had been diluted. Such was the desperate need to make good the losses of the first days of the Somme Campaign, men were rushed to the depleted battalions. Many of the new drafts were fresh from training, while others were from different divisions and regiments. For instance between 16 and 21 July 1916, 518 other ranks, roughly half the fighting strength, joined the 10th Notts & Derbys, the Sherwood Foresters, in five separate drafts. This included a draft from the South Staffords and another made up of veterans from the 9th Notts & Derbys who had fought at Gallipoli. Trained men were needed and the latter group, as trained men from the battalion's own geographical region, would have been a doubly welcome addition to the unit. Similarly, a large draft of men from the Norfolk Regiment had recently joined the 7th Borders.

At this point in the campaign when new men arrived they had little or no time to be assimilated into their new units before they were sent into the line and the officers had little time to get to know the new men under their command. This caused some problems and discontent throughout the 17th Division, as it did in other divisions. A soldier's family was the section and his home the platoon. Time was required to allow the new men to get used to their new units. Without this time to assimilate and train, the combat efficiency of the battalions, already shaken by their experiences at Quadrangle Support Trench, would be even further reduced.

There had been severe losses among the officers of the 17th Division, right up to the rank of brigadier-general. Second lieutenants, lieutenants, captains and majors had all become casualties and in one way or another, the battalion commanders had suffered as well. Although, if the absence of eight of the twelve colonels made any difference to the tour in Delville Wood remains to be seen.

As far as battalion commander casualties went the 50th Brigade fared better than the other two brigades. Only the 10th West Yorks had lost their C.O. Lieutenant-Colonel A. Dickson[13] had been killed in action, along with his second in command and many of his men, at Fricourt, on 1 July. That whole battalion had to be practically re-constituted in the days following the opening of the Somme Campaign. Lieutenant-Colonel Cecil A. Rowley remained with his 6th Dorsets, Lieutenant-Colonel Fife remained with his 7th Yorks and Lieutenant-Colonel Clive was still with his battalion, the 7th East Yorks.

Of the brigades, the 51st suffered the worst; it had 100% of its battalion commanders absent. Lieutenant-Colonel Norrington the C.O of the 7th Borders, had seemingly vanished without trace and that battalion was under the command of Major Reginald Strutt Irwin with ex-Territorial Force officer, Major J. H. Bowe as his 2 i/c.[14] Lieutenant-Colonel Forrest of the 7th Lincolns had gone home and his battalion was to be commanded by Major F. E. Metcalfe. Lieutenant-Colonel Barker of the 8th South Staffords had been taken ill on 13 July and sent to a hospital in the rear so the battalion was commanded initially by Captain Farwell and then Captain C. H. Manger. Lieutenant-Colonel Banbury of the 10th Notts & Derbys had left on 26 July after being promoted to Brigadier-General and given command of the 61st Brigade.[15] Therefore, the battalion was initially commanded in the field by Captain L. Gilbert.

The 52nd Brigade was missing three of its colonels. Major G. P. Westmacott was in command of the 9th Northumberland Fusiliers and he was nursing a wound received during the operations in the previous tour of duty. His C.O., Lieutenant-Colonel H. Bryan was unavailable, though why was not recorded. Major George Leslie Torrens had the command of the 10th Lancashire Fusiliers, Lieutenant-Colonel Thomas Stewart Herschal Wade[16] the battalion

---

13 Lieutenant-Colonel A. Dickson, C.O, 10th West Yorks. Formerly of the 1st South Lancashires.

14 Norrington did not return to his battalion.

15 Brigadier-General Banbury was one of two battalion commanders of the 17th Division to be promoted to General Officer rank during the war.

16 Lieutenant-Colonel Wade, D.S.O., returned to the command the battalion and by 1918 he had been promoted to Brigadier-General.

C. O was absent, and no reason for the absence was given in the war diary. Lieutenant-Colonel E. G. Harrison of the 12th Manchesters, had been badly wounded[17] and Major Philip Mathew Magnay,[18] formerly of the 1st Royal Fusiliers, had taken over on 8 July. Lieutenant-Colonel George Edward Wannell,[19] the C.O of the 9th Duke of Wellingtons was still with his battalion.

Dysentery was rife among the men of the 17th Division, as it was throughout all units on the Somme battlefield, and every day men were sent back to the hospitals with the sickness. Influenza had also made an appearance in the trenches and so, it appeared, had measles.

The 17th Division was in the hands of the newly appointed Major-General Robertson and the Division's senior, experienced, Brigadier-General Fell had been dismissed on 6 July. His brigade, the 51st, was now commanded by the recently arrived novice Brigadier-General G. F. Trotter. The 50th Brigade was commanded by Brigadier-General W. J. T Glasgow, who had been in charge since March 1916 and who had been physically affected by the heavy losses to his brigade in July. The third Brigadier-General, J. L. J. Clarke, 52nd Brigade G.O.C., who had been in post since March 1916, may also have been troubled by the events of July. In any case, as will be seen, he did not seem inclined to push his men hard at Delville Wood and treated his men with a good deal of sympathy.

---

17 Lieutenant-Colonel Harrison, C.O, 12th Manchesters. He did not return to his battalion and he retired from the Army with a full pension.

18 Promotion had come very quickly for Philip Magnay, the son of Sir William and Lady Magnay. He was a second lieutenant when he went to France, somewhere between 12 and 24 September 1914 and his appointment to the 12th Manchesters saw him promoted to Lieutenant-Colonel. He was Mentioned in Despatches three times, on 16 June 1916, on 4 January 1917 and posthumously on 22 May 1917. Magnay was killed in action on 13 April 1917 during the Battle of Arras.

19 Lieutenant-Colonel Wannell D. S. O., had been with the battalion since it had come out to the Western Front in July 1915. He had been Mentioned in Despatches on 16 June 1916. Later in the war he would move on to be a Lieutenant-Colonel in the Monmouth Regiment and would survive to live in Scarborough.

The High Command

The situation in the Somme Campaign in August 1916 was not simple or straightforward. Peter Simkins said in a conversation with the author, that operations at High Wood and Delville Wood in July and August 1916 were really the aftermath of the battle for the German second line. While conducting these operations, General Sir Douglas Haig, G.O.C. of the B. E. F and his Fourth Army Commander, General Sir Henry Rawlinson also had to prepare for the assault upon the German Third line. To compound the situation, Haig and Rawlinson both had to deal with the French Army and they had some difficulty with this. The French Army was on the right of Rawlinson's Army and operations here, at the interface between the two formations, had to be co-ordinated. Co-operation by both of the Allies was not always assured or easy.

It is not the intention of this book to provide deep analysis about Sir Douglas Haig or the other generals who appear in these pages. Yet, sketches of three of the generals, Haig, Rawlinson and Horne are required, if only because their orders and wishes directed the events in which the troops of the 17th Division were involved. All three men were in their fifties, both Haig and Horne were religious Scotsmen and Rawlinson was an Englishman. Haig was a cavalryman, Rawlinson an infantryman and Horne was an artilleryman. Haig was married, as was Rawlinson; Horne married and started a family after the war.

Sir Douglas Haig is still a man who invites debate and controversy and many still have an opinion of him. His character and reputation have been under attack since the 1920s and that attack gained momentum when Mr Lloyd George published his *War Memoirs*[20] in the 1930s. But in recent years there has been an academic push to re-examine him as a man and a soldier and redress the balance. Some of this work has revealed him in a different light and shows that far from being a donkey, he was a capable and modern general who embraced modern technology and who saw its potential. To some, still, he was a callous butcher and others believe that he was a

---

[20] D. Lloyd George, *War Memoirs of David Lloyd George,* (Odhams Press Ltd, 1933. Re-printed 1938)

misunderstood man who did his best in the circumstances. In some literature he is the murderer of thousands but as the man who had a pivotal role in the British Legion and the Poppy Appeal, he is quietly forgotten. There have been reams written about Haig, from Denis Winter's attack upon him in the book *Haig's Command*[21] to the stoic defence of him in John Terraine's *Douglas Haig The educated soldier*.[22] There are enough books available to suit everyone's theories of Haig.

The view that he was a callous murderer who was oblivious to the conditions at the front is wrong. The image of him (portrayed by Geoffrey Palmer) sweeping toy soldiers into a dust pan in the final episode of *Blackadder Goes Forth*,[23] to demonstrate his callous attitude to his troops, belongs more to that other piece of entertainment, *Oh, What a Lovely War*,[24] than it does to historical fact. In their balanced book *Douglas Haig War Diaries and Letters 1914 – 1918,* Gary Sheffield and John Bourne wrote, "His diary frequently records his admiration for the achievements of his 'amateur' soldiers and an appreciation of their suffering."[25] That he was privileged there is no doubt.[26] "Haig

---

21 D. Winter, *Haig's Command,* (First published, Viking 1991. Re-printed, Penguin 1992)

22 J. Terraine, *Douglas Haig The educated soldier,* (Hutchinson & Co. Ltd, 1963)

23 *Blackadder Goes Forth,* written by Richard Curtis and Ben Elton. BBC World Wide Ltd. It must be recorded that while the show may be historically inaccurate it was written as entertainment and as such is still hugely enjoyable and a firm favourite of the author.

24 *Oh What a Lovely War.* A Theatre Workshop production directed by Joan Littlewood; first performed in March 1963.

25 Sheffield & Bourne, *Douglas Haig War Diaries and Letters 1914 – 1918,* p.42

26 John Bourne wrote to the author, "Haig. I checked his Royal credentials. His favourite sister, Henrietta Jameson, introduced him into the Prince of Wales's circle in the 1890s. Her husband, Willy Jameson, shared the Prince's expensive enthusiasm for yachting. Edward VII made Haig an ADC (Extra) in 1902. I've checked the list of ADCs in the Army List. It appears that they are 'handed over' when the monarch changes. There were already 60 ADCs when Haig was appointed, one of the first appointments made by the new King. It is difficult for us lowly, humble chaps quite to know what is going on here, but it seems that being made an ADC (Extra) was an honour rather than a job. Most of the ADCs, who presumably had ADC-type jobs to do, were 'courtiers', but those who had proper jobs to do, like Haig, seem to be 'extra'. Plumer and Robertson were also ADCs, as was your chum Pilcher. Spens, Broadwood, Alderson, Hubert Hamilton, Birdwood, Keary, Fitton, Forestier-Walker, MacBean and Heneker, all of whom served in the Great War as generals at various levels, were

was welcomed in royal circles, especially those of Edward VII, from early in his career."[27] but these facts in no way made him perfect and like the generals on both sides, he was not a super-hero. His H.Q *was* a chateau but he often visited his generals and men and he was criticised for both having a chateau H.Q and interfering with the military affairs of his subordinates. But, he was, in the jargon of the time, "Johnny-on-the-spot", the man to whom the task of being Britain's top soldier had fallen.

Haig's devotion to the 'wearing-out' battle, or attrition, has earned him much criticism but he was a thoroughly trained staff officer who had helped Lord Haldane reform the British Army and Territorial Force in the years before the war. John Terraine said that Haig had learned and believed in the four phases that had to be passed through in order to achieve victory in battle:

1. The manoeuvre for position.
2. The first clash of battle.
3. The wearing-out fight of varying duration.
4. The eventual decisive blow.[28]

The problem for Haig, posterity and popular opinion was that the third phase lasted an awfully long time and cost so many casualties. It has been suggested that he was a schemer and an intriguer; he was certainly ambitious. In his dealings with others Haig could lack generosity, be touchy and demonstrate prickly pride and vanity. Equally he could be courteous, was generally interested in people of all walks of life and he had time for other people. Sir Winston Churchill said of him, "He might be, he surely was, unequal to the prodigious scale of events; but no one else was discerned as his equal or better."[29] He also said of Haig and the war, "the Great War owned no master; no one was equal to its vast and novel issues; no

---

also ADCs to Edward VII or George V or both. Haig disappears from the list of ADCs by 1905. For almost the whole of the period he was an ADC he was in India as IG Cavalry (1903-6)." Dr. J. M. Bourne, 2012.

27 Sheffield & Bourne, *Douglas Haig War Diaries and Letters 1914 – 1918*, p. 12

28 Terraine, *Douglas Haig The educated soldier,* p.48

29 W. Churchill in Terraine, *Douglas Haig The educated soldier,* Acknowledgements, p. xiii

human hand controlled its hurricanes; no eye could pierce its whirlwind dust-clouds."[30] Gary Sheffield and John Bourne wrote, "He was an excellent man to work for, demanding but appreciative. For this reason, his reproaches – when delivered – were accordingly stinging."[31]

By and large, Haig and Rawlinson had a good working relationship and they seemed to have a friendship. Their frequent meetings were often productive. Like Haig, Rawlinson had been involved in the re-organisation of the army before the war; in Rawlinson's case he had assisted with training and education in the army. Although it has been suggested that Rawlinson was frightened of Haig, Peter Simkins says there is little evidence of that in Rawlinson's diaries.[32] He was, perhaps, nervous of Haig, and he certainly knew when he had annoyed the General, or was about to. Rawlinson was also probably well aware of how much that his continuation as an Army Commander relied upon his chief. In his relationship with Haig, Rawlinson demonstrated an "equable temperament" and had a "subtle and malleable attitude to his dealings with Haig."[33] Rawlinson also had a knack of being able to distance himself from the worries and cares of the day and he slept well at night. Perhaps these were useful attributes for a battlefield general? All things taken into consideration, 1916 was not an easy year for Rawlinson and despite their friendship Haig, from mid-July on, was becoming increasingly annoyed with the way Rawlinson's Fourth Army was operating. He had a habit of putting his own advancement ahead of others and to his subordinates Rawlinson could be cold and hard. Be that as it may, as August wore on Haig became increasingly irritated with Rawlinson's lack of close supervision of his Corps Commanders. One of those Corps Commanders was XV Corps G.O.C, Lieutenant-General Horne. He had been Haig's artillery advisor when the latter commanded I Corps and was a protégé of Haig's. So far, 1916 had not been an easy year for Horne either.

---

30 W. Churchill, *The World Crisis 1911 – 1918,* (First published, Charles Scribner's sons, 1931. Re-printed, First Free Press, 2005), p. 653

31 Sheffield & Bourne, *Douglas Haig War Diaries and Letters 1914 – 1918,* p.15

32 P. Simkins, *Haig and His Army Commanders*, p. 85 in B. Bond & N. Cave, *Haig A Reappraisal 70 Years On.* (Leo Cooper, 1999)

33 P. Simkins, *Haig and His Army Commanders*, p. 85 in Bond & Cave, *Haig A Reappraisal 70 Years On.*

It is possible, when one considers Haig's growing irritation with Rawlinson's command style, that Haig knew the XV Corps commander, Horne was, at the very least, partially to blame for the piecemeal operations of July. But, in late August, he chose to tear a strip of Rawlinson rather than the subordinate; delivering "a terse reminder of the duties of an Army Commander, making it clear that he was not impressed by the want of close supervision by Rawlinson of his subordinates."[34] It could be, as John Bourne suggested in a conversation with the author, that because Horne was Haig's protégé, Haig would be uncomfortable dressing him down. That being the case, perhaps Haig hoped that the 'carpeting' would go down the chain of command from Rawlinson to Horne; saving him the trouble. If this was indeed the case then it was a display of underhand and unpleasant behaviour by the Commander in Chief but not entirely out of character.

Horne is an enigmatic figure in the literature of the war. In Haig's diary for the period there is little or no sign of any criticism of Horne; save one slight disagreement about the ability of the 51st (Highland) Division's G. O. C., Major-General Harper.[35] Horne is almost invisible in Robin Prior and Trevor Wilson's book about Rawlinson, *Command On The Western Front.*[36] He is equally translucent in John Terraine's *Douglas Haig The educated soldier.* He is absent from many well-known books about the Somme battle.

Martin Middlebrook writing in his seminal book *The First Day On The Somme* is in no doubt as to Horne's behaviour in July 1916. He refers to Horne as a "demanding task master" who put Major-General Pilcher under "relentless pressure".[37] As has already been mentioned, Pilcher was dismissed by Horne for not pushing his division hard enough and considering Haig's poor opinion of

---

34 P. Simkins, *Haig and His Army Commanders*, p. 86 in Bond & Cave, *Haig A Reappraisal 70 Years On*

35 G. Sheffield & J. Bourne, (Eds), *Douglas Haig War Diaries and Letters 1914 – 1918,* (BCA, 2005), p. 210

36 R. Prior & T. Wilson, *Command On The Western Front The Military Career Of Sir Henry Rawlinson 1914 – 1918*, (Blackwell Publishers, 1992. Re-printed Pen & Sword, 2004)

37 M. Middlebrook, *The First Day On The Somme,* (First published, Allen Lane, 1971. Re-printed, Penguin 1994), p. 259

Pilcher, this dismissal must have pleased him. Pilcher protested to Horne about the piecemeal attacks that the latter was ordering but his words fell upon deaf ears. Pilcher was naturally upset about his dismissal and it still rankled after the war. In a post-war letter to Brigadier-General Edmonds, the Official Historian, he said

> *If I had obeyed the Corps more literally, I should have lost another two or three thousand men and achieved no more. I was, as you know, accused of a want of push, and consequently sent home. It is very easy to sit a few miles in the rear and get credit for allowing men to be killed in an undertaking foredoomed to failure, but the part did not appeal to me and my protests against these useless attacks were not well received.*[38]

In the July 1916 war diaries of XV Corps and the 17th Division, Horne is very much present and there is plenty of evidence that he *was* putting pressure upon the Major-Generals of the 17th and 38th Divisions in July 1916. He ordered piecemeal attack after piecemeal attack on Quadrangle Support Trench, up narrow, blocked trenches and over the open into the path of heavy machine guns and crossfire from un-secured flanks. Each time the ill-considered, uncoordinated assaults failed and the casualty list grew.[39] There is evidence, however, in the August war diaries of the XV Corps and the 17th Division that he handled the 17th Division and Pilcher's replacement, fellow Scot, Major-General Robertson, very differently. In September, Horne was promoted to the command of the First Army, so he cannot have done that much wrong in the eyes of the chief and it does seem that he matured as a General. Of Horne, John Terraine said that he was a competent gunner and a quiet, retiring man who shunned publicity,[40] but in this lecture, Terraine said no more.

---

38 TNA. PRO: CAB 45/190.

39 TNA. PRO. WO 95/921. War Diary, XV Corps. TNA. PRO. WO 95/1981. War Diary, 17th Division and W. Osborne, *Quadrangles,* (Exposure Publishing, 2007. Second Edition, Salient Books, 2010)

40 J. Terraine, 1991 Lecture, *British Military Leadership in the First World War*, p. 46 in A. Clayton (Ed), *1914 – 1918 Essays on Leadership & War by John Terraine,* (Trustees of The Western Front Association, 1998)

Orders and Plans

Haig conceded that losses on the Somme in July had already been higher than they should have been, but these losses would not affect the Army's ability to continue the offensive.[41] On 23 July he informed Rawlinson that in his army area he wanted to consolidate on the left and in the centre and improve things on the right.[42] Rawlinson then held a conference with his Corps commanders on 31 July. He ordered XIII Corps to prepare for an offensive against Guillemont on the right just as Haig wanted but he then told the commanders of III and XV Corps to adopt an offensive posture on their front lines in the left and centre of the Fourth Army Front.[43]

On 1 August Haig wrote that he believed proof had been given to the world that Verdun and the opening phase of the Somme Campaign had shown that the Allies were capable of combating the enemy's finest troops and pushing them from the strongest positions. The Germans had suffered heavy losses and the application of steady pressure would soon tell and defeat them, therefore the British offensive should be maintained. He would push his attack where the general situation and preparations made success possible otherwise he would not attack. He expected to continue the offensive into autumn. The next day he had to admit that the German Army units facing the British on the Somme had recovered well from the chaos of July and now British attacks had to be made after "careful and methodical preparation".[44] Haig now envisaged that a major set piece attack would take place in September.[45]

---

41 Sheffield & Bourne, *Douglas Haig War Diaries and Letters 1914 – 1918,* p. 213 - 214

42 Prior & Wilson, *Command on the Western Front, The Military Career of Sir Henry Rawlinson 1914 – 1918,* p. 216

43 Prior & Wilson, *Command on the Western Front, The Military Career of Sir Henry Rawlinson 1914 – 1918,* p. 216

44 Sheffield & Bourne, *Douglas Haig War Diaries and Letters 1914 – 1918,* p. 213 - 214

45 Sheffield & Bourne, *Douglas Haig War Diaries and Letters 1914 – 1918,* p. 31

Reinforcing plans that he had already outlined, Haig told Rawlinson to help the French who were on the British right flank. Haig wanted them to get forward, come into line with his troops, and therefore eliminate the Longueval-Delville Wood Salient. In order to help the French, Haig wanted Rawlinson's Fourth Army to take Guillemont, Falfmont Farm and Ginchy on the right of Delville Wood. None of these objectives could be taken without careful preparation he warned Rawlinson. Preparations on the right should get under way immediately and the attacks made when the commanders on the spot felt that everything had been done to deliver success. Haig did not want Rawlinson to launch any serious attacks from the front line held by III and XV Corps, Munster Alley to Delville Wood.[46]

Haig sometimes exercised his command with a light touch; he outlined his broad plans and most of the time allowed his subordinates to handle the details. He wanted the divisions of the III and XV Corps to prepare for an offensive on the left and in the centre but the decision to launch a serious offensive here was to be Haig's alone, not Rawlinson's. This part of the line, for now, was to be stationary and in a state of preparation for an offensive. Observation of the German lines on the British left and in the centre should be improved where possible. Positions that had been taken had to be consolidated, fire steps in captured trenches reversed to face the correct way, new assembly, communication and front line trenches had to be dug. Redoubts and trenches in the rear had to be prepared and strengthened in case of a serious counter-attack and lines of communication, tracks, roads, railways and light tramways had to be maintained to aid the flow of men and munitions to and from the front.

46 Prior & Wilson, *Command on the Western Front, The Military Career of Sir Henry Rawlinson 1914 – 1918,* p. 217

THE STORY

Prelude

Delville Wood now formed a salient in the German line and it was considered vital for forthcoming operations that the British hold this exposed position. It was under constant German observation and surrounded on three sides by a four-mile arc of artillery. The area was devastated and steeped in gas and the trenches reeked of urine and the unburied corpses that lay everywhere one looked. The front line was not a continuous trench line; it was made up of sections of trench, small pits, shell holes and fallen trees. Barbed wire was strung between the splintered tree trunks. Artillery, machine gun, rifle and sniper fire was constant.

On 21 July orders arrived for the 17th Division to move up to the front line. On 27 July and now on the north side of the river Ancre below Albert the Division was on three hours notice to go into the line. There was a ceremonial parade on this day and instead of Lieutenant-General Sir Henry Sinclair Horne who should have officiated, Major-General Philip Rynd Robertson, the new Divisional G.O.C, presented medal ribbons to men who had earned decorations during the battle to take Quadrangle Support Trench. The Division had rehearsed the parade and it began at 6.00 pm. According to Hilliard Atteridge, the formation's first historian, the whole division was drawn up on three sides of a square for the parade and Robertson used this moment to address his new command. He said

> *Officers, N.C.Os, and men of the 17th Division, - The Corps Commander had hoped to be here himself today to present the Military Medals*[47] *to the N.C.Os. and men of the Division, but he is very sorry that owing to press of work he is unable to come.*
>
> *As this is the first opportunity I have had of speaking to you on parade, I would like to tell you all how very proud I am at finding myself in command of such a fine Division, whose reputation stands very high in the British Army. I have heard from many how well the Division had always fought, and especially how splendidly they did during the first ten or twelve days of the present battle, and it is with the fullest confidence that I look*

---

47 The Military Medal was introduced in March 1916.

forward to the time when you will again meet the enemy, and am certain that you will then add to the laurels already gained by the 17th Division.

The N.C.Os. and men who are now to receive decorations have been brought to notice for special acts of gallantry and devotion to duty, and the names of others have been forwarded for rewards to higher authority; besides all these I know that there are many officers and men who have done most gallantly, but whose deeds are unrecorded. In every big battle this must be so, but every one of you whether rewarded or not has the satisfaction of knowing that it is your individual efforts which, combined, all go to build up the fine reputation of the Division, and also that each one of you has done his duty well, for the British Empire and a great and just cause.[48]

It is an interesting speech. True, he was giving them a pep talk and perhaps a 'bit of flannel' but he was also echoing what others in the British Army thought about the 17th Division at the time. It was well regarded and had a reputation for being a fighting division. It is a view that has been somewhat lost in the years after the war.

On 30 July orders arrived for the Division to go into the line. The following day Brigadier-General J. L. J Clarke, G.O.C 52nd Brigade, now the Division's senior Brigadier-General, received orders to go forward, but those orders were changed in favour of a move on the morning of 1 August.

On 31 July Fourth Army H.Q noted that the army was relying upon aircraft and pigeons more than ever as the main methods of communication. Each Corps in the army had received 150 'French Lamps' for communication with aircraft and a request for four hundred more pigeons per Corps had been sent in. Later in the afternoon signal rockets were issued to the divisions. These were to be used to send S.O.S signals to the artillery and a test was scheduled for 11.00 am the following day.

At 12.50 pm, Fourth Army H.Q issued orders about the movement of troops. Because of the hot weather the divisions should not "march their troops during the heat of day."[49] All reliefs and changes of billets and bivouacs were to be carried out in the morning,

---

48 P. R. Robertson in Hilliard Atteridge, *A History of the 17th (Northern) Division*, p.145

49 TNA: PRO WO95/431. War Diary, Fourth Army, August 1916.

evening or night. Captain Bernard Charles Mozley, A Company commander of the 6th Dorsets, recorded that in the days before they returned to the line, the weather was hot and oppressive.[50] The men were paraded in the mornings and then only for a short time to keep them out of the heat. In the afternoons, the officers exercised their horses, riding out to Heilly and Mericourt to look up old friends and comrades in other units. During the day the men of Lieutenant-Colonel Wannell's 9th Duke of Wellingtons had taken advantage of the fine weather and gone bathing. This was followed by training in the art of bayonet fighting. The mud, so deep and glutinous in early July, had been baked hard and dust clouds betrayed any movement to watching artillery observers and aircraft.

Shortly after lunch, on 31 July, at the 80th Brigade, R.F.A., H.Q, Dernancourt,[51] Lieutenant-Colonel George Ambrose Cardew[52] was sitting in his tent writing out recommendations for men to receive awards for the actions of the previous month. As he wrote, he received a message stating that the 17th Division was to go back into the line near to their former positions on the following evening. There appeared to Cardew to be an unseemly rush to get the Division back into the front line, it really was not ready to go back into the fighting. The message also summoned him to 17th Division H.Q. at Ribemont-sur-Ancre. At the time the Divisional artillery was without a commanding officer because Brigadier-General Ouseley, the 17th Division C.R.A, had been wounded in July. As the senior

---

50 IWM 01/45/1. Captain B. C. Mozley, D.S.O. Papers held at the Imperial War Museum.

51 Dernancourt was a large and busy rail head that not only provided accommodation but handled a huge amount of war material and munitions required by the Somme Campaign.

52 Lieutenant-Colonel Cardew, C.M.G., D.S.O., like all eligible regular officers had been mobilised in 1914 and had headed to France as C.O of the 6th Division's Ammunition Column via Waterford in Ireland and Cambridge in England. He was relieved of his command after only seven days in France and only two of them at the front. A catalogue of errors and problems convinced his divisional commander that Cardew could not maintain discipline in the ranks or manage his horses. Cardew was soon found work with the 17th Division and took over the fledgling 80th Brigade, R.F.A. He seems to have mended his ways and he was personally brave, being Mentioned in Despatches on 15 June 1916 and earning the D.S.O. Along with dining out and socialising he also enjoyed the odd bit of looting.

artillery colonel, Cardew had already represented the 17th Division at a meeting of other divisional C.R.As and was continuing to do the job. The 17th Division obviously required a new C.R.A and Cardew felt that the job should be his.

He left his recommendations and rode to the Divisional H.Q in his motor car. On arrival Major-General Robertson and Colonel Collins, the Divisional G.S.O.1, briefed him about their plans for holding the line at Longueval and Delville Wood. After the meeting Cardew, Brigadier-General Glasgow, G.O.C 50th Brigade, and an officer called Phipps motored over to Heilly where they met with Cardew's friend and mentor, Brigadier-General Ernest Wright Alexander V.C., the G.O.C Royal Artillery, XV Corps.[53] Cardew made a point of asking Alexander why the 17th Division was going back into the line with what appeared to be undue haste. Even if he did know the reason Alexander could not explain to Cardew why it should be so. Yet considering General Haig's orders that the centre of the Fourth Army line, Delville Wood, should remain stationary and no offensive was expected there in the near future, it was probably not surprising that the 17th Division should return to the front rather than a fresh one. It was not expected to launch a major attack. In fairness to Cardew he was probably unaware of Haig's intentions. XV Corps recorded that the 17th Division was returned to the line to free up fresh troops.[54] Presumably to free up those fresh troops to train and prepare for the forthcoming operations against the German third line. Lieutenant-Colonel Clive of the 7th Yorks was relieved that they were returning to the line because, in his opinion, the men were suffering from boredom. On 23 July five of his soldiers had got dead drunk and another, a nineteen-year-old early Kitchener Volunteer, Lance Corporal James Hamilton, had drowned in the River Somme.[55]

---

53 Later Major-General Ernest Wright Alexander, V.C.

54 TNA: PRO WO 95/922. War Diary of XV Corps. August 1916.

55 The personal diary of Lieutenant-Colonel Fife, *Soldiers Died in the Great War* and Ancestry.com. Hamilton's Medal Index Card records him as entering France and Flanders on 13 July 1915. This means he had been part of the Advance Party that went out to France before the main body of the 17th Division crossed the Channel on 15 July 1915. The card also records that he was a private. Perhaps he had just been promoted before he died, or his rank was not recorded.

After dining at Heilly, Cardew, King, the Brigade Major, and a few other officers went up to the ruined village of Fricourt. Here they met with Brigadier-General A. H. Hussey the C.R.A of 5th Division, Brigadier-General Blane the C.R.A of 33rd Division and Brigadier-General Oldfield the C.R.A of the 51st (Highland) Division. They discussed the situation but Lieutenant-Colonel Cardew decided that, in his own opinion, the Generals were of little help. He did note that the whole area around Fricourt was being strafed by the German artillery, even more than it had been in July and that the weather was hot and the ground dusty. He returned to his H.Q at Dernancourt to prepare for the move forward to the line. At midnight on 31 July he wrote a letter to his wife and then he wrote up his diary for the day.[56] All units of the 17th Division prepared to move back into the line and Divisional H.Q closed down, moving forward to Bellevue Farm near the town of Albert. The war grumbled on and that night the eastern sky was illuminated by a fireworks display of hanging flares, colourful lights, rockets and the lightning flash of detonating shells.[57]

---

56 IWM 86/92/1. Lieutenant-Colonel G. A. Cardew, C.M.G., D.S.O. Papers held at the Imperial War Museum.

57 An un-named officer in Hilliard Atteridge, *A History of the 17th (Northern) Division,* p. 147.

Chapter One: 1 August

At dawn, a mist lay over the battlefield but as the sun rose higher in the sky the heat of another summer day burned it away. For the rest of the day the weather was exceptionally fine. The staff at 17th Division H.Q, at Bellevue Farm near Albert, recorded that the 52nd Brigade had moved up into the line to take over from Major-General Reginald Byng Stephens'[58] 5th Division. It was also noted that the Divisional artillery had moved up into position. On their left, facing High Wood, was the 51st (Highland) Division and on their right was the 2nd Division of Lieutenant-General Congreve's XIII Corps.

The 17th Signal Company began the busy task of sorting out the communications. A testing station was set up at Bellevue Farm; there was a signal office and exchange at Fricourt and another office and exchange at Pommiers Redoubt.[59] Wireless stations were set up at a site southeast of Bazentin-le-Grand and at Montauban which kept up communication with the units at Fricourt. Pigeons were kept in the front line for the companies who had no telephone lines to their Brigade H.Q. The pigeons would also serve if telephone lines were broken; which was often the case.

The battalions of the 50th Brigade were camped at Dernancourt. The 10th West Yorks and the 7th Yorks, the Green Howards, were in camp there and continued with their training. New drafts arrived for both battalions. Fourteen men joined the 10th West Yorks and after a new draft of officers and men joined the 7th Yorks it was recorded that their ration strength on this day was thirty-one officers and 611 other ranks. The battalion was nearly two hundred men short of its fighting strength of eight hundred. The 10th West Yorks was practically a new battalion, having lost so many men in July. At their

---

58 Stephens had been the Lieutenant-Colonel of the 2nd Battalion, in November 1914.

59 This redoubt, a fortified network of trenches, was situated on the Mametz – Montauban Road behind Pommiers Trench. Both former German positions the trench and redoubt had been captured by elements of the 53rd and 54th Brigades, 18th (Eastern) Division, on the morning of 1 July. In August both positions served as concentration centres for troops coming into and going out of the line as well as being home to signallers and various command posts.

bivouac the men of the 50th Brigade Machine Gun Company took the opportunity to work on their equipment and weapons and the men were given the chance to replace any missing pieces of kit.

The 10th Notts & Derbys and 7th Borders, of 51st Brigade, received orders to move forward from Buire to bivouac near Pommiers Redoubt. Guides had been sent out during the morning to find the route to Pommiers Redoubt in preparation to meet the battalion when it moved forward. The 51st Brigade was going forward to the Pommiers Redoubt area to support the 52nd Brigade, which was in the process of taking over the front line.

On the previous evening, as part of the relief of the 5th Division, Brigadier-General Clarke, G.O.C of 52nd Brigade and one of his staff had gone to see Brigadier-General M. N. Turner, G.O.C 15th Brigade, at his H.Q, to arrange the relief of their section of the line. Turner's H.Q was situated in a deep dugout in Montauban Alley and from there several communication trenches branched off and led to the site of the village of Longueval. Turner's brigade was holding the line west of Delville Wood, Longueval Village and part of the line running up to High Wood.

5.00 am

It was noted at 52nd Brigade H.Q that the relief of the 5th Division by the 17th Division had begun. The Brigade began the march to Fricourt from the rear area and came under the command of G.O.C of 5th Division. The 9th Duke of Wellingtons left their bivouac near Dernancourt and marched to Fricourt. The ruined village was being shelled when they arrived and the area was crowded with troops so the units of 52nd Brigade were forced to move a short distance away in an attempt to avoid casualties. The 10th Lancashires recorded that they had been placed in 52nd Brigade reserve. At their bivouacs on the side of the Albert–Amiens Road the 52nd Brigade Machine Gun Company paraded prior to moving off to Fricourt. Their orders were to travel across country via the village of Meaulte then to follow the Albert–Becordel Road up to Fricourt.

6.45 am

The 6th Dorsets, of 50th Brigade, paraded at the Dernancourt railhead and then marched the short distance to Bellevue Farm. This brigade, under the command of Brigadier-General W. J. T Glasgow, was moving forward to Bellevue Farm, where the Divisional H.Q was situated, to wait in reserve.

7.00 am

Fourth Army H.Q received a report that enemy shellfire was heavy and continuous both on and behind the British front line in the Longueval area. At Dernancourt the men of the 7th East Yorks, of 50th Brigade, took part in physical training, which was followed by company training. After this, as the day became warmer, they rested and waited for orders to move up to Bellevue Farm. The 77th Field Company, R. E, left Dernancourt. The dismounted men of the Company went to Mametz and the mounted men went to Becordel.

Lieutenant-Colonel Cardew and a group of his gunner officers from 80th Brigade, R.F.A rode through the shelling up to Montauban. Once there they scouted around for suitable gun positions for the Brigade's 18-pounder field guns. Cardew was not particularly pleased with the position chosen for his batteries but he and his officers did their best. Once they had chosen what Cardew dismissively referred to as "indifferent positions" he and his officers rode off to Fricourt to meet with Brigadier-Generals Blane and Hussey.[60]

7.30 am

The staff at XV Corps H.Q scrutinised all of the intelligence information that they could to get a picture of what was going on in and behind the German lines. They noted that the British Divisions on its front were facing, from West to East, the 31st (Reserve) Infantry Regiment of the 18th (Reserve) Division and the 75th and 76th (Reserve) Infantry Regiments of the 17th (Reserve) Division. A German officer, captured in the Delville Wood area, had told his interrogators that there was a good deal of chaos behind the German lines. Battalions were being pushed into the front line without any regard to which regiment or division they came from. Behind the

---

60 Imperial War Museum. (IWM:) Unpublished papers, Lieutenant-Colonel Cardew C.M.G, D.S.O, 86/92/1.

German lines construction work was underway, new trench systems were being dug and wired and existing positions strengthened. The German trench line was being doubled from Warlencourt-Eaucourt to Flers, the defences around Eaucourt L'Abbaye were being strengthened and a new line had been begun from Warlencourt to Gueudecourt and on to Leuze Wood. Ginchy was also being strengthened.[61]

Two men of the German 75th (Reserve) Infantry Regiment had been captured by III Corps on the left of XV Corps; the information that they gave to their captors was passed on to XV Corps. Both men were fairly new to the front having arrived in mid July from a recruit depot. They said that Switch Trench that ran from High Wood and behind Delville Wood was well constructed and was furnished with dugouts. These, they said, were only shrapnel proof. The prisoners told their interrogators that the morale of the German forces in this area was good.[62]

Prisoners captured later said that the German line near Delville Wood was poor. It had been badly knocked about by shellfire and was only five feet deep. The wire in front of the line was stretched between tree stumps and was about three feet high; it was between three and eight strands thick. In contrast, the state of the Flers Line was good and it was well provided with deep dugouts. One platoon of infantry held the front line and three platoons were held in reserve in the support trenches behind. The men were well provided with ammunition and Klugel grenades.[63] It was said that each gruppe had two hundred thousand rounds allotted to it and each man carried one hundred and fifty rounds. The 77mm guns of the German 29th Field Artillery were in position behind the Flers line. Two machine gun companies had eight guns in the line. Sometimes they were all in the front line, other times three were situated in dugouts in the support trenches. The gun teams could move position and set up

---

61 TNA: PRO WO 157/469. War Diary, XV Corps Intelligence Summaries, August 1916.

62 TNA: PRO WO 157/469. War Diary XV Corps Intelligence Summaries, August 1916.

63 The Klugel Grenade, model 1913, was a segmented iron ball with a brass fuse, once the fuse was ignited by pulling a loop, the black powder charge ignited about seven seconds later.

wherever they were needed.[64] The men were well provided with food but because of the shelling it came forward at irregular intervals. There was no fresh drinking water available but the troops had been issued with mineral water and coffee was plentiful. Iron rations were only to be consumed when they were needed.[65]

The German companies were reported to be at full strength but only 130 to 150 men from each company were available to defend the front line. The rest of the men were required to provide labour for the entrenching work that was going on in the Warlencourt – Gueudecourt line. The companies were made up of regulars, reservists and recruits, the youngest of which came from the 1915 class.[66]

8.00 am

Warning orders were received by the 8th South Staffords informing them that the 51st Brigade was to move forward from Buire at 6.00 pm. In the absence of anyone senior, the veteran Captain A. W. Farwell had assumed command of the battalion; such had been the officer casualties at Quadrangle Support Trench.

9.00 am

The 6th Dorsets arrived at Bellevue Farm and were given a grassless, dusty field as a bivouac area. Captain Mozley remembered that the battalion H.Q Mess was set up in an old gun pit, while he and the officers of A and B Companies managed to secure a dugout for their mess.[67] Those men without tents simply slept on the ground with their greatcoats as covers. They were to remain here for three days.

The 52nd Field Ambulance marched out of Dernancourt towards the front line. They followed the cross-country route through Meaulte,

---

64 But surely not carrying so much ammunition.

65 TNA: PRO WO 157/469. War Diary XV Corps Intelligence Summaries, August 1916.

66 TNA: PRO WO 157/469. War Diary XV Corps Intelligence Summaries, August 1916.

67 Imperial War Museum (IWM): Unpublished papers Captain B. C. Mozley, D.S.O. 01/48/1.

Fricourt and Mametz and headed for the Mametz-Montauban road. Meanwhile Major J. Ferguson, the commanding officer of the 51st Field Ambulance, travelled by motor car to the Divisional Casualty Collecting Station to take over the station from the 14th Field Ambulance of the 5th Division. The Quartermaster, Sergeant Major, Wardmasters and Dispensers travelled with him.

This Collecting Station consisted of a wood and canvas hut and two small marquees, which were all situated on a triangle of ground where the Fricourt – Albert Road and the Fricourt–Meaulte Road joined. It was surrounded by artillery wagon lines. Horses passed through the Station to get to the water troughs; this and the constant traffic on the roads made it a very dusty and busy spot. Water for the Station was drawn from tank-lorries in Becordel village twice a day and was scarce. Ten motor vehicles, all old civilian charabancs, were attached to the station to evacuate sitting cases to the 34th and 45th Casualty Clearing Stations at Vecquemont. The Advanced Dressing Station was on the Mametz–Montauban Road, which had an Advanced Collecting Post in the Caterpillar Ravine, another name for 'The Gully' or Caterpillar Valley. The personnel of the 52nd Field Ambulance manned both of these positions.

9.30 am

Having just arrived from their bivouac on the Amiens - Albert Road the 52nd Brigade Machine Gun Company assembled on ground next to a mine crater near Fricourt.

10.00 am

Carrying parties of the 52nd Brigade battalions were loaded up with bombs and stores to be taken to the front. The transports then moved off to an area one mile to the south west of Albert where they were placed under the command of the Brigade Transport officer. A 52nd Brigade camp was set up here for different battalion details and the Quartermaster's stores. Camps and horse lines for different units were everywhere.

In August 1916 Guy Chapman, an officer in the 13th Royal Fusiliers, was stationed in the transport lines in Happy Valley,[68] to the south east of Mametz Wood. He described the transport lines saying that the area seemed to hold millions of men and animals. The long lines of traffic raised dust clouds that turned to gold in the hot, summer sunlight. He described the place as a meeting place, a market place, the point where divisions met, going forwards and those going back.[69] This whole area, like other positions in the rear, invited intense interest from the German Air Service. Consequently the ground was steeped in tear gas and was often shelled.

Officers from the 9th Northumberlands and 9th Duke of Wellingtons, 52nd Brigade, went up to the front line to inspect the trenches that their men would eventually take over.

10.20 am

The 17th Division, so recently in heavy fighting, was in need of rest and re-organisation. This fact had not escaped the notice of the higher command. It was well known at Fourth Army H.Q that the Division was in a bad way, it had taken heavy casualties and the battalions had a number of untried troops and, as has been noted, some battalions were without their colonels. Fourth Army made it known to XV Corps H.Q that the 17th Division must soon come right out of the line in order to bring up a fresh division. Before this, the Division had more work to do. XV Corps H.Q informed 17th Division that they would probably have to take over Delville Wood and the trench running south of the wood on the night of 2/3 August.

11.00 am

Reports came in to Fourth Army H.Q from III Corps ground units saying that four German aircraft were cruising un-hindered over Mametz Wood, behind the British lines.

---

68 Happy Valley was also known as The Valley of Death and Death Valley. It lies north of Mametz Village, very near the site of Quadrangle Support Trench.

69 G. Chapman, *A Passionate Prodigality* (First published, Ivor Nicholson & Co, 1933. Reprinted, Ashford, Buchan & Enright, 1993) p. 106

There was nothing in the report about anti-aircraft guns engaging them or the Royal Flying Corps intercepting them. They were fired upon by machine guns but evidently that failed to discourage or even harm them because they remained over Mametz Wood for an hour. These aircraft were either spotting for their guns or photographing the British positions. The Tommies on the ground must have wondered where the R.F.C were. The notion that the air force was 'nowhere to be seen' was common to both sides. In his book *The Friendless Sky Alexander* McKee wrote that the German infantry in August 1916 on the Somme said, "the English were the only fliers they ever saw. *Where were the German air heroes?* demanded the German soldiers in letters home; were they perhaps at home, being decorated?"[70]

11.30 am

The 52nd Brigade's concentration area in and around Fricourt was being shelled and considering the proximity of Fricourt to Mametz Wood this was probably as a result of the prowling German aircraft. So in order to minimise casualties Brigadier-General Clarke ordered the 52nd Brigade Machine Gun Company and two battalions to move further back into a field a short way down the Fricourt Road.

Noon

Despite the shelling, Lieutenant-Colonel Cardew, not often concerned by hostile shelling, and his companions lunched briefly with Brigadier-General Hussey amid the ruins of Fricourt Village.[71] In the sky above, after an hour's un-interrupted and profitable work, the German machines peeled off and headed for their aerodrome, mission accomplished and with no loss. Considering the concentration of British troops and paraphernalia on the ground the aviators must have gained some very useful intelligence for their Generals.

---

70 A. McKee, *The Friendless Sky*, (First published, Souvenir Press, 1962. Re-printed, Nel Paperback, 1972), p. 62

71 IWM: Cardew 86/92/1.

It was a busy time for the 52nd Brigade Machine Gun Company. After moving as instructed, orders arrived concerning their part of the relief of the 15th Brigade, which was holding the line west of Delville Wood and Longueval Village and a portion of the line leading up to High Wood. The 52nd Brigade Machine Gun Company would relieve the 13th Brigade Machine Gun Company of 15th Brigade. The 52nd Brigade Machine Gun Company recorded that its machine guns were to be distributed as follows:

D Section was to be placed with the 9th Duke of Wellingtons on the right of the Brigade front. Number thirteen and fourteen guns under Second Lieutenant Mason were to go into Piccadilly Trench and Longueval Village. Number fifteen and sixteen guns under Second Lieutenant Moon were to be placed in the north west corner of Delville Wood.

C Section, under Lieutenant John Somerville Gowring, was to be placed with Major Westmacott's 9th Northumberlands on the left of the Brigade front. Number nine gun under Lance Corporal Frank Tradewell was to be set up on the left in the front line trench. Number ten and twelve guns under Sergeant Mayhew[72] were to be placed in Strong Point A. Number eleven gun under Corporal Barnes was put into Strong Point B. The four guns of B Section, under Second Lieutenant John King Michell, were to be in support in George Street. This trench was immediately in front of the old German second line. A Section, with four guns, under Second Lieutenant McInnes was to be held in reserve near the Company H.Q in Montauban Alley.

At the 17th Divisional Collecting Station on the busy junction of the Fricourt-Albert-Meaulte roads, Major Ferguson of the 51st Field Ambulance completed the admin work of the hand-over by formally taking responsibility for the Station's Admission and Discharge Book. All he needed now was his staff and transport. Meanwhile, their colleagues of the 52nd Field Ambulance arrived at the Mametz – Montauban road.

---

72 Very possibly Sergeant David J. Mayhew.

1.00 pm

During the day the 80th Brigade, R. F. A, moved from Dernancourt and headed for their new positions chosen for them by Cardew and his officers, in the valley south of Montauban. Similarly the 81st Brigade, R.F.A, left the rest area and proceeded to a new position south-west of the village of Montauban. The 81st Brigade, R.F.A, H.Q was to be set up in Pommiers Trench. The 79th Brigade, R.F. A, marched to the wagon lines near Meaulte and from there proceeded to the front line. They had orders to relieve the 166th Brigade, R.F.A, of the 33rd Division.

The main body of the 51st Field Ambulance, doctors, orderlies, bearers and other staff left camp and headed for the Divisional Collecting Station under the command of the Scotsman Captain Alfred David Gorman, M.D. A Section, a tent sub-division of the unit, had already set off for the Station under Captains Walker, M.D and Cotter, M.D.[73]

Shortly after lunchtime the R.F.C was busy. Spotting aircraft flew over the lines working closely with the gunners. With the aircrew's assistance twenty-five enemy targets were engaged, eighteen of which were enemy gun batteries. As usual enemy aircraft were also active over the lines. Nine German aircraft were seen flying very high over the front and the R.F.C did attempt to engage but only managed five inconclusive dogfights. One British machine was reported to have been hit by anti-aircraft fire and was seen by the troops at the front to fall from the summer sky.[74]

1.30 pm

The tent sub-division of A Section, the 51st Field Ambulance, under the command of Captains Walker and Cotter arrived at the 17th Divisional Collecting Station and began to erect their tents on the

---

73 Cotter would be Mentioned in Despatches on 28 November 1917.

74 The report does not say if the aircraft crashed or not. The only R.F.C casualty on the Western Front for this day was Captain William Assheton Summer, M.C, of 22 Squadron. That was a reconnaissance squadron and was operating over the Somme at this time. The Squadron flew FE2s an aeroplane which had a crew of two.

crowded, dusty ground. With the arrival of some of his staff the C.O of the 51st Field Ambulance could now officially take responsibility for any patients that were brought into the Collecting Station.

2.00 pm

By now the relief of the 15th and 95th Brigades, of the 5th Division by 52nd Brigade was under way.

The 52nd Field Ambulance took over the Advanced Dressing Station near the Mametz- Montauban road. Three doctors, Captains Daniel Dougal,[75] Bury, and Ballen, along with a bearer division went on from the Advanced Dressing Station to the bearer post in the Gully on the eastern end of Caterpillar Wood. Once there they sent squads of bearers to the aid posts in the quarry north of Montauban and in the sunken road that ran between Bazentin-le-Grand and Longueval. They now had a chain of medical facilities in place capable of moving casualties away from the fighting.

2.15 pm

Lieutenant-Colonel Cardew and his officers arrived back at Dernancourt after lunch with Brigadier-General Hussey at Fricourt. Still un-officially minding artillery affairs for the Division he did not go forward to catch up with his own artillery brigade. Instead he retired to his tent, read a couple of letters and ate a slice of cake. Afterwards he relaxed and wrote two letters home.[76]

2.20 pm

An advance party of the 8th South Staffords were sent forward to Pommiers Redoubt.

---

75 Dougal had been Mentioned in Despatches on 15 June 1916, he would later be promoted to Major and win the M.C.

76 IWM: Cardew 86/92/1.

2.30 pm

Ten minutes later the 9th Duke of Wellingtons moved out of the Pommiers Redoubt area, Lieutenant-Colonel Wannell went ahead of them with an advance party to take over the H.Q dugout at Longueval Village and the company commanders travelled independently of their companies. One company went ahead of the main body to take over the trench stores. The heat had increased and the men suffered as they marched, particularly those carrying heavy loads.

What remained of Longueval was burning when the advance party arrived to set up the battalion H.Q. Anything that was remotely flammable was on fire and the dugout allocated to them as H.Q was a burnt-out hole. Searching around the area the men found another one but it had to be cleared of corpses before it could be used. The two companies instructed to take over the front line moved into old trenches running south from the 'Quarry' and waited there for the guides to take them into the line.

When these guides from the 1st Norfolks arrived they proved to be useless because they had no clear idea where the front line actually was. Having said that, *no one* really knew where the front line was. For troops used to defined lines of trenches this was a novel and disturbing situation. The two companies of the 9th Duke of Wellingtons decided that they would try to find the 1st Norfolks, and the front line themselves and a search began through the shell holes and small, wrecked posts. The men of the Duke of Wellingtons did not know at the time but the 1st Norfolks were in a bad way, they had been in the thick of it and had lost some 429 men since 21 July. The Duke of Wellingtons' did finally get into position and contact was made with the battalions on the left, right and in support. Runners were exchanged between the battalions and a chain of orderlies was established that stretched back to 52nd Brigade H.Q in Montauban Alley.

The line that the 9th Duke of Wellingtons had taken over was roughly established along the edge of the wood, well clear of the village and posts had been pushed out clear of the wood, forward of the so-called established front line. Reconnaissance revealed that these posts were abandoned or blown in. They formed a line that was made up of hardly more than a series of shell holes that ran inside the wood. The actual front line was well behind this rough line and some distance from the edge of the wood. A patrol discovered that the front line of the battalion on the right was actually level with their support positions. Lieutenant-Colonel Wannell decided that it was impossible to refer to his positions as a front line. There were no real trenches, just a series of shell holes and scrapes dug by individual men wherever they were able.

The conditions that the troops found in the front lines were bad. Lieutenant William Norman Hoyte, a 10th Notts & Derbys man on the 51st Brigade staff, remembered that the front line was as bad as they had ever seen. Constantly active artillery had stopped any clearance of the battlefield and the corpses of men and animals lay unburied and rotting in the open air.[77] The stench, the fat flies and the filth was awful, all made worse by the very hot summer weather.[78]

3.00 pm

The sections of the 52nd Brigade Machine Gun Company moved off from their field near Fricourt to take up their allotted forward positions. The marching order was B Section, led by the commanding officer, Major Lintott, followed by D then C and A at half-hourly intervals. H.Q staff, under the command of the Sergeant Major, travelled with A section.

3.30 pm

Captain Gorman, M.D and the main body of the 51st Field Ambulance arrived at the Divisional Collecting Station.

---

77 Hilliard Atteridge mentioned that sometimes, rarely, un-official truces were arranged by both sides to bring in casualties and bury the dead. (See p. 155 of the Divisional History.) There were no such truces recorded by 17th Division units while the formation was in the line at Longueval and Delville Wood.

78 W.N. Hoyte, in M.T.F.J. McNeela, ed, 10th (S) Battalion *The Sherwood Foresters The History Of The Battalion During The Great War,* (First written, 1920s. Printed by Naval & Military Press, 2003), p. 18

4.00 pm

Before A Section of the 52nd Machine Gun Company could move, a bomb accidentally detonated in the field near Fricourt wounding a number of men. Lieutenant A. H. Killick, Private A. R. Press of the 52nd Machine Gun Company,[79] Privates T. Dodds and J. Pickles of the 9th Northumberlands, both of whom were attached to A Section, were all wounded, as was an unfortunate horse. It could have been that these men were putting detonators in hand grenades before going up to the line. Accidents with Mills Bombs were very common.

The transport of the 51st Field Ambulance arrived at the crowded 17th Divisional Collecting Station.

4.30 pm

The staff of 52nd Field Ambulance reported that they had completed the take over of all aid posts from the 15th Field Ambulance. They recorded that casualties were to be moved as follows: Bearer squads and wheeled stretchers would bring casualties from the front and the bearer post in the quarry north of Montauban to the bearer post in the 'Gully' at the eastern point of Caterpillar Wood. From here, horse ambulance wagons would carry them to a point on the Montauban Road where the Ford vans would pick them up and take them to the Advanced Dressing Station. Horse transport, quartermaster and four chaplains were left at the 52nd Brigade Transport Lines south-west of Albert under the command of Lieutenant Watson. Three horse ambulance wagons, two Ford Vans, four large carts and two water carts were stationed at the Advanced Dressing Station. One riding horse was evacuated from the front because it had been injured by a bomb on the journey to the front, possibly as it passed through the assembly area in the field near

---

[79] All four men recovered from their wounds. Lieutenant Killick and Private Press survived the war but so far it has not been possible to ascertain the fate of Privates Dodds and Pickles. Dodds may have joined the 1/8th D.L.I and been killed in action on 5 November 1916.

Fricourt Village. A small Wolsley van[80] and its driver were also evacuated but no reason was given why. Which of the two was defective was, sadly, not recorded.

4.45 pm

The 7th East Yorks received their orders to move forward to Bellevue Farm on the following day.

5.00 pm

The 9th Northumberlands, 52nd Brigade, moved into the neighbourhood of Pommiers Redoubt. They had orders to be ready to go forward from there and relieve the 15th Royal Warwicks in the front line.

Further back, the 7th Borders, 51st Brigade, marched from their bivouacs one mile north-west of Buire. They were under orders to proceed to Pommiers Redoubt. Two men were wounded as they marched.

6.00 pm

Elements of the 51st Brigade arrived at Pommiers Redoubt to relieve the 95th Brigade, 5th Division, after marching from Buire. The various units went into support in and around the Redoubt. The 7th Yorks and Lancs, the Divisional pioneers, left their camp on the slopes a mile north-west of Dernancourt and headed for Fricourt.

The Divisional artillery continued to deploy on the gun line. Having the whole area under observation and probably aware that a relief was underway their colleagues of the German artillery welcomed them with sustained fire. 81st Brigade, R.F.A, who had already deployed, reported that the Brigade area was shelled during the afternoon and that the shelling carried on into the night. The 78th Brigade, R.F.A, arrived from Dernancourt and took over positions in

---

80 The Wolseley Company was owned by Vickers & Sons and, among other road vehicles, built specialist vehicles for many different tasks. These were known by the name of 'Wolsely'.

front of Longueval from the 162nd Brigade, R.F.A. Two guns from B Battery were attached to A and C batteries so that they could operate tactically as two six gun batteries. 79th Brigade, R.F.A, began arriving at the gun line. Lieutenant-Colonel Cardew's 80th Brigade had by now arrived at the valley south of Montauban. They were given targets in and around Orchard Trench. It had been recently discovered that this trench had been recently dug and occupied by German troops.

After tea, Lieutenant-Colonel Cardew rode in his car to 17th Division H.Q at Bellevue Farm. Here, he was shown an order that greatly upset him; the 5th and 17th Divisional artillery were to be combined and placed under the command of Brigadier-General Hussey. After the duties that Cardew had performed during the day and on the previous day he, no doubt, thought that he was to be promoted to command the 17th Divisional Artillery. Later, in his diary, he put a brave face on things but his disappointment was evident. Upon leaving Bellevue Farm, where he accepted an invitation to dine at the 17th Divisional Artillery Mess, he motored straight to Fricourt and sought out Brigadier-General Hussey, C.R.A of the 5th Division, to find out what he knew about the proposed amalgamation. Brigadier-General Hussey appeared baffled and could not help Cardew; he had heard nothing but doubted that it was true. Lieutenant-Colonel Cardew then telephoned Brigadier-General Alexander to ask his opinion of the situation. Alexander told him that he, too, was doubtful that such an order had been issued.[81]

That evening, things became a little more confusing. Shortly after tea Major Sutton[82] was suddenly called away from the 78th Brigade, R.F.A, to take over temporary command of the 80th Brigade R.F.A, because it was without a commanding officer. It was understood at 78th Brigade, R.F.A, that Cardew had been called to Divisional H.Q to act as the temporary C.R.A.

---

81 IWM: Cardew 86/92/1.

82 This was probably Major Frederick Sutton, D.S.O, originally of the R.G.A and then B Battery, 81st Brigade R.F.A. He returned to the R.G.A during the war and was promoted to Lieutenant-Colonel.

6.15 pm

XV Corps sent a situation report to Fourth Army H.Q. The situation was unchanged; there was nothing to report.

6.20 pm

After travelling via the villages of Meaulte and Fricourt, the 8th South Staffords, now under the command of Captain C. H. Manger, began arriving at Pommiers Redoubt. Here they began to take over from the 1st East Surreys. It was recorded that the 52nd Brigade was in the line and the 51st Brigade was in support.

6.30 pm

The 10th Notts & Derbys moved off towards Pommiers Redoubt. Lessons had been learned from the first days of the campaign and only twenty officers went forward with the battalion, the rest were left behind at the Brigade depot near the town of Albert. The battalion had suffered a high number of officer casualties in the Quadrangles episode, and as noted earlier, was commanded at this time by the very capable Captain L. Gilbert.

XV Corps noted that the day had been fairly quiet. Longueval village was still burning that evening. Lieutenant-General Horne ordered that all commanders should improve their methods of signal communication. Also, when out of the line, the divisions should train in night operations, patrolling, following up barrages and practise the establishment of small forward posts.

During the evening aircraft of the German air service tried to cross the lines but were intercepted and driven back by aicraft of the R.F.C. One German machine tried to avoid the British aircraft by attempting to climb to 15,000 feet. Captain Andrews, R.F.C, managed to out climb the German machine attaining a reported 15,800 feet, at which point the German pilot gave up the contest and headed home, unmolested, in the direction of Cambrai.

7.00 pm

The 52nd Brigade H.Q moved forward and was set up in Montauban Alley trench.

At Bellevue Farm Lieutenant-Colonel Rowley and Captain Mozley took on Captain Geoffrey O'Hanlon and Lieutenant A. E. Barton[83] at Bridge after dinner. Mozley remembered that the game ended one rubber all.[84]

After his journey to Bellevue Farm and Fricourt, a baffled Lieutenant-Colonel Cardew drove home to Dernancourt. On his return he had a bath and then went straight bed. He was still unsure if he was going to be promoted or not.[85]

8.00 pm

The Anti-Aircraft unit reported to Fourth Army H.Q that since the previous evening they had seen fifty-one German aircraft, engaged sixteen and nine had crossed the British front line.

The five officers and 203 other ranks of the 93rd Field Company, R. E, were ordered to move into billets west of Mametz. The Sappers were to be billeted in captured, deep German dugouts but the transport had to go to Becordel because the area around Mametz was under shellfire.

The 79th Brigade, R.F.A, H.Q was established; the gun batteries were in the gun line and were coming under fire. Despite this the batteries began to fire registering rounds at Orchard Trench, north-west of Longueval village.

9.00 pm

The 79th Brigade, R.F.A, reported that the heavy German bombardment had ceased.

---

83 Barton would be promoted to Captain and Mentioned in Despatches on 25 May 1917.

84 IWM: Mozley 01/48/1.

85 IWM: Cardew 86/92/1.

10.00 pm

The 78th Field Company, R.E, took over dugouts from the Home Counties Field Company, Territorial Force. Their position was given as two hundred yards west of Mametz.

The German artillery shelled Longueval and what remained of the village continued to burn.

10.15 pm

The 7th Lincolns arrived at Pommiers Redoubt and Trench to relieve the 9th Northumberlands of the 52nd Brigade, who had been ordered into the front line to relieve the 15th Royal Warwicks. Major Metcalfe's 7th Lincolns had a fighting strength of thirty-two officers and nine hundred and fourteen other ranks. It had been reinforced while it was out of the line. Along with new men straight from training, 81 men of the draft had come from the Notts & Derbys and seven men had come from the North Staffords. Eight men had also gone sick.

10.30 pm

The 7th Yorks and Lancs arrived at Fricourt and went into bivouacs in the rubble and old trenches. Here Lieutenant-Colonel Byass set up his battalion H.Q. The 8th South Staffords completed the relief of the 1st East Surreys at Pommiers Redoubt. The night was spent collecting stores from various different dumps.

10.50 pm

Shortly after the 8th South Staffords completed their relief of the 1st East Surreys, the final elements of the 10th Notts & Derbys also arrived at Pommiers Redoubt. Their night was also spent collecting stores from the Divisional and Brigade dumps. Carrying parties were detailed to take the stores forward.

10.52 pm

Fourth Army H.Q, noting the movements of the formations under Lieutenant-General Horne's command, recorded that the 50th

Brigade, having moved from Dernancourt, had its H.Q at Bellevue Farm. The 52nd Brigade had its H.Q in Montauban Alley and the 51st Brigade had its H.Q at Pommiers Redoubt.

11.00 pm

The 52nd Machine Gun Company reported that all guns had got into position. Ominously, a short while later, Captain Cutting reported to Major Lintott that no trace could be found of the two machine guns that had been sent forward in the advance to Posts C and D. These were possibly number fifteen and sixteen guns under the command of Second Lieutenant Moon from D Section that had been sent to the north-west corner of Delville Wood. Captain Cutting told Lintott that, in his opinion, the gun crews had either been killed by shellfire or captured.

Having taken the sections to their forward positions, the 52nd Brigade Machine Gun Company transports, now under the command of the wounded Lieutenant Killick, reassembled at Fricourt. He had orders to lead the transports back to the 52nd Brigade depot. He soon realised that it was too dark to find the Brigade transport lines so the transport teams bivouacked at Bellevue Farm. 31172, Lance Corporal Hendry was wounded in the jaw and arm by shrapnel as he worked at the dump.

11.30 pm

The 93rd Field Company, R.E, completed their move to the villages of Mametz and Becordel. On arrival the men of number four section were sent to Bellevue Farm to work on dugouts.

The Divisional artillery brigades were heavily shelled all night. The noise of artillery fire from both sides was so loud that the men in the front line found it hard to hold a conversation; it was sometimes impossible to hear what the nearest man was saying.

Chapter Two: 2 August

The task for this day was to get in touch with the 13th Brigade of the 5th Division, which the 17th Division was relieving and who were supposed to be stationed in the Wood. But the situation was confused. Posts were isolated and the enemy was close at hand. Local features had been flattened, the smouldering village of Longueval, like many of the others on the battlefield, had been pulverised and reduced to rubble. There were problems with the new men and many were 'green'. The front line was just a series of shell holes and wrecked trenches. Men tried to repair them, shore them up or dig them deeper, fighting against hard ground and tangled tree roots. All the while they were under constant fire. The British advanced posts that had been set up caused a problem for the Royal Artillery gunners because these posts were very close to the enemy and were in danger of being shelled by British guns. The exposed posts could only be withdrawn at night.

1.00 am

Fourth Army H.Q received a report that the German artillery was dropping a gas bombardment on British artillery positions between the Hammer Head, a part of Mametz Wood, and Bazentin-le-Grand. The gunners were forced to don their gas respirators and often had to take cover, seriously hampering their ability to fire back or carry on with their firing schedules.

An officer in a Heavy Artillery Battery in the area at the same time, wrote about a night gas bombardment on positions near his gun line in August 1916. It was eerie he said to see the gun crews working while wearing their gas respirators. They were slow moving, like fiends and demons, ghostly in the gloom. Verbal commands were useless so orders were given by notes scribbled on pads, illuminated by flashlight, or simple pointing gestures by "hooded monsters of the Inquisition."[86]

---

[86] B. Assher, *A Nomad Under Arms*, (H. F. & G. Witherby, 1931), p. 147 The name of the author, Ben Assher, is a pseudonym.

1.05 am

Major Westmacott of the 9th Northumberlands reported to 52nd Brigade H.Q that his men had completed the relief of the 15th Royal Warwicks. He now had A Company in Pear Street, B Company in Pont Street, C Company in reserve and D Company was on the left of A Company to the right of the 1/5th Seaforth Highlanders. The 1/5th Seaforths, of 152nd Brigade the 51st (Highland) Division were in the forward trenches at High Wood. The bombers of the 9th Northumberlands were held in reserve with C Company.

Four Vickers guns of C Section, the 52nd Brigade Machine Gun Company, were in the line and two Stokes guns of the 52nd Trench Mortar Battery were being kept in reserve. Three men were wounded during the relief and the lines were shelled intermittently but the day was generally quiet. Eleven men "were accidentally wounded by (the) explosion of a German trench mortar detonator."[87]

2.00 am

The Germans ceased the gas bombardment on the Hammer Head and Bazentin-le-Grand area.

3.00 am

The 52nd Brigade reported to 17th Division that the relief of 15th and 95th Brigades was complete and that Brigadier-General Clarke was now in command of the sector. The report went on to say that the situation was very confused all along the front line so patrols had been sent out to try and clarify matters.

---

87 TNA: PRO WO95/2013. War Diary 9th Northumberland Fusiliers, August 1916. This was possibly an attempt to get a souvenir that went wrong. Fuse caps, German helmets, bayonets and all other sorts of paraphernalia were popular with the Tommies. Nothing has changed, these are still popular collector's pieces today.

3.20 am

Lieutenant-Colonel Wannell reported to Brigadier-General Clarke that his battalion was in position in the front line. Patrols had returned and informed Wannell that the advanced posts C, D and E had been occupied by the enemy.[88] The patrols had had a difficult time because the area had been heavily shelled. In his report, Lieutenant-Colonel Wannell said that the ground was badly cut up and, because of the state of the so called front line, he had no doubt about his men's ability to hold it if the enemy attacked. In his opinion the German infantry would have a difficult time trying to make any kind of cohesive advance over the broken ground.

He reported the tactical situation as follows. The 9th Northumberlands were on his left up to post B; the 9th Duke of Wellingtons held the line with four Vickers guns and three platoons. One platoon was stationed in a slit trench that connected with Pont Street. Two companies were placed in trenches nearby; one company was stationed in Church Street. The battalion bombers were in Piccadilly along with the Stokes mortars. The 9th Duke of Wellingtons were connected to the right hand battalion, the 22nd Royal Fusiliers, by a series of posts and Lewis gun positions but there was a gap of forty yards between these two battalions. It had been reported to battalion headquarters that there was an advanced post still manned by men of the 1st Norfolks. Brigadier-General Clarke was informed that a patrol had been sent out to find this post. Arrangements had been made with the 9th Northumberlands on the left for patrolling between the two battalions.

3.30 am

A draft of thirty-seven N.C.O's and men joined the 7th East Yorks at the camp near Dernancourt.

---

88 Posts C and D had been manned by gun teams of the 52nd Brigade Machine Gun Company and they had gone missing. They must have been captured or killed before these posts were occupied by the German troops.

4.00 am

The German artillery ceased shelling Longueval but the village continued to burn.

4.30 am

At Dernancourt reveille blew for the 7th East Yorks. The battalions of the 50th Brigade were to prepare to move forward to the line.

At the Divisional Collecting Station the 51st Field Ambulance reported that, as far as casualties were concerned, it had been a quiet night. The men were given orders to spend the day cleaning up their camp and to move the cookhouse; the doctors organised their shifts. Captain Walker took the day duty and Captain Cotter took the night duty.

A number of men from the 7th Yorks and Lancs, the Pioneers, left Fricourt for work in the front line. They had orders to work on a communication trench that was to run from Montauban to Longueval and it was to be the main communication trench for the area. Reliefs moving over the open were under observation and were regularly shelled. The new trench was needed so that troops could travel to and from the front line in a degree of safety. The whole area was littered with corpses, dead animals and the wreckage of transport. The trench crossed the valley between Montauban and Longueval. This area was known to the troops as "Death Valley". The work was divided up between the sections and C Company remained at Fricourt as the divisional reserve.

5.00 am

Having been given half an hour to wake up and get ready for the day the men of the 7th East Yorks went to breakfast. An hour later in the misty summer morning they paraded at Dernancourt and then began the march to Bellevue Farm.

The transport of the 52nd Brigade Machine Gun Corps left Bellevue Farm for the 52nd Brigade Transport Lines. Lieutenant Killick had orders to report to Major Percy Reginald Owen Abel Simner[89] of the 9th Duke of Wellingtons, the O.C of the 52nd Brigade depot. Simner, like Wannell, had been with the battalion since they had come out to France on 15 July 1915 and he was probably the 2 i/c.

6.15 am

The 7th Yorks marched out of Dernancourt to Bellevue Farm and following 17th Division's orders, they left their tents behind. Lieutenant-Colonel Ronald D'Arcy Fife, the battalion commander, [90] was not particularly pleased about this.

6.35 am

The 10th West Yorks paraded at Dernancourt and then began the three-mile march to Bellevue Farm.

7.00 am

The 93rd Field Company, R.E, reported that numbers one and three sections were working on a bomb dump for the 52nd Brigade and the 80th Brigade, R.F.A. Number two section was at the disposal of the 52nd Brigade. During the course of the morning four men were wounded by shellfire.

---

89 By December 1917 Major Simner had become the Lieutenant-Colonel of the 9th Duke of Wellingtons and had earned the D.S.O. He had also been Mentioned in Despatches three times, on 16 June 1916, 4 January 1917 and 18 December 1917. He survived the war to live at 7, Prince of Wales Terrace, Kensington, London.

90 The second son of William Henry and Caroline Jane Fife of Lee Hall, Northumberland. He joined the Yorkshire Regiment in 1887 and retired from the army in 1913. He was recalled with the rank of major and then given command of the 7th Yorks, rising to Lieutenant-Colonel. He was wounded and deafened in 1917, did not properly recover and he had to retire. He 'did his bit' in World War Two, serving as a private in a Home Guard unit that was commanded by his own gamekeeper. He died in 1946. The personal diary of Lieutenant-Colonel Ronald D'Arcy Fife, C.M.G., D.S.O. Courtesy of The National Trust and The Green Howards Museum, Yorkshire.

Following the rest of the 50th Brigade, the 50th Machine Gun Company marched away from their bivouac area at Dernancourt and headed for Bellevue Farm.

7.30 am

The 7th East Yorks arrived at Bellevue Farm, closely followed by the 7th Yorks. As each unit arrived at Bellevue Farm they set up a camp; though in the case of the 7th Yorks that was not easy as their tents were back at Dernancourt. A further draft of one corporal and forty-two men joined the 7th Yorks at Bellevue Farm and the new men were distributed between the companies. This draft had come from the Green Howards' 4th Territorial battalion and Lieutenant-Colonel Fife was very pleased with them. They were physically fit and, importantly to the regionally raised battalions of this time, they were Yorkshiremen.[91]

8.05 am

On arrival at Bellevue Farm the 10th West Yorks were given a field on the south side of the farm for a bivouac. Nearby A and B Companies of the 6th Dorsets attended to their physical training as the columns of 50th Brigade Infantry marched into the camp.[92]

8.30 am

An hour after their arrival at Bellevue Farm the 7th East Yorks began to set up a bivouac in their allotted field. Bellevue Farm and its surrounding area was by now a very busy place.

Sergeants 3752 Somerset and 15045 Andrews arrived from the base and were sent forward to rejoin the 52nd Machine Gun Company in the trenches.

Sergeant Healy and two men of the 13th Brigade Machine Gun Company arrived at 52nd Brigade Machine Gun Company H.Q in Montauban Alley and handed over a machine gun and tripod that

---

91 Personal diary of Lieutenant-Colonel Fife.

92 IWM: Mozley 01/48/1.

they had found abandoned near Post C. This could have been one of the guns that had gone missing on the previous day; interestingly they made no mention of Post C being occupied by German troops. This done, Sergeant Healy and his men joined up with Sergeant Pollard and other men of the 13th Machine Gun Company who had also been relieved and set off to rejoin their unit. Both Sergeants were completely oblivious to the fact that they were leaving two machine gun teams behind. During the morning Major Lintott, C.O of the 52nd Brigade Machine Gun Company, visited his company dump and his gun crews in the line.

9.00 am

Lieutenant-Colonel Cardew arrived at Bellevue Farm in his car and found that he was to report to 17th Divisional H.Q. He duly reported and, to his delight, he was informed that he was to take command, albeit temporarily, of the Divisional artillery. This situation, at least, had been sorted out.

Lieutenant-Colonel Fife was ordered by 17th Division H.Q to send a lorry and a party of men to bring their tents back from Dernancourt. The party returned later with the bad news that another brigade had occupied their tents and refused to hand them over. Lieutenant-Colonel Fife was unsurprised. Later, he walked over to captured German trenches beyond Becourt Wood to have a look around. The area was occupied by heavy guns and howitzers.[93]

10.00 am

The misty morning cleared and the weather was again hot. A light wind blew from the north and some cloud bubbled up. Major-General Stephens of 5th Division gave Major-General Robertson of 17th Division a situation report. The line was said to extend along Pont Street to Duke Street then across Piccadilly to Delville Wood. Posts were 'believed to be' strung out in a line at A) the junction of the trenches in Pear Street, B) the junction of Pear Street and Wood Lane, C) out in front of Wood Lane, D) in North Street, and E) at

---

93 Personal diary of Lieutenant-Colonel Fife.

the corner of Orchard Trench. Maps showed post E out in front of Orchard Trench.

The relief of 5th Division by 17th Division was now complete. The front line posts were apparently taken over and command of the line was officially handed from Major-General Stephens to Major-General Robertson. The staff at 17th Division H.Q noted that posts A and B were relieved with no problem but apparently C, D and E posts were found to be unoccupied by the 15th Brigade and were not taken over by 52nd Brigade. Furthermore, it was recorded in the 17th Division diary that "Posts C, D and E had apparently never been established."[94] Which begs the question what had happened to the two missing machine gun teams? Had they set up elsewhere? What was written in the 17th Division diary is slightly at odds with the situation that the 9th Duke of Wellingtons had reported earlier. They had said that posts C, D and E were occupied by the enemy and not held by the British.[95]

The Divisional artillery was now in position in the gun line and the gunners set about registering their guns. The 81st Brigade, R.F.A, recorded that their target zone was along Orchard Trench and on to Delville Wood. This artillery unit was covering the front of the 52nd Brigade, which held Pear Trench and Longueval village. The Brigade bombarded Orchard Trench and then searched the countryside behind it throughout the day and night.

Orders from XV Corps arrived at 17th Division H.Q. Major-General Robertson was told that his Division was

> *To relieve the left of XIII Corps up to its Eastern boundary on night 4th/5th Aug. The new front of the 17th Div from that date to extend from a point about 200 yards South of DELVILLE WOOD round DELVILLE WOOD to junction of roads S.10.d.8.8 on left.*[96]

Efforts were made, by the 9th Northumberlands and the 9th Duke of Wellingtons throughout the day, to find out what the situation was south of Orchard Trench and on the north western edge of Delville Wood. It was a difficult and dangerous task; German machine gun

---

94 TNA: PRO WO 95/1981. War Diary 17th Division, August 1916

95 See 3.20 am entry.

96 TNA: PRO WO 95/1981. War Diary 17th Division, August 1916

fire and shelling made movement almost impossible. Even the rations, coming up from the rear, could only be got up to the line with extreme difficulty.

There was some considerable doubt in the minds the staff of the 17th Division as to the actual position of the forward posts. To make matters worse the news that German troops had dug and occupied Orchard Trench had only recently arrived at H.Q. Indeed, the trench had been given to the 80th Brigade, R.F.A., as a target the previous evening. That the trench had been dug and occupied by the enemy was considered by the 17th Division staff to be the principal cause for the 5th Division's failure to attack on the night of 30/31 July. It was a nasty surprise; all of Delville Wood had been thought to be free of the enemy, this trench ran along the north-western edge of the wood near the Flers Road. The situation in Orchard Trench would have to be cleared up. Meaning, bluntly, that the enemy had to be ejected and the trench taken. This trench was to become an objective for the 17th Division during this tour of duty.

A derelict armoured cable had been found by the 17th Signal Company in Montauban Alley trench and the signallers brought it back into use between Pommiers Redoubt and 52nd Brigade H.Q, which was situated in a dugout in Montauban Alley Trench. The cable was then adapted and added to in order to improve communications to the units in the front line.

10.40 am

Major-General Robertson reported to Lieutenant-General Horne at XV Corps H.Q that he had assumed command of the front formerly held by 5th Division. This information was passed on to Fourth Army and the staff there duly recorded the change of command between 5th and 17th Divisions at 11.05 am.

11.14 am

Lieutenant-General Horne had been told that the 17th Division was out of contact with the 2nd Division on the right. That division was under the command of XIII Corps, so Horne contacted Lieutenant-General Sir Walter Norris Congreve at XIII Corps H.Q and made him aware of the lack of contact. Horne told Congreve that the 17th

Division were patrolling to try and make contact and requested that XIII Corps order the 2nd Division to do the same.

12 Noon

As shells fell and exploded about a mile away in Albert, the men of the 7th East Yorks completed making their bivouacs at Bellevue Farm.

Brigadier-General Alexander arrived at Bellevue farm to visit Lieutenant-Colonel Cardew. Alexander told Cardew that it had largely been his idea that Cardew should take over the 17th Division artillery because he wanted the Lieutenant-Colonel to "have a show". The burden of higher command soon made itself felt to Cardew as he settled down to a pile of office work. Later he had a series of meetings with Colonel Collins and Major-General Robertson.[97]

During the afternoon Major Lintott of the 52nd Brigade Machine Gun Company visited his guns in the Longueval Sector. These guns and the positions in Piccadilly were heavily shelled and C Section had two guns put out of action with damaged barrels. The machine gunners always had spares available because barrels needed changing after firing about 18,000 rounds[98] so they were swiftly replaced.

2.10 pm

Brigadier-General Clarke at 52nd Brigade H.Q sent a warning order to the 9th Duke of Wellingtons and the 9th Northumberlands. They were to prepare for an attack on Orchard Trench on the night of 3/4 August. The 9th Northumberlands would attack on the left and the 9th Duke of Wellingtons on the right. The enemy had to be cleared out of Orchard Trench and only then would Delville Wood be completely in British hands. Or so it was thought at the time.

---

97 IWM: Cardew 86/92/1.

98 G. Coppard, *With a Machine Gun to Cambrai.* (Originally published, H.M.S.O, 1968. Re-printed, Cassell Military Paperbacks, 1999), p.48

3.15 pm

The 8th South Staffords reported that the ground around Pozieres and High Wood, on their left, was being heavily shelled.

4.15 pm

The artillery of both sides struggled for supremacy and consequently counter-battery fire was heavy all along XV Corps front. In order to deal with the threat that the German guns posed General Rawlinson had informed Lieutenant-General Horne that the guns must fire at full intensity even during the lull in infantry action. It would be a tough task for the gunners. Orders were passed to the batteries giving details for night firing. The batteries covering the 17th Division were ordered to prepare for a bombardment prior to the attack on Orchard Trench. At his H.Q, Lieutenant-General Horne, a gunner by trade, concluded that if he had two more 60-pounder howitzer batteries his counter-battery fire would be far more effective.

4.40 pm

R.F.C machines had been up all day co-operating with the guns. Today twenty-two targets were observed and engaged, seven of which were German gun batteries. Enemy aircraft were reported to be less active than on the previous day. Ten machines had crossed the lines but the R.F.C had only managed two inconclusive dogfights. Crews of reconnaissance machines had reported that fires were burning in Longueval, Combles, Le Transloy and Morval. One R.F.C crew reported seeing a series of big explosions to the south-west of Combles.

5.00 pm

Major Lintott of the 52nd Brigade Machine Gun Company returned to his H.Q in Montauban Alley after visiting his guns in and around Longueval. There he found two hungry, thirsty and exhausted machine gunners waiting for him. Lance Corporals Cotteral and McInnes of the 13th Machine Gun Company had come in from their post out in front of the 17th Division's line. Presumably the two men had passed through the front line and been directed to the 52nd

Machine Gun Company H.Q. Cotteral and McInnes reported that two 13th Machine Gun Company weapons, under the command of Sergeant Potter, were still in an isolated position out in front of the north-west corner of Delville Wood. The crews had had no water or rations for three days.

On hearing their report Major Lintott wasted no time and ordered that rations and water should be sent forward immediately to these gun crews. He then ordered that two crews of Second Lieutenant Mason's A Section, under Sergeant Somerset and Corporal Lee, go forward, relieve the crews and take over the guns. The guns would now come under Mason's command. Aware of the confused nature of this part of the front line Major Lintott contacted Lieutenant-Colonel Wannell of the 9th Duke of Wellingtons and *demanded* an escort of bombers for his two gun teams as they went forward. Then he contacted the C.O of the 13th Machine Gun Company and told him about his waifs and strays. Lance Corporals Cotteral and McInnes went with Sergeant Somerset's men to act as guides. The 9th Duke of Wellingtons sent a situation report to Brigade H.Q. On receiving this message, Brigadier-General Clarke decided to go to the 52nd Brigade Machine Gun Company H.Q and personally interview the N.C.Os of the two gun teams. He also informed divisional H.Q.

5.02 pm

XV Corps contacted Fourth Army H.Q and reported that counter-battery fire was heavy on its front. Having warmed to his plan to obtain some more heavy weapons Lieutenant-General Horne asked General Rawlinson if two more 60-pounder howitzer batteries could be made available to him so that the German guns could be more effectively dealt with.

5.30 pm

Having spent the day registering their guns, the 78th Brigade, R.F.A, began to bombard the enemy front line. Following orders each gun fired one round every two minutes. All batteries of the 79th Brigade, R.F.A., carried out a bombardment of Orchard Trench. Sergeant Downing of A battery and Gunner H. Reid of B battery were wounded by the counter-battery fire that came their way. The 80th Brigade, R.F.A., also began to bombard Orchard Trench.

6.00 pm.

The 17th Division H.Q received the message from 52nd Brigade H.Q. Brigadier-General Clarke told Major-General Robertson about the two machine gun detachments from 13th Brigade, 5th Division, who had just been located in positions just north of the Flers road. They had been cut off from their formation for three days without food or water. These men were at once relieved and as an extra precaution the 52nd Brigade had set up a Lewis gun post near the two Vickers Gun posts.

After a series of meetings held throughout the day and a tour of the front line positions the Commanding Officers of the four 51st Brigade battalions, Major Irwin, Major Metcalfe, Captain Manger and Captain Gilbert, met at 51st Brigade headquarters in Pommiers Redoubt for a conference with their G.O.C, Brigadier-General G. F. Trotter and the Divisional commander, Major-General Robertson.

Pommiers Redoubt had been 'lightly' shelled during the day At this time the redoubt was always under fire and reports were made referring to light or heavy shelling in much the same way as rain fall would be reported. Two men of the 7th Borders had been killed and another wounded. Even though their deaths were recorded as 3 August[99] these men were more than likely Privates, 14925, Frederick Carr and 12845, John Stainton.[100]

Lieutenant-Colonel Fife and Captain Ronald Egerton Cotton[101] walked over to Fricourt to have a look at the positions that the 17th Division had attacked a few, short weeks ago. They concluded that the attacks here had been hopeless from the outset.[102]

---

99 The records do not show any casualties for the 7th Borders on this day. The records are probably wrong.

100 They are buried side by side in Dantzig Alley Cemetery.

101 Cotton had been mentioned in despatches on 13 June 1916. He would later be promoted to Major and be mentioned in despatches again in 1917. By the end of the war he had risen to the rank of Lieutenant-Colonel and after the war he went to live in Argentina.

102 Personal diary of Lieutenant-Colonel Fife.

6.30 pm

Brigadier-General Clarke at 52nd Brigade H.Q dugout in Montauban Alley received a situation report from Major Westmacott of the 9th Northumberlands.

7.00 pm

The 78th Brigade, R.F.A., ceased fire upon the German front line. The Germans promptly began to shell the batteries and the 78th Brigade H.Q.

7.20 pm

General Rawlinson contacted the G.O.Cs of III, X, XIII and XV Corps with a rebuke. It was not considered good enough, he said, to just report 'situation normal' as these reports made it difficult for him to realise the situation at the front. The reports should, in future, at least give some idea of the intensity of the German artillery fire. At the time General Haig was not particularly pleased with the speed at which information filtered back from the Divisions, to Corps, to Army and to him. The quality of the information would have been just as important to him as the speed at which it arrived.[103]

7.23 pm

The Anti-Aircraft unit reported that since the previous evening 117 enemy aircraft had been spotted. Thirty-five had been engaged and ten had crossed the British front line.

7.30 pm

Sergeant Greaves of the 52nd Brigade Machine Gun Company led a ration carrying party up to the guns in the front line. He had been wounded in the back when a shell landed at H.Q. A mule was also badly wounded.

---

103 See Sheffield & Bourne, *Douglas Haig War Diaries and Letters 1914 – 1918*, p. 220

As soon as the 80th Brigade, R.F.A, ceased fire on Orchard Trench the German guns immediately engaged the Brigade with counter-battery fire.

7.45 pm

The 52nd Brigade sent a situation report to Major-General Robertson at 17th Division H.Q.

All day working parties of the 10th Notts & Derbys had continued to carry stores forward from the Divisional and Brigade dumps. On this day Medical Officer Captain L.D. 'Doc' Saunders, left the battalion to take up the command of an Ambulance Train. Captain T.D. Cumberland, R.A.M.C, arrived that day to replace him. Saunders had been with the battalion since it had been raised and was very popular with the men and officers. Lieutenant Hoyte wrote "A few men who had tried the difficult path of the malingerer had cause to fear him, but to all ranks he was the 'good old Doc'…"[104] Lance Corporal Eric Harlow, a stretcher bearer in the 10th Battalion, remembered how 'Doc' Saunders asked him to go with him to serve as his personal orderly. Saunders rated Harlow very highly; the two men had become firm friends during the Battle for The Bluff in the Ypres Salient in February.[105] Working in the regimental aid post Saunders witnessed how on his own initiative, time and again, hour after hour, Harlow had led the stretcher-bearers out into the fighting to bring casualties in. Unknown to Harlow until later, Saunders put him up for a D.C.M., but it was turned down. Instead he was awarded the M.M, when it was introduced. Harlow heartily agreed that he should have been turned down for the D.C.M, and was genuinely baffled as to why he should have received the M.M.[106]

---

104 Hoyte, in McNeela, *10th (S) Battalion The Sherwood Foresters,* p. 18

105 That an officer and an N.C.O should be firm friends may sound impossible but these two men worked closely together in the Regimental Aid Post and were always in the thick of the fighting, where they were needed. They would have got to know each other well and in the fight to save lives niceties of rank were probably, out of necessity, put aside. Harlow and Saunders remained lifelong friends and regularly visited each other after the war. Saunders was often called to be an expert witness by the N. S. P. C. C in child abuse cases.

106 Imperial War Museum (IWM): Unpublished papers, Corporal E. H. Harlow, M.M. 03/44/1.

The offer to go with Saunders was tempting; such a move would mean that he could leave the trenches behind for some time, if not permanently. Lance Corporal Harlow was an articulate, intelligent and well-educated man; he thought long and hard about the offer. Finally he opted to remain with the battalion, deciding that he could not leave his comrades behind; nor could he turn his back on the job that he had volunteered to do. It was not the only opportunity that came his way this month. Officer casualties had been high and men from the ranks were being encouraged to volunteer for a commission. Battalion commanders were instructed to find likely lads to volunteer and Gilbert would have known that Harlow had what it took to be an officer so Harlow was invited to volunteer. He was an old soldier now, an original Kitchener Volunteer who had been with the battalion since early 1915, Harlow turned the job down. He said at the time that he was probably being a fool but he did not want a commission; he knew that an officer's job was not an easy one.[107] Two of his friends from the early days had already gone to be officers; one Charles Crowther Hart[108] had become an officer in early 1915. Another, his great friend and mentor, Sergeant Gimson[109] had gone off quite recently. Later on, Harlow was promoted to Corporal.

Meanwhile, Pommiers Redoubt and the surrounding area were shelled and four men of the 10th Notts & Derbys were slightly wounded. The shelling extended back into Pommiers Trench where the 7th Lincolns were stationed; they had one man wounded.

8.00 pm

17th Division issued a warning order to 52nd Brigade H.Q telling them to be prepared to launch an attack on Orchard Trench on the night of 3/4 August. It is not immediately clear if XV Corps ordered this attack or if it was ordered by Major-General Robertson at divisional level. It bears all the hallmarks of the type of operation

107 IWM: Harlow, 03/44/1.

108 Hart became a lieutenant in the Duke of Wellingtons and was attached to the King's African Rifles. He was killed in action in Africa in November 1917.

109 Sergeant Gimson became a captain in the King's Own Yorkshire Light Infantry and was attached to the 61st Trench Mortar Battery. He was killed in action on the Western Front in August 1917.

ordered by Lieutenant-General Horne in July but, curiously, there is no mention of it in the XV Corps war diary until *after* the event. The Fourth Army war diary mentions the operation after it had happened but only refers to it as an "enterprise",[110] leading one to think that it may have been an opportunistic, but sanctioned at higher level, operation by the 17th Division.

The 78th Brigade, R.F.A., began to shell the area immediately behind the German front line. They maintained a slow, sweeping, rate of fire. The German counter-battery work continued.

The 52nd Field Ambulance recorded that the collection of casualties proceeded normally. By this time six officers and 165 other ranks had passed through the Advanced Dressing Station.

The 17th Division reported to XV Corps that German troops had been seen moving around in Delville Wood and that they had been engaged by Lewis gunners. This event was not recorded in the XV Corps diary but was recorded in the Fourth Army diary on the following day.[111] It could have been very important and maybe more notice should have been taken of the report by XV Corps, particularly in view of matters that were to arise concerning German troops in Delville Wood a few days later.

8.10 pm

Probably mindful of the earlier rebuke about situation reports from General Rawlinson, Lieutenant-General Horne sent a *full* report to Fourth Army H.Q.

8.15 pm

The 9th Duke of Wellingtons reported to 52nd Brigade H.Q that German units were definitely operating in Delville Wood; they also passed this information on the 22nd Royal Fusiliers of 99th Brigade, 2nd Division. The 2nd Divisional staff knew about the German presence but the report from the Duke of Wellingtons supported their own report sent to XV Corps H.Q, 15 minutes earlier. At the

---

110 TNA: PRO WO 95/431. War Diary, Fourth Army Headquarters, August 1916.

111 TNA: PRO WO 95/431. War Diary, Fourth Army Headquarters, August 1916.

time it was believed that German troops had no positions inside the boundary of the wood. The nearest known German trench was the recently dug Orchard Trench, on the edge of the wood.

8.53 pm

Pommiers Redoubt was *slightly* shelled.

10.10 pm

The 52nd Brigade issued orders to the 9th Northumberlands and the 9th Duke of Wellingtons for the forthcoming attack on Orchard Trench. The warning order concerning the attack had been issued at 2.10 that afternoon.

11.00 pm

Fourth Army H.Q contacted XV Corps and said that a prisoner, taken by the French just north of the Somme River, had told Intelligence Officers that the Germans were going to launch a gas attack on the following day. The exact location of this attack had not been specified so all Corps on the Somme battlefield were alerted. The words of one man put the entire Allied force on the Somme on edge.

11.30 pm

Major Westmacott of the 9th Northumberlands received more detailed orders for the attack on Orchard Trench. The attack, along with the 9th Duke of Wellingtons, was to begin early on the morning of 4 August. In what was loosely termed the front line, the 9th Northumberlands began to make arrangements and plans for their attack.

Lieutenant-Colonel Cardew, C.R.A, 17th Division, finally managed to prise himself out of his office at Bellevue Farm and went to his tent. To the thunderous background din of British and German artillery, pounding away in the hot, stuffy night, Cardew settled down to write two letters and his diary. Albert town had been shelled again during the evening and he noted that his 80th Brigade had been shelled and suffered some casualties. As part of his new role he was working very closely with the Divisional staff and Cardew wrote that he found Major-General Robertson and Colonel Collins the G.S.O.1, very friendly and pleasant. The telephones were not working well, he noted and that was causing problems for communication with the divisional artillery brigades covering the front line. On the bright, side his mail had found him. Cardew wrote with satisfaction that he had two letters and a parcel of socks.[112]

In the front line, the 9th Northumberlands continued with their preparations for the attack on the morning of 4 August. Very soon, shells were landing all around them and the battalion started to take casualties. Second Lieutenant E. Howes was killed and Second Lieutenant R. E. Ramsbottom was wounded by the bombardment.

Midnight

Sergeant Potter of the 13th Machine Gun Company reported to Major Lintott at the 52nd Machine Gun Company H.Q in Montauban Alley. He brought with him his command of Lance Corporals Cotteral and McInnes and five other men. Sergeant Somerset and Corporal Lee's machine gunners had found the lost machine gunners and given them food and water. Then, after their first food for three days, Potter's men had handed their machine guns over to Sergeant Somerset's command and made their weary way, through the shellfire, back to Montauban Alley. Potter and his men were completely exhausted but transport was being sent for the privates so they settled down to wait. Potter, Cotteral and McInnes were to be detained a little longer. Brigadier-General Clarke was to interview them personally on the following day.

---

112 IWM: Cardew 86/92/1.

Chapter Three: 3 August

Various parties of infantrymen either worked through the night or went to work in the early morning. The continual artillery fire smashed trenches and dugouts. Trenches had to be dug, re-dug, repaired and fortified. Communications had to be established, re-established and continually repaired. As usual, the infantry had to provide the labour for the Signallers and the Royal Engineers. This often very hard, physical work was extremely unpopular with men either fresh from the fighting or just about to go into the fighting. Sometimes company and platoon commanders simply ignored requests for men to go and labour. For second lieutenants to ignore such orders they must have had, at least, the tacit support of their company and battalion commanders.

The 17th Signal Company made communication arrangements for when the 17th Division extended the right flank to take over from the left hand brigade of XIII Corps. Lines were laid from test points in front of Montauban Alley back, by two routes, to Pommiers Redoubt. One of these routes was another disused, armoured cable. It only ran a quarter of the way to Pommiers Redoubt and had to be lengthened and completed by the signallers. Lines were laid to the two battalions in the front line and there was a precarious junction in the communication line that needed attention. It was noted in their diary that when the 17th Signal Company took over communications in this sector there were no forward telegraph communications available.[113]

The 77th Field Company, R.E reported that they began work on a communication trench and the support line. Sections 1 and 3 of the 78th Field Company, R.E began work upon a Signal Post and look out. This was specifically for visual signalling between Longueval and Montauban. The post had to have a twelve foot nine inch double roof of steel; it was to be eleven feet below the surface with five-foot headroom inside. Steps had to be made up to the observation post at one end and an exit was required at the other. Seventy five percent of the excavation work had already been done

---

113 TNA: PRO WO 95/1994. War Diary 17th Signal Company, August 1916

and the frames and roof material were at the site. Number 2 section of the 78th Field Company, Royal Engineers, was put to work extending the first aid dugout on the Mametz – Montauban Road. The men of B Company, the 10th Notts & Derbys were detailed to work on a forward communication trench. Captain Wheeley was slightly wounded but he remained at duty.

The 93rd Field Company, R.E, reported that the work of the previous day carried on. They noted that the weather was extremely hot and many of the men in the company were suffering from diarrhoea. In many places dead men and animals were left where they lay, expanding and going black in the sun and heat, covered by swarming flies. Captain Guy Chapman of the 13th Royal Fusiliers said that there was a good deal of sickness in the transport lines. In his unit four out of five officers actually went sick with dysentery after a few days of arriving at the front. The flies that fed on corpses swarmed around the men's food when they tried to eat.[114]

2.00 am

Lieutenant L. Whitaker arrived at the 52nd Brigade Machine Gun Company H.Q with a limber from the 13th Brigade Machine Gun Company. He collected the five privates of Sergeant Potter's command and left Potter and his fellow N.C.Os to the mercy of the Brigadier-General.

2.40 am

All batteries of 79th Brigade, R.F.A, began to fire registering rounds at Orchard Trench in order to get the range prior to the attack. A few enemy shells fell around Pommiers Redoubt but a major bombardment did not develop.

3.25 am

All was not well with the 80th Brigade, R.F.A. The German counter-battery fire had done a good job against all elements of the 17th Divisional artillery and the 80th Brigade was no exception. D Battery

---

114 Chapman, *A Passionate Prodigality*, p. 107

of the 80th Brigade, R.F.A, had been forced to limber up its guns and move position. Once in their new position they had to re-register their guns and this would take them out of the fighting for some time. A Battery also had problems. Two guns had to be removed from the gun line because their piston rods had worn out. At this point in the battle a majority of the guns in the British Fourth Army had been in use since the last week of June and were rapidly wearing out. The batteries of 79th Brigade, R.F.A, carried on registration shooting.

3.40 am

The German gunners fired another light barrage at and around Pommiers Redoubt. The 7th Borders were still in Pommiers Redoubt and at some point during the day Second Lieutenant D. C. Sykes of the 7th Borders was wounded and Lance Corporal, 14582, Mark Bardy was killed.

4.00 am

The adjutant of the 9th Duke of Wellingtons noted in the battalion diary that two machine guns, manned by the 1st Norfolks, had been relieved.[115] Interestingly, the Duke of Wellington's adjutant wrote that these two posts had been reported by the Machine Gun officer as blown up and not held. Which machine gun officer made this report was not recorded but evidently the posts *had not* been blown up and Sergeant Potter and his men were proof that they had most certainly been held.[116] There must have been a fair number of wounded men in and around the Duke of Wellingtons' position because the adjutant noted that R.A.M.C orderlies and men of his battalion had worked extremely hard throughout the night moving the wounded away from the front line and on to the dressing

---

115 These were the two machine gun posts of the 13th Brigade Machine Gun Company manned by Sergeant Potter and his men. The 9th Duke of Wellingtons had provided a bombing squad to protect the relief.

116 As the 52nd Brigade Machine Gun Company were co-operating with the Duke of Wellingtons then one must assume that this assertion had been made by an officer from that Company.

stations. By this time in the morning the battalion's section of the line was clear of wounded men.

Elements of the 9th Duke of Wellingtons had pushed forward to occupy Duke Street Trench. Once this had been done Lewis gun teams, protected by bombers, were pushed out in front of that trench. A patrol went out to try to find another post which had been reported to be still manned by the 1st Norfolks. They were unable to find this post but did encounter a German patrol a short distance from the British front line.

With Duke Street secure, a full company of the 9th Duke of Wellingtons now moved forward to try and occupy the line at the northern edge of the wood where it joined up with Duke Street and North Street. In the war diary it was categorically stated that this line *had not been held* by the 1st Norfolks when the 9th Duke of Wellingtons took over from them.[117]

The 78th Brigade, R.F.A., ceased fire on the ground behind the enemy front line. They re-sighted their guns and began a wire cutting operation in front of an enemy strongpoint.

4.30 am

Major Metcalfe, the C.O of the 7th Lincolns, reported that Lieutenant Kendall's C Company had left Pommiers Redoubt and headed for Longueval to provide labour for a digging fatigue. Several heavy shells landed on the battalion position, four men were severely wounded and had to be evacuated.

The 51st Field Ambulance recorded that the bombardment had been heavy all night and the Deputy Assistant Director of Medical Services visited the Station later in the morning. Despite the shelling, the Station received very few patients during the day.

The 7th Yorks and Lancs returned to work on the communication trench between Montauban and Longueval. This time D Company remained behind in Fricourt as the Divisional reserve. During the day B Company had five men wounded by shellfire.

---

117 TNA: PRO WO 95/2014. War Diary 9th Duke of Wellingtons, August 1916

Lieutenant-Colonel Fife decided that, because the 7th Yorks would soon be in action, it would be a good idea to get some training near the front line. This would be good experience, particularly for the newcomers who had not been in action and close to the front line; they could experience artillery fire at first hand. He ordered that the battalion march forward to the old German trenches near Becourt Wood where he had been the day before. These trenches were just a mile behind the current front line and shells were falling and bursting in the vicinity almost all of the time. Once there they began to practice attacking trenches.[118] At this time many of the battalions who had been involved in the fighting in early July were using captured trenches like this in order to give the new and untried drafts a chance to train and also to try and develop attacking methods that might reduce such horrendous casualties in future.

Later on another, larger draft of between 112 and 115 men arrived at the 7th Yorks. They were 'bantams' and in Fife's opinion physically poor specimens, particularly compared to the Yorkshire T.F men. Worryingly, they were almost all practically untrained. They had arrived under the command of Captain Kay. Kay had been away since being wounded at 'the Bluff' in February and Fife was glad to have him back. He was immediately posted to Hare's B Company.[119]

During the day the 50th Brigade Machine Gun Company carried out schemes using combined sights and the Commanding Officer, Captain Bolton, lectured the Company sergeants on the uses of indirect fire.[120]

---

118 Lieutenant-Colonel Fife's personal diary.

119 Lieutenant-Colonel Fife's personal diary.

120 This was firing the machine guns out of the line of sight of a target. The weapons were elevated and then fired up into the air and the bullets would then fall upon the intended target from above much like an artillery bombardment. It was an effective method of keeping enemy infantry under cover and these machine gun barrages were often used in conjunction with artillery operations. There has been some debate about the effectiveness of these barrages, some say that they were not lethal. German prisoners reported that they were deadly.

5.30 am

Lieutenant-General Horne visited 17th Division H.Q at Bellevue Farm and while he was there he went to see Lieutenant-Colonel Cardew who was battling with a pile of paperwork. Cardew recorded that he personally found the Corps Commander to be a pleasant and nice man. The weather was set to be fine and hot once again with a light north-westerly wind.

17th Division issued Operation Order no. 71. 52nd Brigade was ordered "to attack Orchard Trench running from about S.11.d.7.7 to S.11.c.5.8 early on Aug 4th and join up with our trench at S.11.c.0.8. Attack to be made at 12.40 am on Aug 4th after intense bombardment."[121]

On the 17th Division's left flank, men from the 52nd Field Ambulance reconnoitred the 2nd Division bearer post at the northern end of Bernafay Wood, to the rear of Longueval, to see if it would be any use to them. They also looked at the road from Montauban to Bernafay Wood with a view to using it to move casualties. The C.O of the 52nd Field Ambulance asked that the 51st Field Ambulance send fifteen squads forward by 9.00 pm.

One of the 52nd Field Ambulance orderlies had fallen ill and had to be evacuated.

6.00 am

Lieutenant-Colonel Wannell reported that one platoon of his Duke of Wellingtons' held Duke Street between Piccadilly and North Street and they had a post, manned by bombers, out in front of them. One platoon, backed up by a Lewis gun, was posted on the forward edge of the wood near North Street. One Vickers gun was situated in the front line and another was placed in an advanced position in a shell hole, protected by a screen of riflemen and bombers. They had tried to push a company forward, beyond this line, but that attempt had been prevented by intense German shellfire. Positions could not be set up and men who tried to dig in were caught in a barrage that first fell on the British troops and then

---

121 TNA: PRO WO 95/1981. War Diary, 17th Division, August 1916

kept going into the British rear. Shelling was going on day and night; patrolling was difficult. It was recorded that conditions were appalling and the men were quickly exhausted; their problems were compounded by the fact that it was hard to get food and water to the men in the line and the forward posts.

Now that the Duke of Wellingtons had pressed further forward, a soldier of the 2nd King's Own Scottish Borderers, 13th Brigade, 5th Division found his way into one of their forward positions. He reported that he had been manning his post for quite some time and that the 1st Norfolks had failed to relieve him.[122] The 2nd King's Own Scottish Borderers, as part of the 13th Brigade, had relieved elements of the 15th Brigade in the front line on the night of 29 July. They had attacked the Orchards and enemy posts north of Longueval at 3.00 am on 30 July and suffered heavy losses. They had been relieved by units of the 17th Division on 1/2 August. This man had been adrift from his unit for three days. Stragglers in this section of the Somme front were becoming a normal occurrence.

6.30 am

The second in command of the 10th West Yorks led the battalion's company commanders from Bellevue Farm to look at the ground near Fricourt where the battalion had been disastrously engaged on 1 July. They went to see if any lessons could be learned from what happened on that day.

6.50 am

Lieutenant-General Horne sent a situation report to General Rawlinson at Fourth Army H.Q. The right Division, the 17th

---

122 On p.117 of A. H. Hussey and D. S. Inman, *The Fifth Division In The Great War* it is recorded that a machine gun team of the King's Own Scottish Borderers had been left behind in a forward position and was relieved by the 17th Division. This is possibly erroneous and a reference to the machine gun teams of the 13th Machine Gun Company, not the K.O.S.B's. This straggler made no mention of a machine gun team or other men. Indeed, there were mentions of isolated machine gun teams of the 1st Norfolks as well. Undoubtedly, men of many different units had been left behind in isolated positions and it just goes to show how confused the front line situation actually was.

Division, had not yet sent in a situation report to Corps so nothing could be reported from there. The enemy had responded to the British artillery's night shoot by firing back, Mametz and Fricourt Woods had been shelled. The 51st Division, on the left, reported a quiet night.

7.00 am

The 52nd Brigade noted that the situation report sent at 6.00 am by the 9th Duke of Wellingtons had been received.

At Bellevue Farm the 7th East Yorks began physical training.

7.20 am

XV Corps reported to Fourth Army H.Q that German infantry had been seen in Delville Wood at 5.30 pm and 8.00 pm on the previous day.

7.30 am

XIII Corps contacted XV Corps with the information that a German soldier had been captured and had given vital information to his interrogators. Apparently, he had become separated from his unit and wandered from the XV Corps front into the XIII Corps area. He was from the 4th Company, 1st Battalion, 23rd Regiment of the 12th Division. His capture confirmed that this Regiment was in the line between Delville Wood and High Wood. It seemed to the British intelligence officers that the German units were being mixed up. Elements of the 24th (Reserve) Division, 12th (Reserve) Division and the 18th Bavarian (Reserve) Division had been identified in the area. They concluded that the German High Command was being forced to put units into the line that were nearest to the fighting, irrespective of their formations, to try to resist the British attacks.

Physical training ended for the 7th East Yorks and the men were given a one and a half hour break.

8.00 am

The second in command of the 10th West Yorks and his band of company commanders returned to Bellevue Farm. They returned with a plan. They would take the entire battalion back to the original 1 July trenches and re-enact the attack and this time it would be done differently. "In a way that in the light of recent experiences would have been best."[123]

9.00 am

Brigadier-General Clarke visited the 52nd Brigade Machine Gun Company H.Q in Montauban Alley and talked to Sergeant Potter and Lance Corporals Cotterall and McInnes. The Fifth Division History tells us what happened to the machine gunners and how they came to be cut off and it is probably what they told Brigadier-General Clarke.[124] It turned out that the machine gunners had not been abandoned at all; no one knew that they were there. On 29 July the 13th Brigade of the 5th Division had relieved the 15th Brigade in the part of the line now held by the 17th Division. At 3.00 am on 30 July elements of the 13th Brigade launched an attack upon German positions in the Orchards and posts north of Longueval Village and beyond Delville Wood. All objectives on the right of this operation were gained but the attack on the left flank failed. Or so it was thought. Without anyone in the 5th Division knowing the machine gunners had got to the final objective on the left and set up a post. They remained there under British artillery fire and beating off German infantry attacks throughout 30 and 31 July, 1 August and most of 2 August until hunger and thirst convinced them to make contact with the British front line. After the brief interview Brigadier-General Clarke congratulated them on their devotion to

---

123 TNA: PRO WO 95/2004. War Diary 10th West Yorks, August 1916

124 A. H. Hussey & D. S. Inman, *The Fifth Division In The Great War,* (First published, Nisbet & Co Ltd, 1921. Re-printed, Naval & Military Press), p.117. Hussey and Inman got their information slightly confused. They recorded that only one gun team was cut off and that the team came from the King's Own Scottish Borderers. Considering that the 9th Duke of Wellingtons' recorded that the gun teams came from the 1st Norfolks and they themselves were involved in their rescue, Hussey and Inman can be forgiven!

duty and asked Major Lintott to forward a report of recommendation to their Commanding Officer.

After this, Major Lintott began the calculations and arrangements for maintaining indirect fire on the German positions, Tea Trench, Tea Support and Switch Trench. B Section's guns were to lay down indirect fire from their positions in the old German front line during the intense British barrage, prior to the forthcoming attack upon Orchard Trench.

The soldier of the 2nd K.O.S.B went out with a patrol from the 9th Duke of Wellingtons to try and find his old post. He failed to find it and the officers of the 9th Duke of Wellingtons sensibly concluded that he had failed to find his old post because it was in the line recently established by their own men.

It was now crowded at Pommiers Redoubt with men of the 8th South Staffords and the 10th Notts & Derbys crammed into the position. The 8th South Staffords sent B Company to trenches in the rear to try and make some space. Back at Bellevue Farm, the men of the 7th East Yorks began company training.

9.30 am

A draft of forty men arrived at Bellevue Farm and reported for duty with the 7th East Yorks.

10.00 am

General Rawlinson arrived at XV Corps H.Q in Heilly for a meeting with Lieutenant-Generals Horne and Congreve. The Army Commander set out and explained General Haig's plans for further operations. Further down the chain of command the 51st Brigade H.Q staff and regimental officers spent the day in conferences and reconnaissance of the line.

10.15 am

As part of the 51st Brigade preparations to go into the line, Captain Manger of the 8th South Staffords sent Captain Smyly and Second Lieutenant Langton to the front line to gather what information they could.

10.20 am

XV Corps recorded that 17th Division had asked for the heavy artillery barrage to be stopped during the previous night but now the request had been withdrawn. XV Corps recorded that the 17th Division had now managed to establish posts; one fifty yards north of the edge of Orchard Trench, one between North Street and Piccadilly and one identified by map reference S.11.d.5.6.

10.30 am

Orders arrived for the 10th Notts & Derbys to go forward and relieve the 22nd Royal Fusiliers, 99th Brigade, of the 2nd Division in Mine Trench on the following day. The relief was to take place during daylight. The 22nd Royal Fusiliers had been in action from 27 July, had taken serious casualties, and were in need of rest and recuperation.

Captain Manger moved the 8th South Staffords battalion H.Q to an old German dugout. These dugouts were infested with flies and often filled with dead men but many were homely, decked out with panelling, wallpaper, cupboards and curtains.

10.40 am

Lieutenant-Colonel Wannell of the 9th Duke of Wellingtons was forced to report to 52nd Brigade that his battalion was exhausted and "quite unfit to carry out the projected attack."[125] Intensive operations against Quadrangle Support Trench and a swift return to the fighting had fatigued the men. Pushing units forward, patrolling, trying to hold the confused front line, constant shelling and the dreadful state of the ground had told heavily on the battalion. The 17th Division's History records that there had been reports that the 9th Duke of Wellington's had suffered gas attacks and there had been many casualties.[126] Neither the 9th Duke of Wellingtons' nor the 52nd Brigade War Diaries mentioned this gas attack but then there is no mention in the 9th Duke of Wellingtons' diary that they were unfit to

---

125 TNA: PRO WO 95/2009. War Diary 52nd Brigade, August 1916

126 Hilliard Atteridge, *A History of the 17th (Northern) Division)*, p. 153

attack. Gas shells were being fired in the bombardments as a matter of course.

11.30 am

Brigadier-General Clarke understood how bad things were for Wannell's 9th Duke of Wellingtons and ordered the 12th Manchesters to move up from their support positions and prepare to attack the objective instead. The attacking elements of the 12th Manchesters were to move through the 9th Duke of Wellingtons. The companies of the 12th Manchesters not involved in the attack were ordered to gradually relieve the 9th Duke of Wellingtons in the front line. The problem here was that the Manchesters were in no better shape than Wannell's Duke of Wellingtons.

During the morning Major-General Robertson had been with Brigadier-General Clarke at his 52nd Brigade H.Q in Montauban Alley. This was situated on the southern side of Caterpillar Valley. He will have agreed with Clarke's decision to replace the Duke of Wellingtons with the Manchesters. The 17th Division H.Q recorded the changes for the forthcoming attack. The attack on the morning of 4 August was to be made by the 9th Northumberlands on the left and the 12th Manchesters on the right.

11.50 am

Watching the shelling and receiving reports from the front line, it soon became apparent to Major-General Robertson that a British post out in front of Orchard Trench was being shelled by the British guns. He contacted the Heavy Artillery and asked them to cease-fire. The post could not be evacuated until after dark so this hampered the heavy artillery operation in support of the forthcoming assault. What reason Major-General Robertson gave is unclear, in the 17th Division war diary it states that the ceasefire was requested because of the post but in the minds of the heavy artillery officers there was some doubt.

12 noon

The hottest part of the day was approaching and at Bellevue Farm the 7th East Yorks took a break from company training. Lieutenant-

Colonel Cardew recorded that the weather during the day was indeed "fearfully hot."[127]

12.30 pm

The 9th Duke of Wellingtons reported that the shelling was continuing and the fire was coming from the direction of Ginchy. Lieutenant-Colonel Wannell stated that he was now doubtful that an earlier report that his men had made about British shrapnel bursting over the German lines was correct. Patrols had been sent out to see if they could find any more manned posts out in front of the established line. A patrol had discovered what *could* have been a post but all they had found was an abandoned Lewis gun and no living men.

1.10 pm

Senior artillery officers informed Lieutenant-General Horne at XV Corps H.Q that Major-General Robertson had earlier asked for the heavy artillery to cease-fire. That a mere Major-General had requested the cease-fire had probably irritated them. It was not immediately clear to the senior artillery officers *why* Major-General Robertson wanted the heavy guns to stop firing they said. They thought that either British soldiers were in Wood Lane and Orchard Trench or that the wrong trench was being shelled. Lieutenant-General Horne gave his permission for the artillery to cease firing while the situation was cleared up. The reason for Major-General Robertson's request for a cease-fire was the British post out in front of Orchard Trench. He was trying to stop the Tommies in the post getting blown up by their own guns.

1.45 pm

Lieutenant Spicer of the 2nd South Staffords, whose battalion was stationed half a mile away, paid a courtesy visit to the 8th South Staffords.

---

[127] IWM: Cardew 86/92/1.

2.00 pm

The 10th West Yorks paraded at Bellevue Farm ready to march to the old British line at Fricourt and to make the 1 July attack again. They were not to do so. When the leading elements of the battalion arrived at the line they discovered that other British troops were practising bomb throwing in the ground between the old British line and the old German line. Their re-enactment was cancelled.

2.30 pm

Captain Manger paid a courtesy visit to the 2nd South Staffords H.Q.

3.00 pm

The 79th Brigade, R.F.A, carried out the first of 'bursts of fire' on Switch Trench and the ground in front of it.

3.45 pm

Brigadier-General Clarke, of 52nd Brigade, issued further orders to his battalions for the coming attack. The attack was to take place at 12.40 am on 4 August.

4.00 pm

Lieutenant-Colonel Wannell of the 9th Duke of Wellingtons received the message, Brigade Operation Order number 86, from 52nd Brigade H.Q. His battalion would not be attacking, the 12th Manchesters were to attack through them and the 9th Northumberlands were to attack on the left. Arrangements were made with the 12th Manchesters to create a dump of tools and Lewis gun drums for their use. The 9th Duke of Wellingtons were informed that they were required to carry water for the 12th Manchesters and provide guides for them.

4.30 pm

The situation had become a little clearer. XV Corps was informed that there were no British troops in Wood Lane but despite the request for the heavy guns to cease fire, they were still firing and hitting the British front line. Major-General Robertson contacted Lieutenant-General Horne and told him that he was engaging the enemy objective with his own Divisional artillery and would prefer it if the heavy guns did not fire on it again. He wished his attack to have the benefit of surprise.

That Horne allowed Robertson, a divisional commander, such freedom is interesting. Firstly, there does not seem to be any sign of harsh taskmaster Horne who had pushed Major-General Pilcher in July. Secondly, at this time in the war, some corps commanders were loath to allow their divisional generals to use their own initiative. Nor were divisional commanders given much control over artillery units other than their own Divisional Artillery Brigades.[128] Robertson was, perhaps, a more able commander than is generally thought and Horne probably knew of his fighting ability. Robertson certainly proved throughout the war that he was not at all intimidated or frightened by the High Command, he often spoke his mind and he handled the 17th Division well. And perhaps, after the mistakes of the first phase of the campaign, Horne was now learning to use a lighter touch in command, to allow his subordinates to have their head and use their own initiative.

The General of the XV Corps artillery wrote to the 3rd Squadron, R.F.C, on behalf of Lieutenant-General Horne. He pointed out to fliers that they should pay more attention to registering the 60-pounders and 4.7-inch heavy batteries on to enemy gun batteries. He went on to tell them that the heavy howitzers or heavy guns should *not* be used against enemy batteries unless there was some *special* reason.

Pilot Cecil Lewis was flying photo reconnaissance and artillery spotting duties with the 3rd Squadron at the time. On 1 August he wrote in his flying log, "Very hot, consequently long range artillery spotting and photography difficult owing to haze."[129] Some of the senior infantry and artillery officers had little grasp of aerial conditions and the difficulties of the R.F.C's task.

---

128 Miles, Official History 1916 Vol II, p. 569

129 C. Lewis, *Sagittarius Rising* (Greenhill Books, 2003), p.127

By definition, flying over enemy positions was not a particularly safe occupation. On 4 August Lewis wrote in his log, "Went out on photography. Archie (anti-aircraft fire) was so good that I actually felt the puff of hot air when one of the damn things burst. Pretty good shooting!"[130]

The R.F.C did not only have to contend with anti-aircraft fire. Enemy machines were patrolling ready to shoot down the reconnaissance aircraft. Sometime during August, while on a photographic patrol, Lewis and his observer 'Pip' tangled with a German aircraft and came off much the worse for the encounter.

If some of the generals were not entirely well informed of the hazards of flying, it was made certain that the aircrews were well aware of the conditions that the men on the ground faced. During August, Lewis and a group of other fliers were sent forward to see an artillery position in Caterpillar Valley.

> *They were quite snugly settled into the little valley, living in dugouts made of large semi-tubular steel caissons, corrugated and shell-proof. These, standing on a low rampart, made a domed room within, and the sandbagged roof was invisible from the air. They were divided into sections, the entrances, a narrow opening just wide enough for one man to pass between them.*[131]

At Bellevue Farm the 50th Brigade Machine Gun Company had their tea and then carried out drill. After tea, Lieutenant-Colonel Cardew visited Brigadier-General Glasgow at his H.Q and then went to see how his horses were getting along.

5.30 pm

The 78th Brigade, R.F.A., had halted the wire cutting operation and began to bombard the enemy front line.

130 C. Lewis, *Sagittarius Rising*, p.127

131 C. Lewis, *Sagittarius Rising*, p.129

6.00 pm

The 79th Brigade, R.F.A., ceased the bursts of fire on Switch Trench. They recorded that they had been shelled by hostile batteries at intervals throughout the afternoon.

Major Lintott of the 52nd Brigade Machine Gun Company inspected B Section at their support position in George Street. He then visited the H.Qs of the 9th Northumberlands and the 12th Manchesters.

The 51st Field Ambulance received a request to send fifteen stretcher squads forward to form a reserve at the Advanced Dressing Station on the Mametz – Montauban Road. The 52nd Brigade was due to attack at 1.00 am the following day. There was also a request for a motor bus to be sent up at 2.00 am.

6.15 pm

The 93rd Field Company, R.E, noted the arrival of 52nd Brigade operation order number 86 and that it contained no orders for any extra work for them.

6.50 pm

The time of the forthcoming attack was reported to the 9th Duke of Wellingtons to be at 12.40 the following morning. An officer from the Royal Engineers arrived at battalion H.Q with orders to dig wells and open up disused and blown-in dugouts. The 9th Duke of Wellingtons reported to 52nd Brigade H.Q, that the shelling was still heavy and the smouldering village of Longueval was now unrecognisable. Any map references to the village were useless because no streets or features existed.

6.58 pm

Lieutenant-General Horne of XV Corps contacted Fourth Army H.Q and reported that Longueval village, Caterpillar Valley and Mametz Woods were being shelled.

7.00 pm

The 78th Brigade, R.F.A, ceased fire on the enemy front line.

8.00 pm

During his visit to the 12th Manchesters H.Q, Major Lintott learned that there was an enemy machine gun sited at Point D. Major Lintott immediately contacted Mason and ordered him to fire upon this gun, with all of his weapons, as soon as it opened fire. Mason was ordered to knock it out.

The 52nd Field Ambulance recorded that four officers and one hundred and thirty seven other ranks had passed through the Advanced Dressing Station. In anticipation of the coming attack a request for more bearer squads was sent to the 51st Field Ambulance. In response to the request sixty men from 51st Field Ambulance's B and C bearer sub-divisions, under the command of Captains Barclay and Gorman, were sent up to the front.

The 81st Brigade, R.F.A., began an intense bombardment of Orchard Trench in preparation for an attack by the 12th Manchesters. The Germans answered with a very heavy barrage.

8.10 pm

XV Corps noted that a pre-arranged bombardment by 17th Divisional artillery had begun. The 78th Brigade, R.F.A., renewed their bombardment of the enemy front line and the 79th Brigade, R.F.A., bombarded Orchard Trench.

8.45 pm

The 17th Division issued Operation Order No.72 to the 51st Brigade. Brigadier-General Trotter was ordered to relieve the 99th Brigade of the 2nd Division during the night of the 4/5 August.

9.00 pm

The German heavy bombardment was still falling on the British forward posts.

The squads of bearers from the 51st Field Ambulance that had been requested by 52nd Field Ambulance arrived at the front. They were immediately sent to Captain Dougal at his bearer post in Caterpillar Valley.

10.00 pm

Number four section returned to the 93rd Field Company, R.E, after completing their work on the dugouts at Bellevue Farm. For some reason their signaller had remained behind.

The 79th Brigade, R.F.A, bombarded Switch Trench. Once again the German counter-battery fire was effective and took its toll on the gunners of the 79th Brigade. 20995 Gunner G. H. Sorrel, 114770 Gunner W. J Bodin, both of A battery, 24354 Sergeant A. Cook, 103235, Gunner F. Groom, both of B battery, 35078 Bombardier Ware, 12811 Gunner C. H. Parker both of D battery were all killed. Second Lieutenant T. Martin of A battery was shell shocked and the following men were wounded, 60142 Sergeant E. Jones, 70267 Gunner J. Atkins, 20098 Gunner W. Bland, all of A battery, 11563 Gunner H.M. Brown, 11650 Gunner R. Hart both of B battery, 2488 Sergeant J. McGill and 103551 Gunner P. J. Stanhope both of D battery.

The 52nd Brigade Machine Gun Company reported that the Germans had opened a very heavy barrage on the British lines and that gas shells were reported to be falling on the left flank. In the storm of shells and gas the men's morale was failing but the 12th Manchesters were ordered to stand fast.

Fourth Army H.Q later noted that a Gas Alarm had been given because gas shells had fallen on positions in and around Caterpillar Valley.

10.05 pm

The heavy bombardment continued to fall between High Wood and Longueval. An S.O.S flare was launched from Longueval and it was seen and noted by the staff at 52nd Brigade H.Q in Montauban Alley.

10.10 pm

The front line was obviously getting 'jittery' so Brigadier-General Clarke ordered Major Torrens' 10th Lancashire Fusiliers, spread out in dugouts in Montauban Alley, to stand by to move from Caterpillar Valley to Longueval.

10.15 pm

The bombardment was reported to divisional H.Q and the 17th Division staff noted that it was "very heavy hostile artillery fire".[132] The 52nd Brigade reported to 17th Division H.Q that British troops were sending up S.O.S flares; now multiple rather than singular. Brigadier-General Clarke also told Division that the 12th Manchesters had reported that German infantry was attacking Longueval.

10.25 pm

Shortly after this report, 17th Division received a message from the cooler heads of the 9th Northumberlands reporting that the enemy were *not* attacking Longueval but were putting down a very heavy bombardment that included gas shells. Division noted that the 12th Manchesters were having great difficulty getting into position for the attack because of the barrage. The communication trench up which they had to travel, Piccadilly, was being shelled and the battalion reported that it was suffering casualties.

10.30 pm

The heavy German bombardment on the front line suddenly ceased and Major Westmacott of the 9th Northumberlands reported to Brigadier-General Clarke that the situation at the front was quieter. Even so, Longueval was still being lightly shelled and the 9th Northumberlands requested that the British barrage cease. The German bombardment had seriously hampered the 9th Northumberlands' arrangements for the attack. Captain Ellis Milton

---

132 TNA: PRO WO95/1981. War Diary 17th Division, August 1916

Jackson,[133] B Company commander, was wounded as was his acting C.S.M. This was a blow to the operation because B Company was to lead the attack on the left flank. The lull in the heavy artillery fire was short lived.

10.35 pm

A report from 4th Brigade R.F.C., arrived at Fourth Army H.Q. During the day a stream of lorries and horse-drawn wagons had been spotted travelling from Villers-au-Flos to Beaulencourt behind the German lines. Another aerial patrol reported that Switch Trench had been bombarded by the British artillery but it appeared that the trench was undamaged.[134] There was a twelve feet wide track near Switch Trench that looked as if it was used regularly. The edge of Flers road appeared to have been entrenched and a new trench had been dug by the German infantry that ran towards Delville Wood.

10.45 pm

By this time the 12th Manchesters managed to get moving along Piccadilly and a gas warning was issued for High Wood. The 12th Manchesters were still not in position for the attack.

11.20 pm

Despite the setbacks, Major Westmacott, 9th Northumberlands, reported to 52nd Brigade that his battalion's preparations for the attack were back on course and proceeding satisfactorily. He also reported that Captain Jackson, Captain Raymond Vivian Leslie Dallas,[135] Second Lieutenant A. D. Rose and two other ranks had been wounded.

---

133 Captain Jackson had come out to France with the battalion in July 1915, he recovered from his wound and later joined the Royal Engineers. Jackson survived the war.

134 This would have been the fire missions carried out at 3.00 pm and 6.00 pm by the 79th Brigade, R.F.A., and they were still firing at it.

135 Captain Raymond Vivian Leslie Dallas, M.C., was later killed in action on 13 April 1918.

The artillery duel carried on in earnest and the British and German troops in the front lines bore the brunt of the shellfire. The bombardment continued to fall on the 9th Northumberlands with increasing ferocity. Forty men became casualties to the guns. On this side of midnight Privates 5211 R. Hargreaves, 20675 J. Ryder and Sergeant 12884 T. S. Silverton, M.M, were all killed. But the damage was not only being done by German guns, the 9th Northumberlands war diary stated bluntly "the majority of these casualties had been caused by our own shell fire."[136] The three men who were killed by the shells were buried together, in a row.

Westmacott's officers of the 9th Northumberlands planned to attack Orchard Trench with fighting patrols from B Company and they were to be followed up by B Company's other three platoons. A Company was the third line and C Company was in reserve. D Company had orders to go forward when Orchard Trench was secure and dig a trench to the left of it. There was no battalion in support for this attack but the 10th Lancashires were in reserve. The 12th Manchesters, supported by the 9th Duke of Wellingtons, were supposed to be attacking on the right flank but at this time they were still not in position. At this point there was some doubt if the attack was going to go ahead at all.

The 1/5th Seaforth Highlanders of 152nd Brigade, 51st Division, were in the line to the left of the 9th Northumberlands but they were not involved in the attack upon Orchard Trench. The 1/5th Seaforths were involved in a scheme of their own. 152nd Brigade had orders, following that division's policy of "peaceful penetration", to dig a new front line trench some two hundred yards ahead of their current line.[137]

11.30 pm

The 52nd Brigade Machine Gun Company reported that the enemy bombardment had slackened and it was decided that the attack should go in as planned. The shellfire had slackened but not stopped; the 52nd Field Ambulance reported that the heavy guns

---

136 TNA: PRO WO95/2013. War Diary 9th Northumberland Fusiliers, August 1916

137 F. W. Bewsher, *The History Of The Fifty First (Highland) Division 1914 – 1918* (First published, 1920. Re-printed, Naval & Military Press) p. 82

fired all night. So did the 50th Brigade Machine Gun Company, camped at Bellevue Farm, near Albert. They recorded that the artillery was active all night.

Chapter Four: 4 August

Taking advantage of the lull in the German shelling the British troops made their final preparations to attack Orchard Trench. In truth, the 9th Northumberland Fusiliers were in no better shape than the 9th Duke of Wellingtons. The constant shellfire from both sides and the physically demanding work of trying to dig deeper trenches and dugouts for cover had taken a serious toll on the men. Veterans were exhausted and shaken but the new men, straight from Britain, were terrified. This was their first taste of the front line and shellfire and it was horrifying.

12.30 am

The four Vickers machine guns of Second Lieutenant Michell's B Section, 52nd Brigade Machine Gun Company, began indirect fire on the trenches behind the German front line. Firing from George Street each gun fired 3,000 rounds of ammunition as they swept over Tea Trench, Tea Support and Switch Trench. Their task was to cause mayhem in the German rear trenches and force the troops there to keep their heads down, thereby stopping them from reinforcing the small garrison in their front line.

12.35 am

Right on time Cardew's Divisional Artillery opened fire on their target. The field guns and howitzers of the 78th, 79th, 80th and 81st Brigades began a short, but intense, barrage on Orchard Trench.[138] The German troops had a good idea what to expect; they may have even known that the attack was coming and they were very well prepared. As soon as Cardew's divisional guns opened fire flares were launched from the German positions. As the first ones soared into the night they were followed by more and yet more. This constant series of flares lit up no-man's-land and the British front

---

[138] The 79th Brigade soon changed its target and fired upon Switch Trench once more.

line positions like day. Anything that the British did could now be clearly seen.

12.40 am

Adhering to the firing timetable, Cardew's divisional artillery lifted the barrage to positions two hundred yards behind Orchard Trench to allow the British infantry to attack and to block any German reserves that may be coming forward. As the British barrage lifted the German guns began accurate counter-battery fire and the 80th Brigade, R.F.A., suffered badly. Three guns of A battery and one of C battery were put out of action. Orders arrived stating that one Forward Observation Officer had to be stationed with every battalion H.Q. Even though the 78th Brigade, R.F.A., had gone ahead with their part of the operation they recorded that the infantry attack had been postponed. A few hours before this had looked likely. On the other hand, the 79th Brigade, R.F.A., recorded that the attack went ahead.

When the barrage lifted the fighting patrols of the 9th Northumberlands left their trenches and shell holes and were immediately met by a furious German barrage of gas, high explosive and shrapnel shells and machine gun fire. The British infantry could not press their attack and had no choice but to fall back to the start line.

The 12th Manchesters had been unable to move forward along Piccadilly communication trench as arranged. To make up lost time and to get to the front line in time for the attack they had gone forward over the open and suffered a number of casualties as they did so. When they finally arrived they managed to launch their part of the attack and were immediately illuminated by the flares fired by the German troops. Because gas shells were falling the order had been passed to don their gas helmets.[139] When they attacked they got caught by a German barrage. Most were disorientated by the barrage, the bright flares, the gas, their gas helmets and, as it turned out, a liberal dose of rum; the attack descended into chaos and the units became mixed up. Only a few men managed to get forward.

---

139 TNA: PRO WO 95/1981. War Diary 17th Division, August 1916.

There was confusion about the Manchester's part of the attack and not much written about it appears to have survived. Indeed, the 12th Manchester's war diary for the month has been lost, all bar one uninformative sheet. What appears to have happened, piecing together what little information that exists from the 17th Division history, Cardew's diary and comments made in the 9th Northumberlands' war diary is this: The men, many of whom were new, and who had not been under fire before, let alone in an attack, were terrified and had been given an extra rum ration. They were very drunk before the attack began. Some of the men, led by two second lieutenants and a sergeant major, did begin the operation but were checked by shell and machine gun fire and immediately went to ground. Captain William Manstead Benton[140] was then sent forward by the battalion H.Q to find out what was going on, rally them and re-organise them for the assault. As he tried to get them moving he was hit in both legs, then the senior second lieutenant tried to lead the attack and he was hit and killed, then the junior second lieutenant tried to get them going and he too was hit and killed. These two officers were second lieutenants Norman Harry Blythe and William Ralph Osborne Moulton.[141] After all of the officers were hit, the sergeant major, using his experience and common sense, brought the men back into the British lines. This un-named sergeant major who brought the frightened men back in undoubtedly saved lives. In addition, someone must have known that Benton was still alive and reported the fact because a fuss was soon made about getting him back in.[142] It is possible, considering the fact that Benton was still

---

140 William was actually the former Reverend Benton and now, remarkably, a combat officer. According to his medal index card he had been a reverend, a second lieutenant and chaplain in the Royal Marines when he had gone to the Western Front on 28 August 1914. In February 1915, he resigned his commission with the Marines and resigned as a chaplain to take up a combat commission. The New Armies gratefully accepted his services and he joined the 12th Manchesters.

141 Which of the two was senior is hard to tell; according to 19 year old Blythe's medal index card he had arrived at the battalion on 26 June 1916. When Moulton arrived was not recorded but his medal index card shows that he did not merit the 1915 Star; therefore he had arrived at the battalion after December 1915.

142 IWM: Cardew 86/92/1. Hilliard Atteridge, *History of the 17th (Northern) Division,* p.154 and TNA: PRO WO 95/2013. War Diary, 9th Northumberland Fusiliers, August 1916

alive, that he may have ordered the sergeant major to lead the men back to the British lines. Coming so close to the battalion's last time in action, when the Kitchener Volunteers were led into virtual destruction at Quadrangle Support, this was a sad return to the fighting. It did look like a re-run of the costly, piecemeal attacks of July.

As the attack by the 9th Northumberlands and 12th Manchesters began, the communications had failed. The heavy barrage cut the telephone wires and effectively stopped runners getting through. Battalion H.Qs were out of touch with the attacking troops and 52nd Brigade was out of touch with the battalions. Neither 52nd Brigade nor Divisional H.Q's could get any information of any kind for three hours.

Lieutenant-Colonel Cardew got up early and went to his office to talk on the telephone to Brigadier-General Harrison at XV Corps H.Q. The noise of the 17th Division attack was loud and he could hear it at Bellevue Farm. After completing his telephone call, he returned to bed.[143] In his billet nearby, Lieutenant-Colonel Fife tried to get some sleep but the noise of the artillery kept him awake.[144]

1.25 am

Operation orders arrived at the 8th South Staffords H.Q. Captains Burnett and Massey, Lieutenant Day and Second Lieutenants Stanley and Griffiths went forward to look at the line at Montauban and Delville Wood.

3.05 am

Captain Tanfield commanding the attack for the 9th Northumberlands, managed to get a message through to battalion H.Q. He informed his commander that the attack had failed to reach the objective and that he was reorganising his men. Tanfield did not say if he was going to renew the attack or not. In the event, he did not.

---

143 IWM: Cardew 86/92/1.

144 Personal diary of Lieutenant-Colonel Fife.

4.00 am

Casualties began to come into the 52nd Field Ambulance Advanced Dressing Station at a steady rate, but in no real numbers. The 51st Field Ambulance, at the Divisional Collecting Station, recorded that the artillery fire from both sides had been heavy all night but they too recorded that very few patients had passed through up to this time.

4.30 am

It was now daylight and the 79th Brigade, R.F.A., ceased firing on Switch Trench. 81st Brigade, R.F.A, registered on various different targets during the day.

The 7th Yorks and Lancs went to work on the communication trench. This time A Company remained behind at Fricourt. One N.C.O and twelve men from A Company went to a dump to load and unload equipment and materials.

4.35 am

News arrived at 17th Division H.Q, saying that both attacks by the 9th Northumberlands and the 12th Manchesters had failed.

5.00 am

Brigadier-General Clarke at 52nd Brigade H.Q received a situation report of six points from Major Westmacott of the 9th Northumberlands. The six reasons for the failure of the attack did not make comfortable reading.

1. *The men did not know their officers and fifty percent of them were new soldiers who had never been under shellfire before.*
2. *The enemy's flares had lit up the troops before they had assaulted and made them visible targets.*
3. *The enemy barrage of shells and machine guns was impenetrable.*
4. *The right flank was exposed.*

5. *A group of Manchesters had crossed over the right flank of the Northumberlands and then disorganised the right flank by falling back to the British front line.*
6. *Many of the new men were demoralised by the British shelling before the attack began.*[145]

The 9th Northumberlands recorded that the battalion suffered seventy-three casualties. Records show that in fact only two men had been killed on 4 August.

5.30 am

Major King came into Lieutenant-Colonel Cardew's tent at Bellevue Farm and gave him a report about the attack. He told Cardew that it had been a complete failure and it seemed that the Germans appeared to have known all about it. King also informed Cardew that only a short while earlier Lieutenant Alan Scrivener Lloyd of C Battery, the 78th Brigade R.F.A., had been killed and Second Lieutenant R. J. Yeatman of the same unit had been badly wounded.[146]

Lieutenant Lloyd, Second Lieutenant Yeatman and a signaller had been in a Forward Observation Post when they came under artillery fire. Both men were wounded but despite Yeatman's efforts to save his life, 27-year old Lloyd died twenty minutes after being hit. Both officers were awarded the M.C, for their actions on this morning. Only one other man of the 78th Brigade R.F.A., was killed in action on this day; Gunner Harold Brakes, from H.Q, 78th Brigade R.F.A. He was most likely the signaller with Lloyd and Yeatman in the Forward Observation Post. Gunner Brakes is buried in Quarry Cemetery, Montauban. Robert Julian Yeatman recovered from his wounds and went on to be the co-author of the renowned book *1066 and All That.*

The 77th Field Company, R.E., continued their work on the communication trench and the support line. Their wagons were employed ferrying stores and materials from a dump in the rear to

---

145 TNA: PRO WO 95/2013. War Diary 9th Northumberland Fusiliers, August 1916

146 IWM: Cardew 86/92/1.

one that had been set up at Fricourt. The 78th Field Company, R.E., reported that the Signal dugout and first aid post extension had been completed. Number 4 section was working with two companies of infantry on the communication trench between Montauban and Longueval. The 93rd Field Company, R.E., reported that the work carried on as before. Number two section was working on the 12th Manchesters' H.Q. Number four section was employed working at the 52nd Brigade H.Q. The weather was, again, extremely hot. Four more men had been wounded but they remained at duty.

During the day, the 50th Brigade Machine Gun Company carried out advanced stage machine gun tactics at the Camp at Bellevue Farm and two officers from the company rode over to Pommiers Redoubt to reconnoitre the gun positions held by the 51st Brigade Machine Gun Company.

5.20 am

Lieutenant-Colonel Wannell reported to 52nd Brigade that the Duke of Wellingtons' attack had failed to reach the objectives. They also reported that there were a large number of 12th Manchesters in their front line and these could not get back to their positions during daylight. Somehow, a few prisoners had been taken and they were sent down the line.

5.35 am

The 52nd Brigade ordered the 10th Lancashire Fusiliers to be prepared to move off at once. The 10th Lancashires duly moved up to a support position.

6.00 am

Major Lintott, 52nd Brigade Machine Gun Company, visited the gun teams of his C Section positioned in the front line on the left flank.

The R.F.C reported to XV Corps H.Q that a fierce fire had been seen burning by reconnaissance crews at Eaucourt L'Abbaye and a good deal of traffic had been observed on the Villers-au-Flos to Beaulencourt road. Throughout the day the R.F.C flew registration, signalling and photographic patrols but despite the fact that the weather was fine and dry, the conditions were apparently not good for aerial work. Perhaps it was too hazy. The weather was indeed fine and dry and later in the day Lieutenant-Colonel Cardew recorded that the weather was "fearfully hot…again."[147]

6.40 am

The 52nd Brigade sent a situation report to 17th Division H.Q and the news of the failed attacks was confirmed. Major-General Robertson was told that the 12th Manchesters had been late getting to their assembly position. Though they did deploy for the attack they were at once heavily shelled and only a small number of men reached the German wire. The barrage disorganised the attack and the attacking men had been forced to wear their gas helmets because the enemy had fired gas shells.

When the news of the attack filtered up to Lieutenant-General Horne, he and his staff did not fail to notice the behaviour of the Manchesters. It was noted, briefly, with no fuss and no particular surprise, that though their casualties were not severe the 12th Manchesters were disorganised; so much so that they had to be withdrawn from the front line.[148] The 12th Manchesters had lost twenty men, all killed in the action.

Major-General Robertson received further information about the 9th Northumberland's attack, which had been broken up by the heavy barrage. It appeared that the enemy were totally prepared for the coming attack. When the British bombardment began, so did the German one. When the 9th Northumberlands attacked, machine guns and rifles opened fire from Orchard Trench and few of the Northumberlands managed to get across no man's land.

News of the failed attack soon reached the troops camped at Bellevue Farm and Lieutenant-Colonel Fife made a note of it in his diary. He was more concerned with the orders that he had just

---

[147] IWM: Cardew 86/92/1.

[148] TNA: PRO WO 95/922. War Diary XV Corps, August 1916

received for the 7th Yorks to move forward to Pommiers Redoubt that evening.[149]

6.50 am

XV Corps sent a report about the attack upon Orchard Trench to Fourth Army H.Q and General Rawlinson's staff noted the failure.

7.00 am

Brigadier-General Clarke ordered the 9th Duke of Wellingtons to remain in their present position. He then ordered Major Torrens to send two companies of his 10th Lancashires to replace the 12th Manchesters in close support in the old German second line.

At Bellevue Farm the 7th East Yorks, of 50th Brigade, began their morning physical exercise.

7.10 am

Major-General Robertson ordered the 50th Brigade forward from Bellevue Farm to Pommiers Redoubt. Captain Mozley noted that the company commanders of the 6th Dorsets went forward to the Redoubt to make a reconnaissance of the trenches there.[150]

Throughout the day the howitzers carried out a slow rate of fire on Orchard Trench They paid special attention to certain points in the German line but the Forward Observation Officers reported that it was difficult to get decent observation for firing on Orchard Trench east of North Street. No observation could be got from Pear Street or from the ground in front of it, except from the junction of Pear Street and Wood Lane. Observation of the German line was somewhat difficult at this time.

---

149 Personal diary of Lieutenant-Colonel Fife.

150 IWM: Mozley 01/48/1.

7.30 am

At Bellevue Farm the 7th East Yorks ceased physical training and had a one and a half hour break before they began company training.

8.00 am

Up to this point the 51st Field Ambulance had one hundred sitting cases come through the Divisional Collecting Station. The flow had begun at 4.00 am but had tailed off and the remainder of the day was quiet.

9.00 am

The 7th East Yorks began Company training.

The 79th Brigade, R.F.A, was given a new S.O.S barrage zone, further to the east and north of Delville Wood. They were ordered to continue day and night firing on Switch Trench and the area to its rear. The ammunition allotments were as follows: during the day the 18-pounders could fire 500 rounds and at night time 625 rounds. By day the 4.5-inch howitzers could fire 330 rounds and at night time 166 rounds.

Captain Dougal reported to 52nd Field Ambulance H.Q that his bearer post in the Gully (Caterpillar Valley) was clear of all casualties by 9.00 am.

10.00 am

Earlier in the morning the 10th West Yorks had received their orders to move into the Divisional Reserve. A party consisting of one officer and N.C.O from each company and an N.C.O each from the bombers and signallers had gone ahead as the advance party. They had orders to take over Pommiers Redoubt from the 10th Notts & Derbys. When, at 10.00 am, they arrived at Pommiers Redoubt, it was discovered that the 10th Notts & Derbys were actually in Pommiers Trench. The N.C.Os remained to complete the hand over and the officers went back to the battalion.

The 79th Brigade, R.F.A, was informed of the failure of the infantry attack. As well as their operations against Switch Trench, they were ordered to keep up desultory fire on Orchard Trench, the ground to the rear of that trench and on Tea Trench. 98650 Gunner H. Bacon of H.Q and 21162 Gunner A. Jenkinson of A battery were both wounded.

Major Lintott, 52nd Brigade Machine Gun Company, arranged reliefs for his gun teams. The remainder of A Section under Second Lieutenant McInnes was to relieve the two guns of D Section in Longueval. Second Lieutenant Moon was to remain in command of the two guns of 13th Company previously manned by Sergeant Potter. B Section was to move out of George Street and relieve C Section in the front line. D Section, under Second Lieutenant Mason, was to be in reserve at Company H.Q, which was now in Piccadilly.

Major King, Lieutenant-Colonel Cardew's right-hand man, turned in after having had a busy night and morning. Lieutenant-Colonel Cardew recorded, somewhat tartly, that Major King stayed in bed until 3.00 pm leaving him to do *all* of the office work. Cardew was kept busy writing plenty of orders and arranging for numerous barrages but he still found time to have a chat with Brigadier-General Hussey of the 5th Division Artillery.

10.22 am

The 9th Duke of Wellingtons sent a situation report to 52nd Brigade H.Q. One Vickers gun was in position forward at Post E, one was at the corner of Duke Street and North Street and one in Delville Wood itself. Stokes Mortars were stationed in Piccadilly ready to move when they were needed. One platoon was stationed in Duke Street between Piccadilly and North Street. Four platoons were placed between North Street and Post E in seven posts and backed up by four Lewis guns. The advanced post was still manned by a Vickers gun team and protected by riflemen and bombers. The battalion bombers were stationed in Piccadilly as was the Machine Gun Company H.Q. Two platoons were in support along North Street. Four platoons were in a column running from the fields to the south of Longueval village to its southern edge. One platoon was in support astride North Street. The reserve company was in the trench that ran around the church in the village. This company provided carrying parties for the front line units. Water was being supplied by a water cart situated in the Quarry. The C.O reported that his men's morale was fair and he was confident that, if attacked, the battalion could hold the line but he did add that his men were exhausted.

10.30 am

The 9th Duke of Wellingtons' position stretched well into the XIII Corps area and they asked that the onus of keeping in touch should lie with the 1st Berkshires who were alongside them and held Delville Wood. Wannell said that *his* patrols had suffered heavy casualties and had other work to do besides just keeping touch.

10.35 am

A further report was sent by the 9th Duke of Wellingtons stating that an enemy post had been spotted very near to Post E. His men had observed that the German post was defended by a machine gun and about twenty men. The German front line, Orchard Trench, was thought to be held strongly during the night and by snipers and machine guns during the day. They reported that the shelling had eased and recorded that they had been instructed to send all men of the 12th Manchesters back to their original positions and to clear their wounded. It was also noted that the 12th Manchesters were to be relieved by the 10th Lancashires.

11.00 am

The 52nd Field Ambulance recorded that three officers and one hundred and fifty one other ranks passed through the Advanced Dressing Station in the Gully.

12 Noon

Captain Manger of the 8th South Staffords attended a conference at 51st Brigade H.Q.

At Bellevue Farm the 7th East Yorks ceased Company training. Orders came into H.Q for the battalion to move forward to Pommiers Redoubt and Trench to relieve the 12th Manchesters.

The Commanding Officer of the 52nd Field Ambulance visited the bearer post in Bernafay Wood and arranged for one officer and seven squads of bearers from the 51st Field Ambulance to be accommodated there. Their job was to clear 51st Brigade casualties from the Wood to the 52nd Field Ambulance Advanced Dressing Station. Two cars and two wheeled stretchers of the 52nd Field Ambulance were detailed for this duty.

1.00 pm

Brigadier-General Clarke sent a message to Major-General Robertson informing him that his 52nd Brigade was fit enough to hold the present position until the night of 5/6 August.

2.00 pm

The C.O of the 52nd Field Ambulance sent instructions to Captain Barclay of the 51st Field Ambulance. Barclay was to inspect the medical dugout in Bernafay Wood where the A.D.M.S had ordered that another Advanced Dressing Station be set up.

Responding to the request by the C.O of the 52nd Field Ambulance the 51st Field Ambulance sent up three horse drawn ambulances. They were to work between Caterpillar Ravine (or the Gully) and the Advanced Dressing Station near Montauban. They also sent forward five wheeled stretcher carriers. It was all that could be spared.

In the afternoon Brigadier-Generals Alexander and Harrison of XV Corps visited Lieutenant-Colonel Cardew at the 17th Division H.Q at Bellevue Farm.[151]

During the afternoon Major-General Robertson travelled to Pommiers Redoubt and held a meeting with his three brigade commanders. They discussed the orders received by the 17th Division from XV Corps on 2 August. These referred to the re-organisation and the extension of the division's line into Delville Wood. Two brigades, the 51st and 52nd, would now hold the division's front and the 50th Brigade would be in reserve at and around Pommiers Redoubt.

---

151 IWM: Cardew 86/92/1.

4.40 pm

XV Corps ordered an aerial reconnaissance of the area.

4.45 pm

Orders for the 8th South Staffords arrived at their H.Q giving them instructions to relieve the 1st Kings Royal Rifle Corps in Longueval Alley

5.00 pm

Captain Gorman and seven bearer squads from the 51st Field Ambulance were sent to the bearer post at Bernafay Wood to make it an Advanced Dressing Station.

5.45 pm

Having moved forward in companies the 10th Notts & Derbys completed the relief of the 22nd Royal Fusiliers near Mine Trench.

6.00 pm

Captain Barclay and his twenty bearers returned to the 17th Divisional Collecting Station. Captain Barclay reported to his commanding officer that the Assistant Director of Medical Services had ordered that another Advanced Dressing Station be set up in Bernafay Wood. The chosen site was a dugout that at present was occupied by the 6th Field Ambulance. Captain Barclay had inspected the dugout on the orders of the commanding officer of the 52nd Field Ambulance and by arrangement with the commanding officer of the 6th Field Ambulance. Captain Gorman and seven bearer squads had already been sent there for duty. Rations, drugs and stores had to be sent there later in the evening. Three motor cars, one a Ford, arrived at the Divisional Collecting Station on loan from the 53rd Field Ambulance.

6.20 pm

A patrol of the 9th Duke of Wellingtons began preparations to go out into no-man's-land to try and rescue any wounded men of the 12th

Manchesters that they could find. It was known that Captain Benton of the 12th Manchesters had been hit and was lying wounded in a shell hole in no-man's-land but where he was no one actually knew.

6.30 pm

Brigadier-General Clarke ordered the two remaining companies of the 10th Lancashires to move forward to the old German second line from their current position in Montauban Alley.

6.40 pm

The 50th Brigade Machine Gun Company left Bellevue Farm and travelled to the front via tracks through the rubble of Fricourt and Mametz Villages. The Company second in command was left behind at the Brigade depot at Bellevue Farm. The transport lines were situated at a place called 'Wing Corner'.

6.45 pm

It was noted at Fourth Army headquarters that the back areas on the XV Corps front were quieter and there were fewer German aircraft up at the time.

7.00 pm

The 10th West Yorks paraded and then marched to Pommiers Trench. When they reached their new positions they organised themselves as follows. Battalion Headquarters was set up on the extreme left of the line, then came D, B and A Companies. C Company, the Signallers and the Bombers were situated behind this line.

The 17th Division noted that the 50th Brigade H.Q had moved to Pommiers Redoubt.

7.30 pm

XV Corps recorded that guns firing 20 cm shells had bombarded Mametz Wood and Montauban and 6-inch guns had shelled the crossroads in Mametz Village. This crossroads had received a good deal of attention from the German artillery. The German gunners knew that this was an important point in the lines of communication behind the British lines.

The 6th Dorsets left their dusty camp at Bellevue Farm and marched to Pommiers Redoubt. They marched in companies to Fricourt and then from there they went on as platoons. Captain Mozley said that as they left Fricourt the Germans fired whizz-bangs at the road the platoons were using. Despite this unwelcome surprise, only one man, a Lance Corporal, was slightly wounded.[152]

During the evening Major-General Robertson personally collected Lieutenant-Colonel Cardew and took him to his hut for a meeting. There Major-General Robertson and G.S.O.1, Colonel Collins, briefed Cardew on the broader tactical plans for the 17th Division's time at the front.[153]

8.00 pm

Divisional Operation order No. 73 was issued ordering 50th Brigade to relieve the 52nd Brigade on the night of 4/5 August. The order also contained information for the re-adjustment of the front line, which would be held by the 17th Division after taking over Delville Wood from the 2nd Division. The boundary between the two 17th Division Brigades in the line after the completion of reliefs would be North Street – Piccadilly as far as the junction with Sloane Street – Longueval – Montauban Road. Once the relief was complete the 17th Division would have two brigades in the line, one, the 51st Brigade, with two battalions in the line in the right sector and one, 50th Brigade, with one battalion in the line in the left sector. The 52nd Brigade would go into reserve.

The 7th Lincolns left Pommiers Redoubt to relieve the 23rd Royal Fusiliers in Montauban Alley where they would become 51st Brigade reserve. The 7th Lincolns' diary recorded that one man had been wounded and that Major Metcalfe had fallen sick and had been evacuated; Captain T. A. Preddie had taken over the battalion.

---

152 IWM: Mozley 01/48/1.

153 IWM: Cardew 86/92/1.

The 50th Brigade marched from Bellevue Farm to Pommiers Redoubt to take over the positions vacated by 51st Brigade. Some units of the Brigade were accommodated in trenches around Pommiers Redoubt but there were so many troops there other units had to bivouac in the open. 50th Brigade H.Q opened at Pommiers Redoubt and 50th Brigade set up a depot near Bellevue Farm.

Just before Captain Mozley and his men arrived at Pommiers Redoubt, they witnessed an intense artillery barrage going on around Pozieres, away on their left. He and the men watched as S.O.S rockets of all different colours mingled with Verey Lights and shell bursts. Mozley commented how extraordinary this scene was in bright summer daylight.[154]

The 7th Yorks left Bellevue Farm and moved forward to Pommiers Redoubt going into the divisional reserve. Captain Kay, who had only just returned to the battalion, took over B Company because Lieutenant H. K. C. Hare, the company commander, had been sent to hospital with influenza. The battalion transport and eight officers were left behind at the 50th Brigade Depot. One corporal reported for duty with the battalion.

8.30 pm

The 7th East Yorks left Bellevue Farm for Pommiers Redoubt.

The 50th Brigade Machine Gun Company arrived at Pommiers Redoubt and the men were settled into whatever cover they could find; shell holes and trenches. There would soon be some room for them because the 7th Borders were preparing to move out and go up to the line. The artillery continued to fire.

9.00 pm

Moving out by companies the 7th Borders left Pommiers Redoubt and went forward to relieve the 1st Royal Berkshires in the line in Delville Wood.

---

154 IWM: Mozley 01/48/1.

9.15 pm

By now, the 7th Yorks began arriving at Pommiers Redoubt from Bellevue farm. They had had a difficult journey because their guides became confused and got lost. Lieutenant-Colonel Fife blamed their confusion on the noise of the artillery that had increased in intensity and the muzzle flashes that illuminated the night. He said that the tremendous bombardment was covering attacks by III Corps and the ANZACS.[155] On the left small scale, localised operations against Intermediate Trench and Munster Alley by 34th and 23rd Divisions of III Corps had been going on since 2.30 am. Further to the left, beyond III Corps, in what had originally been meant as a co-ordinated operation with III Corps, the 2nd Australian Division of the Reserve Army attacked in strength at 9.15 am to the south east of the Albert – Bapaume Road.[156] When he arrived at the Redoubt, Fife went in search of the H.Q dugout.[157]

9.25 pm

Preparation for the 9th Duke of Wellingtons' patrols was now complete. Any wounded that were brought in were to be placed in dugouts in Piccadilly. They would then be moved from there down the line to the Quarry.

10.00 pm

The 52nd Brigade received orders from 17th Division H.Q for their relief. The 51st Brigade was to take over from them on the night of 5/6 August.

The 8th South Staffords moved forward to relieve the 1st Kings Royal Rifle Corps and they were guided by Second Lieutenant Allen. A and C Companies moved to Longueval Alley; B and D Companies went to Montauban Alley.

---

[155] Personal diary of Lieutenant-Colonel Fife.

[156] H. R. Sandilands, *The 23rd Division 1914 – 1919,* (First published, William Blackwood & Sons, 1925), p. 88 – 89. J. Shakespear, *The Thirty Fourth Division 1915 – 1919,* (Re-printed, Naval & Military Press), p. 68 - 69

[157] Personal diary of Lieutenant-Colonel Fife.

10.30 pm

Back at Bellevue Farm Cardew returned from his meeting with his Divisional General and sat down in his tent to write his diary. He recorded that he had got along very well with Major-General Robertson and his G.S.O.1, Colonel Collins. The weather was now cold and away on the left III Corps were putting in a night attack. The six and twelve-inch heavy guns positioned in the Meaulte area were firing in support of the operation and the blast of the guns could be physically felt at Bellevue Farm.[158]

10.50 pm

All of the stray 12th Manchesters were reported to be clear of the 9th Duke of Wellingtons' positions and the situation in the line was much quieter. As the 9th Duke of Wellingtons prepared to send out another patrol, a soldier jumped out of the German position and rushed across to the British lines to surrender. He fell into the 9th Duke of Wellingtons trench and was promptly bayoneted by a Tommy. Fortunately for the German soldier the bayonet wound was not fatal; he was taken prisoner and patched up. He gave his name as Karl Winter.[159] After this little interlude the patrol got going.

11.05 pm

A patrol returned and made a report. Their information was passed on to 17th Division H.Q. The portion of Orchard Trench east of North Street was only held by snipers during daylight but it was heavily manned after dark. It appeared to be much like the British front line, made up of a series of posts and shell holes. Also, the patrol reported that the enemy had been seen moving up in single file from the direction of Flers. The British line was therefore moved up to the edge of the wood from where fire could be brought to bear. A good many enemy soldiers had been killed as they moved up to Orchard Trench.

---

158 IWM: Cardew 86/92/1.

159 TNA: PRO WO95/469. War Diary XV Corps Intelligence Summaries, August 1916.

11.30 pm

The last of the 6th Dorsets arrived at Pommiers Redoubt and there they passed what they called 'a quiet night'. By now the 7th East Yorks had also all arrived at the Redoubt.

As the 7th Borders attempted to relieve the 1st Royal Berkshires in Delville Wood three men were killed. Acting Corporal, 14012, George Robert Jackson, Lance Corporal, 18385, Walter Higginson and Private, 12801, Charles Johnston.

Night of 4/5 August

The 51st Brigade began to take over Delville Wood from the 2nd Division's 99th Brigade. The 7th Borders went into the wood, the 8th South Staffords and the 7th Lincolns were posted in Longueval and Montauban Alleys. The 10th Notts & Derbys were kept in reserve and 52nd Brigade Machine Gun Company reported that their reliefs were completed. The 52nd Field Ambulance reported that the Advanced Dressing Station was shelled during the evening and night. There were no casualties but several tents were damaged, as was one of the Ford cars.

Chapter Five: 5 August

1.00 am

Lieutenant-Colonel Fife's men finally settled in to the area in and around Pommiers Redoubt. It had taken no little time to unload their transport.[160]

1.30 am

The 8th South Staffords completed the relief of the 1st Kings Royal Rifle Corps and Captain Manger paid a visit to XV Corps Headquarters.

3.30 am

C Company of the 8th South Staffords, crammed into Longueval Alley, came under shellfire.

4.00 am

The batteries of 79th Brigade, R.F.A., registered on their new S.O.S zone during the day. They recorded that the situation was fairly quiet and that the enemy artillery was less active than on previous days. The 81st Brigade, R.F.A., recorded that the British heavy artillery bombarded Orchard Trench. A message from the Director of Medical Services at Fourth Army H.Q in Querrieu arrived at the 17th Divisional Collecting Station. It stated that the commanding officer of the Station, Major Ferguson, was to report to the D.M.S, at Fourth Army H.Q at 9.30 am. This meeting may well have been called to inform Ferguson that he was soon to be replaced as the C.O of the 51st Field Ambulance. That said, Ferguson, who was keeping the unit war diary at the time, made no mention of the reason for this summons.

---

160 Personal diary of Lieutenant-Colonel Fife.

4.15 am

After a great deal of difficulty, and under what the diary keeper of the 7th Borders called "extraordinary difficulties", the 1st Royal Berkshires were relieved in Delville Wood. The battalion discovered that the trenches were incomplete and unconnected and shellfire had hampered the operation. Five men were killed; Lance Corporal, 13132, Matthew Hutchinson and Privates, 22491, Samuel Inman, 18364, George Jackson, 17309, Thomas Jones and 23120, George Pearson. Twelve men were also wounded during this difficult relief.

Once they had completed the relief Major Irwin sent out patrols with orders to listen for any enemy activity. They returned with reports that the German troops were "strongly established" all around the northern edge of the wood. Sniper fire was constant and the strength of their positions caused Irwin to conclude that the German infantry must have been in position for some time before his battalion's arrival in the line. The strength of the enemy positions did not worry him unduly because he did not seem to expect to go onto the offensive. His men's primary task was to improve and strengthen the front line and communication trenches. There was a gap in the front line of 250 yards, a not inconsiderable hole in the British line and he had orders to dig a trench to fill that gap and connect up the line on the right and left. The work would have to be done under the cover of darkness and he set his men to work. Thirteen more men were wounded as they worked.

4.30 am

For the Royal Engineers and Pioneers construction and digging carried on. They were aided by none too enthusiastic infantry units. The 77th Field Company, R.E, continued their work on the communication trench and the support line. The 78th Field Company, R.E, operated a shift system on the communication trench from Montauban to Longueval, one section and one infantry company worked while the other section and another infantry company widened the section just dug. They were shelled and one man, Sapper, 59162, Alfred Henry Le Maitre was killed and two others wounded. The 93rd Field Company, R.E, reported that the work continued on the H.Q dugouts.

The 7th Yorks and Lancs went to work on an old German communication trench. They were converting the trench to a useable, sunken service road. They were also 'zig zagging' the trench because recent experiences had shown how lethal straight trenches were. This time A Company was employed to bury a communication cable. The work was considerably delayed by enemy shelling. During the day five men were wounded and two were killed by the shelling. Privates, 12391, Phillip Power and 12744, Luke Townsend were buried by their comrades alongside the communication trench that they had been working on.

5.00 am

A 9th Duke of Wellingtons' patrol returned to their lines and reported that they had failed to find Captain Benton. Other patrols were still out looking for him and any other wounded.

5.25 am

XV Corps noted that the artillery of both sides had been busy throughout the night. The 9th Northumberlands reported to 52nd Brigade H.Q that the situation at the front was normal. At this moment, considering that there were numerous British patrols out and about, no man's land was dominated by the British and the German troops were not attempting to contest this fact.

6.30 am

The 17th Division noted, optimistically as it turned out, that the relief of 99th Brigade, 2nd Division had been completed and that during the night 50th Brigade had relieved 52nd Brigade. The Divisional front had now been adjusted and was now thus: In the right Brigade sector, two battalions were in the line and two were in support. In the left Brigade sector one battalion was in the line, two were in support and one Brigade was in reserve. Up at the front it was not really that simple, 52nd Brigade had not yet been relieved, the 9th Duke of Wellingtons and 9th Northumberlands were still in the front line. The handover of the front from the 52nd Brigade to the 50th Brigade would take time.

The 17th Signal Company noted that the 50th Brigade H.Q, was located in Pommiers Redoubt because Montauban Alley was now considered untenable and unsafe. The trench was overcrowded with troops and their concentration there attracted a great deal of artillery fire.

The 10th Lancashires were relieved by the 10th West Yorks of the 50th Brigade and the 10th Lancashires moved into Pommiers Redoubt.

XV Corps recorded that the 17th Division had taken over Delville Wood from XIII Corps as ordered. The front line was held by the 51st Brigade on the right, 52nd Brigade was still on the left and 50th Brigade was in reserve at Pommiers Redoubt. Lieutenant-General Horne had one of his staff send a message to remind the R.F.C that they had been waiting for reconnaissance photographs of their XV Corps' portion of the front for three days and that it was imperative that these photographs be delivered.

A patrol finally came across Captain Benton in no-man's-land; he was alive and they brought him in. Benton had lain out there for thirty hours with no food or water and he was in a very bad way. He was taken down the line to Heilly Casualty Clearing Station where he died of his wounds on 17 August 1916.

6.56 am

Fourth Army H.Q noted that the situation on the XV Corps front was normal. The artillery was active on both sides of the lines.

7.30 am

Karl Winter had been taken to 'the Cage.'[161] Though he was suffering from a bayonet wound, prisoner Winter was interrogated by XV Corps officers. He could not locate the position of his trench for his captors but he could tell them that the 31st (Reserve) Infantry Regiment was on the left of his unit, the 84th (Reserve) Infantry Regiment. He was an officer's servant who had only been in the area since 26 July. Until two days ago he and his officer had been based at battalion H.Q which, again, he could not locate. When a company

161 Temporary, divisional POW holding area.

commander had been wounded a replacement was required so Winter had accompanied his officer to the front line. The German troops in the front line were not drinking plain water, he told the British officers, instead they were issued a ration of soda water or they drew a ration of coffee before they went into the front line.

It was noted in the XV Corps Intelligence Summary that German troops were busy working on their trenches behind their current line. They were working hard to prevent the British occupying the ridge between High Wood and Pozieres. Among other work a switch trench had been dug from the old German second line along the rear of the ridge. It ran behind Delville Wood and into High Wood and on to the windmill in Pozieres. The aviators reported that this trench had been well constructed and was well wired.

Number 3 Squadron, R.F.C, reported that the Germans were doubling their trench line from Warlencourt to Gueudecourt. The excavations were not yet complete but the lines to be dug were marked out and wire had been laid.

After his breakfast Lieutenant-Colonel Cardew met with Brigadier-General Hussey and then took a ride in his car to visit the 80th Brigade R.F.A. The Germans were shelling the area behind Montauban and this hampered his efforts to find his old Brigade's H.Q. He eventually discovered it in a deep, unventilated German dugout. When he descended into the dugout, he found everyone asleep. The lack of ventilation made him realise how lucky he was not to be sharing this accommodation!

After waking the artillery officers up Cardew went around the 80th Brigade gun batteries and then headed off to 52nd Brigade H.Q. Here he learned of the disturbing but unofficial events of the 52nd Brigade attack on the night of 3/4 August. He was also told that the staff at 52nd Brigade H.Q doubted the reports about shelling and gas shells sent back by the infantry before the attack. His informant on the staff said that the shelling had not been bad that night and that there had in fact been *no* gas shells fired at the British infantry. Both the 9th Northumberlands and the 12th Manchesters would have vehemently disagreed with this. After this interesting visit, because his car had gone back to H.Q, he had "a long, hot walk to Fricourt."[162]

8.25 am

Fourth Army H.Q recorded that the 17th Division had completed the take over of a portion of the XIII Corps' front.

9.00 am

The 9th Northumberlands evacuated Pear Street, the front line, so that the heavy artillery could bombard the German front line, Orchard Trench. During the shelling, which went on for a few hours, several of the British shells hit Pear Street. The men of the 9th Northumberlands, who were watching the bombardment and already holding a somewhat prejudiced view of the British artillery, concluded that the Forward Observation Officer obviously had little idea about the exact position of the British trenches.

9.05 am

B Company of the 8th South Staffords had to move along Montauban Alley to try and make room for A and C Companies who were crowded together in Longueval Alley. The shelling would have given the officers cause for concern in the overcrowded trenches. All four companies were ordered to dig their trenches deeper.

9.20 am

The 17th Division, along with 33rd Division, which was shortly due to come into the line and relieve the 51st Division on the left, was instructed by XV Corps to make a reconnaissance and have a scheme ready for the creation of a proper line from the left boundary near Bazentin-le-Grand to the right boundary at Longueval. The C.R.E of 33rd Division was preparing proposals so that Corps could push on systematically. It had been decided that two pairs of communication trenches were required.

---

162 IWM: Cardew 86/92/1.

The question of relieving the front line during daylight hours had arisen and Lieutenant-General Horne had decided to allow his divisional commanders to choose the best time for relief. While giving them the freedom to choose he did point out that they should take no unnecessary risks during the reliefs.

9.30 am

The senior officers of the 6th Dorsets visited 50th Brigade H.Q at Pommiers Redoubt for a meeting with Brigadier-General Glasgow and to receive their orders. The officers learned that their battalion was to relieve the 9th Northumberlands in the front line trenches that evening.

9.37 am

A large number of corpses were still lying in Trones Wood, so A and C Companies of the 8th South Staffords were ordered to the Wood on a fatigue. The Tommies were ordered to move the bodies out of the wood, bury them in pits and then cover them with quick lime. Bernard Martin, a second lieutenant who served in the Somme Campaign, remembered with horror that the whole shell blasted area on the approach to Delville Wood was covered with corpses. Under constant observation no one could bury them; a single burial party would invite immediate shellfire so they remained where they were. The troops had to pick their way through the rotting dead on a daily basis[163] and with familiarity they became immune to the sights and smells.

9.44 am

The G.S.O.1 of the Fourth Army Staff who was visiting the 17th Division, reported back to his H.Q that there were a large number of German observation balloons up behind the German lines. The 80th Brigade, R.F.A., had reported that they had counted nine German balloons.

---

163 B. Martin, *Poor Bloody Infantry, A Subaltern on the Western Front 1916 – 1917*, (John Murray, 1987) P. 91

Lieutenant-Colonel Fife arrived at 50th Brigade H.Q to receive a briefing about plans for the next few days from Brigadier-General Glasgow. He asked if there was any news about the attacks made by III Corps and the ANZACS but nothing was forthcoming. After his meeting Fife went for a walk to examine the positions around Trones Wood. It was not a particularly safe trip because the German artillery was dropping shells all around the area in what Fife thought was a random manner.[164]

10.00 am

Arrangements were made by the 9th Duke of Wellingtons' C.O, Lieutenant-Colonel Wannell, for a system of guides and runners to aid the relief of his battalion by the 10th Notts & Derbys. These elaborate arrangements were approved by Brigadier-General Clarke at 52nd Brigade H.Q.

The 52nd Brigade Machine Gun Company received orders that the 52nd Brigade was to be relieved by the 50th Brigade.

11.00 am

B and D companies of the 8th South Staffords who were crowded into Montauban Alley were intermittently shelled by 5.9-inch guns.

The 52nd Field Ambulance recorded that seven officers and eighty-eight other ranks passed through the Advanced Dressing Station. Doctors Captain E. P. Blashki and Lieutenant J. Watson had been transferred, sick, to the 51st Field Ambulance.

11.25 am

The weathermen made a report to Fourth Army H.Q. The forecast was north-east or north wind, blowing to 10 mph. There would be some cloud in the afternoon but with bright intervals. Becoming warmer the temperature for the day was 70° to 75° F. It would be 55° F overnight and 75° F tomorrow.

---

[164] Personal diary of Lieutenant-Colonel Fife.

11.30 am

Major-General Robertson telephoned XV Corps and reported that five German kite balloons were clearly visible. In his opinion they were probably spotting for the German batteries that were shelling the Caterpillar Valley area.

Noon

Captain Bolton, the commanding officer of the 50th Brigade Machine Gun Company, 50th Brigade, accompanied by four of his officers, visited Major Lintott in the 52nd Brigade Machine Gun Company H.Q in Montauban Alley to discuss the impending relief. Between them they arranged it for 3.30 pm. The two guns out on the right, formerly of the 13th Brigade Machine Gun Company and now manned by the 52nd Brigade Machine Gun Company, would be taken over by the 51st Brigade Machine Gun Company. A little inter-divisional re-organisation took place, 3748 Sergeant Smith of the 52nd Brigade Machine Gun Company was promoted to Colour Sergeant and appointed as C.Q.M.S to the 51st Brigade Machine Gun Company. He took up his new appointment during the afternoon.

The ground between Bernafay Wood and Caterpillar Wood was subjected to a heavy German bombardment, no doubt guided by the observers in the balloons.

During the afternoon, the Company Commanders of the 6th Dorsets went forward to inspect the trenches held by the 9th Northumberlands in preparation for the evening relief. On their way forward Mozley and his fellow officers had to go 'over the open', traversing fairly high ground and past the decomposing corpses of British cavalry horses that had been killed on 14 July when the German second line had fallen.[165] On their return from the front line, when they reached the same spot, they were forced to run for their lives because the Germans shelled them again. Obviously the German gunners had the horses 'zeroed'. Despite this attention

165 Mozley was referring to the attack made by a squadron each of the 7th Dragoon Guards and the 20th Deccan Horse. See Appendix 3.

Mozley and his comrades all made it back to Pommiers Redoubt safely.[166]

Gunner Austin J. Heraty of the 80th Brigade, R.F.A., recalled that he saw these cavalry horses when his gun team travelled along the ridge in late July. He remembered that as he rode by the carcasses he noticed that they were not gun team horses and that the stench was awful.[167]

12.17 pm

XV Corps contacted Fourth Army H.Q and informed the staff there about the five kite balloons initially reported by Major-General Robertson. With a Brigade relief going on, troops had to move across Caterpillar Valley that afternoon and Caterpillar Valley was coming under shellfire. Therefore the Fourth Army H.Q staff decided that something had to be done to bring the observation balloons down.

12.45 pm

The 52nd Brigade issued the orders to the battalions and the machine gun company concerning the relief that night. At the same time operation orders came in to the 50th Machine Gun Company from 50th Brigade referring to the relief of the 52nd Machine Gun Company.

1.00 pm

Major Ferguson of the 51st Field Ambulance returned to the Divisional Collecting Station after his visit to Fourth Army H.Q at Querrieu. He noticed that despite the heavy artillery fire there was "little doing" at the Station in the way of incoming casualties. A little while later the D. D. M. S of XV Corps visited the Station. Noticing

---

166 IWM: Mozley 01/48/1.

167 A. J. Heraty, *A Duration Man A Staffordshire Soldier in the Great War* (Churnett Valley Books, 1999), p.62. Heraty was wounded while serving his gun during an artillery exchange with 5.9 Howitzers on 23 July 1916. He was shipped back to Britain and when he recovered he was sent to another R.F.A brigade.

that a number of vehicles were standing idle he promptly ordered five motor buses to return to their respective H.Qs, as there was little work for them to do at the Station. News came through that Captain Barclay had been awarded the M.C. Water, rations and forage was sent forward to the medical staff and horses at the Advanced Dressing Station in Bernafay Wood.

2.55 pm

The 9th Duke of Wellingtons provided the 52nd Brigade Machine Gun Company with a fatigue party to carry the guns down the line as they were relieved.

During the afternoon Lieutenant-Colonel Fife continued his 'Cook's Tour' of the Somme Battlefield and visited the old German trench line opposite Carnoy.[168]

3.00 pm

Using the elaborate arrangements devised by Wannell of the 9th Duke of Wellingtons, the 10th Notts & Derbys began to take over the front line at Longueval.

The 7th East Yorks were warned that they would probably have to move up Montauban Alley at about 7.00 pm. Company officers were ordered to reconnoitre the positions that the battalion would occupy and report to 52nd Brigade H.Q on the way forward.

The first section of the 50th Brigade Machine Gun Company left Pommiers Redoubt to begin the relief of the 52nd Brigade Machine Gun Company. The Company H.Q was set up in Montauban Alley. A Section and half of D Section were also stationed in Montauban Alley. B Section moved into the support line, George Street, and spread out along the trench. These guns would be able to put indirect fire onto Switch Trench and High Wood as well as giving covering fire over the ground between George Street and High Wood. Two guns of D Section went to Longueval and into the front line. One was placed at the corner of Duke Street and Piccadilly. From here the gun could sweep the ground between

168 Personal diary of Lieutenant-Colonel Fife.

Piccadilly and North Street. The other gun covered Piccadilly. C Section went up to Pear Street. Number one gun was set up to enfilade Orchard Trench, number two gun was to enfilade Wood Lane, number three gun could enfilade Tea Lane and also Orchard Trench, number four gun had the duty of sweeping Orchard Trench and Wood Lane.

3.30 pm

The 7th East Yorks received orders to relieve the 12th Manchesters in Montauban Alley at 7.00 pm and Second Lieutenant Goodwin was appointed 50th Brigade Intelligence Officer. They were informed by 50th Brigade H.Q that every effort had to be made to salvage derelict material. Ammunition, bombs and weapons had to be collected and taken back by the limbers that brought up the rations. The battalion began to collect up the abandoned equipment that lay around them and sent it back to the Brigade dump.

4.00 pm

The heavy bombardment of Orchard Street, the German front line, ceased and the 9th Northumberlands were able to re-occupy Pear Street.

A Company of the 8th South Staffords, now returned from the gruesome task of disposing of corpses, crowded into Longueval Alley and were promptly shelled by 77 mm guns.

5.15 pm

The first platoon of the 10th West Yorks paraded and moved forward to go into close support. The remainder of the battalion moved off after them at intervals of two hundred yards. Their route forwards was roughly seven hundred and fifty yards up Pommiers Redoubt and the Montauban Road, then they turned left and crossed Montauban Alley where they came to a quarry. Here the platoons picked up the guides who led them forward to their destination; a line on the right of Bazentin-le-Grand and on the left of Longueval.

When the 10th West Yorks arrived at their allotted positions the battalion commander set up his H.Q in an old German dugout. D

Company spread out on the left, A Company went out in front, C Company set up on the right and B Company went behind them.

5.30 pm

52nd Brigade sent a situation report to 17th Division.

6.00 pm

H.Q and the reserve sections of the 52nd Brigade Machine Gun Company were relieved and they marched to the trenches on the south side of Pommiers Redoubt. Major Lintott showed Captain Bolton of 50th Brigade Machine Gun Company around the H.Q, the dump, front line and support trenches.

6.30 pm

7th East Yorks of 50th Brigade moved into Montauban Alley as part of their relief of the 52nd Brigade.

The Germans shelled Montauban Alley. The war diary of the 7th East Yorks recorded that the shelling killed one man and wounded another. There is no other record of a man of the 7th East Yorks being killed on this day. Official records show that only three men died between 5 and 7 August. Two were killed in action and one died of his wounds.

7.50 pm

Fourth Army recorded that the 17th Division reported that the artillery fire on Delville Wood was slackening. As a matter of concern, eleven German observation balloons had been seen during this day and there had been an increase in German air activity.

8.00 pm

As they settled into their close reserve positions between Bazentin Le Grand and Longueval the 10th West Yorks were shelled. There was no reported damage or casualties.

8.30 pm

The 10th West Yorks of 50th Brigade completed their relief of the 10th Lancashires.

The 50th Brigade Machine Gun Company reported that the relief of the 52nd Brigade Machine Gun Company had been completed and all guns were in position. The Company Sergeant Major was put in charge of an advanced dump near Green Dump. Men from the Sections were sent here to collect rations and water and also to deliver messages. The messages would then be taken by fresh orderlies to Company H.Q. Communication was also kept up by an orderly stationed with the transport. A signal station had also been set up at the dump which was in contact with the 50th Brigade Signal Company. One other rank was wounded during the relief. Captain Bolton inspected the guns in George Street during the evening and the Germans guns continued to shell Caterpillar Valley. The balloons had still not been dealt with.

The men of the 6th Borders began to leave Pommiers Redoubt to go forward and relieve the 9th Northumberlands. Inevitably, when Captain Mozley's men reached the dead cavalry horses they were shelled and forced to take cover. They were held up for a short time but suffered no casualties and when the German gunners lost interest they carried on.

8.45 pm

D Company of the 8th South Staffords collected rations and carried them forward to the 7th Borders who were occupying the shell holes and shallow trenches in Delville Wood.

9.00 pm

The 50th Brigade H.Q moved to Montauban Alley from Pommiers Redoubt. It would seem that no one could decide which was the more crowded and/or dangerous position. The 7th Yorks remained at Pommiers Redoubt.

Considerable enemy air activity was reported to XV Corps H.Q, as was the increasing presence of German observation balloons. XV

Corps contacted the R.F.C and asked them to try and do something about the balloons.

It might well be thought that the big, stationary gas filled balloons, tethered to 10 ton winch lorries, were 'sitting ducks' for aircraft but operations against balloons were not very popular with the aircrews on either side. Such a task was often regarded as "heroic madness"[169] but that said, if ordered to do so, the aircrews would attack the balloons. Some pilots, like American Second Lieutenant Frank Luke, Jnr, even tried to make a career out it.[170] The observation balloons were vital to the artillery and in good, clear weather they provided stable platforms that had a splendid view of the battlefield. They were important, expensive pieces of kit and their crews, both air and ground, were very well trained. In the basket below the gas bag, the observers were in contact with the ground and the gun batteries via cable telephone. Being so expensive and so important, and above all stationary, the balloons were well defended by batteries of anti-aircraft guns and flights of scouts.[171] Any pilot lining his aircraft up to fire at a balloon presented a good target himself. Peter Hart wrote in his book *Bloody April* that "there was never a suitable opportunity [for attacking a balloon] that did not entail severe risks for the attacking pilot."[172] American pilot, Captain J. C. Vasconcelles, said of balloons, "I think they're the toughest proposition a pilot has to meet. Any man who gets a balloon has my respect, because he's got to be good or he doesn't get it."[173] Even if the pilot did open fire and hit the target, they were not always that easy to bring down. Said Lieutenant Alan Dore of 43 Squadron, R.F.C, of trying to shoot down an Allied balloon that had broken free of its mooring (its crew

---

169 N. S. Hall, *The Balloon Buster,* (First published, Liberty Weekly, Inc., 1928. Re-printed, Corgi, 1967), p. 73

170 Second Lieutenant Frank Luke, Jnr, was killed in action on 29 September, 1918.

171 Fighter aircraft.

172 P. Hart, *Bloody April Slaughter In The Skies Over Arras, 1917,* (Weidenfeld & Nicolson, 2005), p. 150

173 Captain J. C. Vasconcelles in N. S. Hall, *The Balloon Buster,* (First published, Liberty Weekly, Inc., 1928. Re-printed, Corgi, 1967), p. 75

had bailed out), "I put one hundred bullets into the gasbag, but apparently without effect."[174]

But the aircraft could not be everywhere at once and they had numerous tasks to perform. Aerial reconnaissance and photography were two of the most important and theses services were always in demand by the generals. The photographs had finally arrived from the R.F.C, at XV Corps H.Q. Lieutenant-General Horne's reminder had worked. They were sent on to the 17th Division and in the evening the divisional staff and Major-General Robertson examined the aerial reconnaissance photographs of Orchard Trench. Any information that could be gleaned was vital.

10.30 pm

Lieutenant-Colonel Cardew sat down to the ritual of writing letters home and writing his diary. The weather was cold, he noted, and the guns were quiet. After his morning visit to his old command and 52nd Brigade H.Q he had stayed in. Major King had visited the 78th and 79th Brigades, R.F.A. Cardew had heard that a show around Martinpuich had been very successful and that significant ground had been taken.[175]

11.00 pm

The relief of the 52nd Machine Gun Company was completed. All sections were now in trenches at Pommiers Redoubt.

All of Captain Mozley's A Company, 6th Dorsets, had finally managed to get into their new trench, Pont Street, that ran from Longueval Village to High Wood, and the relief was eventually completed during the early hours of the next day. There were no alarms that night and Captain Mozley and his men spent a relatively quiet night. A Company held a part of the line that was actually a support trench to C and D Companies who were stationed in Pear Street.

---

174 Lieutenant A. Dore in Hart, *Bloody April Slaughter In The Skies Over Arras, 1917,* p. 175

175 IWM: Cardew 86/92/1.

11.30 pm

In the support line, George Street, B Section, 50th Brigade Machine Gun Company, watched as High Wood was exposed to heavy shrapnel and high explosive shelling. They noted that they saw five red rockets launched from that area.

11.55 pm

The 9th Duke of Wellingtons and the 10th Notts & Derbys reported that the relief had been completed. Wannell's arrangements for guides and runners had worked very well. There were very few casualties; two men of the Notts & Derbys, Privates, 41390, Edmund French and 38360, S.H. Lammin, were killed. Two platoons had been held up at Longueval because they were forced to take cover from a heavy bombardment.

Midnight

The 50th Brigade recorded that the enemy began to shell Montauban Alley. Corps noted that this shelling was considerable.

The 7th Lincolns reported that Montauban Alley and the village of Montauban were heavily shelled all night. Second Lieutenant R. A. Eadie, who had only joined the battalion on 27 July, and four men were killed and thirteen men had been wounded. Some awards for actions in the previous tour at Quadrangle Support Trench arrived. Lieutenant D. A. Jones received the D.S.O, R.S.M Whiting and 15184, Private Harriett both received the D.C.M.

The 80th Brigade, R.F.A., suffered severe counter-battery fire and several dugouts were blown in. Lieutenant Houghton was shell-shocked. When the shelling abated, Lieutenant Carver of D battery was evacuated to the wagon lines, officially because he was sick. In truth Carver was shell-shocked and in an even worse state than Houghton. Cardew later remarked that Carver's nerves were indeed shattered.[176] One man, 108909, Gunner Pleavin was killed, thirteen men were wounded and four guns were put out of action.

---

[176] IWM: Cardew 86/92/1.

Operations for 78th Brigade, R.F.A., continued as the day before. They carried on firing and they too came under counter-battery fire. One man, 70807, Gunner, Masterson was killed.

It was the same story for the 79th Brigade, R.F.A. They carried on firing all day and night on a variety of targets, back area, roads, and communications and the enemy artillery was active all day. Lieutenant J. D. Dutton was posted to the Brigade to command B battery. Major H.A.G. Chamber was evacuated to England, sick. 4506 Corporal Philip Ravenscroft went missing. There is no record of a Corporal Philip Ravenscroft being killed, so he was either found, captured or totally vanished. His medal index card does not record that he died or was captured.

During the day the 81st Brigade R.F.A., registered on new targets.

Night of 5/6 August

The peace that Lieutenant-Colonel Cardew had recorded in his diary at 10.30 pm was soon shattered as the Germans began a heavy barrage of the British rear areas. A great many gas shells mingled with the high explosive shells.

The 52nd Field Ambulance reported that Caterpillar Wood and Valley, and the road leading to Montauban and Longueval were heavily shelled throughout the night. The dugouts at the bearer post in the valley were hit. One of the dugouts was hit badly and completely blown in. Men rushed to try and dig the occupants out. 51523 Private E. A. Davies M.M, was pulled out alive. Wounded and confused, he was sent to the hospital. The further efforts of the rescuers were to no avail, they could not get deeper into the smashed dugout. 72851 Private H.E. James, 76938 Private J. Dunkerley, 41504 Private W. Askew and 41542 Private C.S. Gluckstein M.M, were buried so deeply that it was useless to try and get them out. 42076 Private Parry was also wounded during the bombardment and he too was sent to hospital. Only a few days before, on 27 July, Gluckstein and Davies had been awarded the ribbons for the M. M, by Major-General Robertson for their bravery during the attacks on Quadrangle Support Trench in early July.

B Section, 50th Brigade Machine Gun Company, sent in a report to Company H.Q. They reported the red rockets and the shelling of the front line in High Wood. They also reported that they had employed two guns in traversing, indirect fire on Switch Trench and its rear area until midnight and had expended two thousand rounds of ammunition. The gun teams had worked on improving their positions and making two alternative gun emplacements to the right of the present ones. They had suffered no casualties.

C Section, 50th Brigade Machine Gun Company, sent their report to Company H.Q. They had withdrawn the guns from the front line during the British bombardment. They suffered a direct hit from a shell; one man, Private Crawford, was killed and two were wounded. One of the wounded remained at duty. Corporal Sturgeon displayed great coolness when the shell fell and he set a good example to his men. His immediate recommendation for a D.C.M was turned down because the evidence given was not considered strong enough proof of his bravery.

The 81st Brigade, R.F.A., reported that they came under heavy fire throughout the night. Second Lieutenant Robert Moore Bowman of C battery was killed and Captain F. B. Benham was severely wounded when their dugout was hit. Second Lieutenant Bowman was buried at Carnoy military cemetery.

Once again the noise of the guns kept Lieutenant-Colonel Fife awake.[177]

---

177 Personal diary of Lieutenant-Colonel Fife.

Chapter Six: 6 August

The weather exceptionally fine. Early in the morning Major King left 17th Divisional Artillery H.Q at Bellevue Farm and headed for the front line. Lieutenant-Colonel Cardew remained at H.Q and worked in his office all morning.[178]

12.45 am

The relief of the 9th Northumberlands by the 6th Dorsets was completed. The 9th Northumberlands moved off to Pommiers Trench to become the Divisional reserve. When they arrived the company rolls were checked and all deficiencies were indentured for.

1.30 am

Twenty wounded men of the 8th South Staffords were evacuated from the trenches. A wire came into their H.Q informing them that Captain E.W. Wood had been awarded a bar to his M.C, Captain Gibson had been awarded the M.C and Private S. Lee had been awarded the D. C. M. Once again, these awards had been made for bravery during the actions between 1 and 11 July at Quadrangle Support.

2.00 am

The relief of the 52nd Brigade by the 51st Brigade was completed. Three battalions of 52nd Brigade were concentrated as divisional reserve near Pommiers Redoubt. One battalion bivouacked near Quesnoy. 52nd Brigade H.Q was set up in Fricourt. They remained in reserve and took the opportunity to re-organise.

---

[178] IWM: Cardew 86/92/1.

2.20 am

The 6th Dorsets of 50th Brigade completed the relief of the 9th Northumberlands in the front line, Pear Street. The Brigade now had the 6th Dorsets in the front line, the 10th West Yorks in close support and the 7th East Yorks and 7th Yorks in reserve. The 50th Brigade Machine Gun Company had six guns in the front line with four in support and six in reserve. The Trench Mortar battery had six guns in the front line, and four in reserve. The front was covered by the 80th and 81st Brigades R.F.A. The 93rd Field Company, R.E., under Captain William James Nesbit Glasgow,[179] was responsible for the work at the front.

The 50th Brigade war diary recorded that it was a quiet day despite the shelling of Montauban Alley. Brigadier-General Glasgow noted that there was no communication trench to the front line, Pear Street, and there was no communication with the Brigade on the right flank. The only way to the front line was via Thistle Street and then across one hundred yards of the open to the west end of Pear Street. The Pioneers, the 7th Yorks & Lancs were continuing to work on a communication trench, called Y& L Alley in their honour, but it was not yet finished. Orders had been issued for the completion of YL Alley and the 10th West Yorks were instructed to improve the old German second line. The 6th Dorsets were ordered to improve Pear Street. The 7th Yorks sent a working party to YL Alley in the reserve area.

It was originally intended that the 6th Dorsets would do a two-day tour of duty but relief was cancelled because of ongoing operations. The 6th Dorsets recorded that, because they had enjoyed a fairly quiet time, a good deal of good work done. They dug a trench across the front of Pear Street Trench and named it Dorset Trench. Second Lieutenant Vernon was wounded while this trench was being dug. Several useful patrols were sent out.

In Pont Street Captain Mozley took stock of his position. He had the Seaforths of the 33rd Division on his left. This battalion faced the German position of High Wood and men were in the process of

---

179 Captain Glasgow, whose family lived in Buenos Aires, Argentina, had earned the M.C, and had been Mentioned in Despatches by the time he was killed in action on 7 October 1916.

digging a sap from their portion of Pont Street towards the wood. Pont Street was very narrow and uncomfortable and to make matters worse it was not continuous. There was a break in it of about 150 yards where there was no cover at all. Captain Mozley ordered his men to begin digging to widen and lengthen the trench. The German gunners fired off a large number of whizz-bangs in A Company's general direction. Captain Mozley remembered that it was frontal fire that landed on the road and was harmless to his men. He remarked that it was lucky that it was not enfilade fire.[180]

3.00 am

The Company commanders of A, B and C companies, the 8th South Staffords inspected the positions in Delville Wood.

4.30 am

The 7th Yorks and Lancs carried on the work of the previous day. As far as depth was concerned the communication trench, YL Alley, was completed. B Company was shelled and one man from B Company and four from D Company were wounded.

5.00 am

As the German barrage eased, the two platoons of the 9th Duke of Wellingtons managed to get clear of Longueval. Captain Gilbert of the 10th Notts & Derbys noted that the front line that his men had taken over was just a series of roughly joined shell holes with no connection between the front and support lines. They set about attempting to improve their positions but the broken ground and heavy shelling made such work impossible. The battalion H.Q was set up in Longueval but it was soon moved because a shell scored a direct hit on a bomb dump that was situated close to entrance of the shelter. H.Q was re-opened in a deep dugout on the southern edge of Delville Wood. The new H.Q was far from ideal. This shelter had only a single, deep shaft to allow passage in and out and, to make

180 IWM: Mozley 01/48/1.

matters, worse the entrance to the shaft was in full view of German troops in Guillemont.[181]

The 78th Field Company, Royal Engineers, expected a company of infantry to arrive for work but they failed to show up. The communication trench from Montauban to Longueval had been dug through and it was down to the required depth but it still needed widening and trimming. 50th Brigade promised that more infantry would report for work that night. In the meantime the commanding officer of the 78th Field Company marked out a support line. A Section was to be put to work on it the following day. He requested that a company of pioneers or infantry be provided to work with the section. Another of his sections went to work on dugouts for a Field Artillery Brigade but they were not required because the 93rd Field Company were doing the job. One man of the 78th Field Company was evacuated to the casualty clearing station with shell shock.

6.00 am

All elements of the 9th Duke of Wellingtons were now reported to be clear of the front line trenches and had moved down to Pommiers Redoubt.

In the front line in Delville Wood Major Irwin's 7th Borders had been hard at work throughout the night improving and strengthening the trenches. Irwin also made sure that he always had patrols out in no-man's-land. The diarist recorded that three men had been killed and nineteen more wounded as they had worked. Records show that four men were killed on 6 August: Lance Corporal, 18422, James Heenan and Privates, 12187, Henry Ashmore, 14933, George Morris and 23251 Frank Rance.

7.10 am

XV Corps sent a situation report to Fourth Army H.Q. There had been intermittent shelling of the 17th Division's front all night. The area to the west of Montauban suffered particularly heavy shelling.

---

181 Hoyte, *10th (S) Battalion*, p. 18

The XV Corps intelligence officers were given translations of a German letter that had been picked up either in a trench raid, or taken from a corpse or from a prisoner. In the letter, dated 21 April 1916, the writer told the soldier how bad things were back at home. Food, particularly meat and sausage was scarce; the women of Elberfeld had stormed the town hall and berated the mayor about the situation. Several of the desperate women had been arrested by the police. Every time scarce commodities went on sale in the shops there were thousands waiting to buy and the police were always present. A poor hermit had already died of starvation and even if people had money there was very often little to buy. The writer wearily declared that the war should come to an end. Such news from the German home front would have delighted the British intelligence officers. It was another sign that German morale was close to breaking point. Whatever the news meant to the British, the news would have been terribly worrying and depressing for the front line soldier, Otto, who had originally received the letter.

Later in the morning Lieutenant-Colonel Fife, the C.O of the 7th Yorks, visited Brigadier-General Glasgow at 50th Brigade H.Q to see if he could get any news. Glasgow and Fife were friends, and Glasgow treated Fife as his 2 i/c. When Glasgow was on leave Fife ran the 50th Brigade and just prior to the opening of the Somme Campaign, Glasgow had nominated Fife as his successor should anything happen to him. Pilcher had agreed with and endorsed this arrangement.[182]

8.45 am

Number 3 Squadron, R.F.C., reported that an enemy balloon was up in the air at Grevillers and more were being winched up at Le Transloy and Thilloy. Also, the enemy seemed to have dug new trenches to the north of Longueval and to the south east of Delville Wood near Waterlot Farm.

---

182 Personal diary of Lieutenant-Colonel Fife.

11.00 am

The 52nd Field Ambulance recorded that five officers and one hundred and thirty three other ranks had passed through the Advanced Dressing Station. Doctors Captain Blashki and Lieutenant Watson had both fallen ill and had been evacuated to the hospital.

Noon

The 51st Field Ambulance recorded that it had been a quiet night and morning despite some of what the C.O called "promiscuous shelling"[183] of the neighbouring wagon lines and bivouacs during the night. Up to noon thirteen officers and four hundred and thirty two other ranks had passed through the station. Earlier in the morning Captains Barclay and Walker had gone to the Advanced Dressing Station at Bernafay Wood and found that all was well there.

12.45 pm

Elements of the 51st Brigade made an interesting but unexpected and unpleasant discovery. Not only were German troops in Orchard trench on the edge of the wood but they had also been located in the northern end of Delville Wood. The 10th Notts & Derbys had sent out patrols and one had discovered German posts just inside of the wood, to the right front of the 10th Notts & Derbys' right company. The patrol had been sent to reconnoitre the corner of the small orchard and Orchard Trench. It came under fire from their right rear from about the junction of Flers Road and positions inside Delville Wood. German troops were back in the wood. Their presence was immediately reported to 51st Brigade H.Q and the news was not taken very well. It had been thought that Delville Wood was completely clear of German troops. On hearing this news Major-General Robertson ordered 51st Brigade to send patrols out at once to ascertain where the flank of this enemy trench rested.

During the afternoon men of the 80th Brigade, R.F.A., set about trying to repair their four damaged guns. Three were repaired on the

---

183 TNA. PRO: WO 95/1996. War Diary, 51st Field Ambulance, August 1916

gun line but one was so badly damaged it had to be sent back to the repair depot at Heilly.

Lieutenant-Colonel Fife had a walk around his companies. He was shown a Divisional order that said four of his officers, Wilkinson, Lamb, Roper and Duncan had all been awarded the M.C. The R.S.M walked over to Quadrangle Support Trench and found the grave of 34 year old, Lieutenant George Duncan Macintyre. Macintyre had died of his wounds after being wounded on 9 July while serving with the 7th Yorks. The R.S.M returned with some of the lieutenant's letters that he had found scattered around the grave.[184]

1.25 pm

Operation orders from 51st Brigade for the 8th South Staffords arrived at their H.Q. They were to relieve the 7th Borders in Delville Wood.

2.00 pm

Captain Manger of the 8th South Staffords and the Battalion Medical Officer visited the 7th Borders in their positions before they relieved them.

No. 5 Squadron, R.F.C, reported to XV Corps H.Q that an aerial patrol had seen heavy traffic on the roads behind the German lines.

2.30 pm

In Pommiers Redoubt the 7th East Yorks were ordered to send a working party of one hundred and fifty men to 50th Brigade H.Q at 5.00 pm

During the afternoon the transport and ambulances of the 52nd Field Ambulance at the bearer post in the Gully, Caterpillar Valley, had to move because the post had been virtually destroyed by the bombardment during the night. They moved to a covered trench half a mile away to the south-west.

---

184 Personal diary of Lieutenant-Colonel Fife. Macintye is buried in Gordon Dump Cemetery.

Major King returned to the 17th Divisional Artillery H.Q at Bellevue Farm after his visit to the Division's section of the front line. He found Lieutenant-Colonel Cardew suffering from a severe headache and about to go to bed.[185]

3.00 pm

The Army Commander, General Rawlinson, visited XV Corps H.Q to make his wishes known for action to be taken on the following day in support of XIII Corps.

During the day information had come into XV Corps H.Q about a new type of shell that the Germans had used against a French unit on the night of 2/3 August. It appeared to be a new high explosive shell that threw out sparks and a great amount of smoke when it burst in the air. Sparks from one of the shells instantly set light to a bundle of rags that were lying in the French trench and a greatcoat that was lying on the parapet was covered in phosphorescent spots. These spots remained even after the cloth had been brushed. Any material touched by these sparks became extremely flammable. It was believed that cloth and combustible objects would burst into flames if subjected to friction or heat well after being exposed to the sparks. The spots remained on the men in the trench and made them clearly visible as they moved around. XV Corps was told to warn the divisions about this shell and keep all trench stores of ammunition and rockets well under cover.

No. 5 Squadron, R.F.C, reported to XV Corps H.Q that more heavy traffic had been spotted on the roads behind the German lines facing the Corps.

At Bellevue Farm Lieutenant-Colonel Cardew had just managed to drop off to sleep when he was awoken with the news that a general wanted to see him. Unimpressed, Cardew roused himself to meet the general. He found two generals waiting for him, Brigadier-General Alexander and Major-General C.E.D. 'Buddy' Budworth. Cardew had met Budworth before but in his diary he claimed that he did not recognise the man at first.[186] Which is strange, because the

---

185 IWM: Cardew 86/92/1.

186 IWM: Cardew 86/92/1.

Major-General was on the Fourth Army staff and was General Rawlinson's trusted artillery advisor.[187] Perhaps Cardew's headache was causing him trouble.

5.00 pm

Verbal discussions had gone on between Lieutenant-General Horne and the Major-Generals of the 17th and 33rd Divisions with reference to plans for the attack upon Orchard Trench and part of Wood Lane. Lieutenant-General Horne informed both of his Major-Generals that XIII Corps was intending to attack Falfmont Farm while the French, on the far right, attacked Maurepas. Lieutenant-General Horne suggested that the G.O.Cs of the two divisions should consider fixing their attack for the same time and date. The 33rd Division was in the process of relieving the 51st (Highland) Division in the line on the left of the 17th Division.

Divisional H.Q received a telegram from 51st Brigade reporting that the 7th Borders had also reported the presence of the enemy in the north-west corner of Delville Wood. It confirmed the patrol report sent earlier by the 10th Notts & Derbys. The German troops had re-occupied an old trench and connected it, across the Flers Road, to Orchard Trench. Major-General Robertson duly reported this development to XV Corps H.Q and divisional orders were sent to Brigadier-General Trotter for his 51st Brigade to arrange for the clearance of the wood. According to Lieutenant Hoyte "the higher command at the time decided that it was the fault of the 51st Brigade that the enemy were inside the wood, and this resulted in a certain amount of recrimination and uneasiness."[188]

No one should really have been surprised, the 9th Duke of Wellingtons had reported to 52nd Brigade that German units were operating in the wood on the evening of 2 August. The importance of their report does not seem to have been heeded, it could well have been missed. There is no specific reference to the German presence in the wood in the 52nd Brigade war diary for 2 or 3 August, other than the acknowledgement of a situation report. Nor is there a

---

187 Major-General 'Buddy' Budworth was credited as being one of the first advocates of the artillery 'creeping barrage'.

188 Hoyte, *10th (S) Battalion,* p. 19

reference to the report in the 17th Division's war diary for 2 or 3 August. To be fair, at the time, the staff officers of the 17th Division and 52nd Brigade had been pre-occupied by the forthcoming attack upon Orchard Trench. It may well have been thought that a successful attack upon Orchard Trench would deal with any German units in the wood, even so a German presence in the wood does seem to have been ignored. XV Corps made no note of it either. The incident *had* been reported and was recorded by Fourth Army on 3 August but even at Army level it did not seem to engender any urgent action.

Hoyte went on to say that documents captured later proved that German forces had indeed been in the wood well before the 51st Brigade went into the front line.[189] They had in fact been there for some time and their positions were far better established, maintained and defended than the British, on their discovery, had originally thought. The presence of German troops in Delville Wood threatened to destabilise the careful preparations for the forthcoming operations that General Haig required. Would the Germans be preparing for a serious counter-attack in this sector or digging in for another dogged defence of the wood? Either way, in the jargon of the front line, the situation needed clearing up.

The 17th Division recorded that the 51st (Highland) Division on the left had been relieved by the 33rd Division.

The working party from the 7th East Yorks, made up from men of A and B Companies and under the command of Lieutenant Holroyd, arrived at 50th Brigade H.Q. They were put at the disposal of the 78th Field Company, Royal Engineers and were put to work on the communication trench that ran between the battalion and Longueval.

The 50th Brigade was notified by the 7th East Yorks that the main Montauban-Mametz road was subjected to shelling and Montauban Alley had been shelled between 11.00 am to 3.00 pm. Routes forward were being reconnoitred by the intelligence officer. The war diary recorded that casualties from the previous night's shelling were three men killed and two wounded. Two men of the 7th East Yorks, 12100, Private Leigh and 11/125, Private Wells are recorded as being

---

189 Hoyte, *10th (S) Battalion,* p. 19

killed on this day. 15285, Sergeant Woodward died of his wounds on the following day.

5.20 pm

Fourth Army issued the objectives for the XV Corps bombardment (between Delville Wood and High Wood) and the objectives and zero hour for the XIII Corps attack. Accordingly, XV Corps sent artillery instructions to 17th Division and these would have been passed to Lieutenant-Colonel Cardew in his capacity as the C.R.A. Identical instructions were also sent to the 33rd Division. The divisional artillery brigades were to assist the operations by XIII Corps and the French by opening a heavy bombardment of the German line in the Division's sector at 4.30 pm on 7 August. They were to shoot for an hour ending at 5.30 pm and then begin a bombardment on the night 7/8 which would increase in intensity between 4.00 am to 8.00 am on the 8th.

After his tea Lieutenant-Colonel Cardew rode out to the wagon lines. Here, he met Lieutenant Carver of the 80th Brigade's D battery. As his former commanding officer Cardew knew Carver well and he was shocked at the man's state. Carver had been sent down the line after the 80th Brigade had come under heavy bombardment during the night. When he met Cardew, Carter was feeble, very nearly crying and had a dreadful look in his eyes. In his pitiful state Carver begged Cardew to send him away from the front. Kindly, Cardew resolved then and there that he would do as Carver asked but the encounter seriously unnerved him.[190]

6.00 pm

The 50th Brigade had been forced to evacuate Pear Street because the divisional heavy artillery had been firing upon the German front line, Orchard Trench. Following the bombardment the staff at 50th Brigade H.Q had ordered that patrols should be sent out to ascertain if the German garrison was still in Orchard Trench. By this time the 6th Dorsets had returned to their positions. They had attempted to take advantage of the heavy bombardment by occupying the junction

---

190 IWM: Cardew 86/92/1,

of Orchard and Wood Trenches but machine gun fire brought this attempt to a halt. They reported that the German garrison was still in place.

6.40 pm

XV Corps contacted the 17th Division and Major-General Robertson was ordered to take steps to clear up the situation in Delville Wood. Lieutenant-General Horne and the XV Corps staff were not at all pleased with the situation.

6.45 pm

The 8th South Staffords received their operation orders and the rations arrived.

7.00 pm

Two horse drawn ambulances returned to the 17th Divisional Collecting Station, one wagon remained at the Advanced Dressing Station in the Gully but the horses and drivers returned with the other ambulances. One heavy horse was slightly wounded.

7.12 pm

XV Corps sent a situation report to Fourth Army H.Q. In it Lieutenant-General Horne told General Rawlinson that the 17th Division had reported that the Germans had moved back into an old trench in the north-west corner of Delville Wood. He told General Rawlinson that an attempt had been made to dislodge them but the attack had been frustrated by rifle grenades. Lieutenant-General Horne went on to say that the situation would be dealt with. He also reported that the British heavy artillery had successfully shelled Orchard Trench and Longueval Alley and the village of Longueval had been shelled by German guns all day.

The 80th Brigade, R.F.A., began 'dusk to dawn' firing. Each battery fired for one hour then another battery took over.

8.50 pm

The 8th South Staffords were informed that they were not now to take over the line from the 7th Borders. No reason was given for the cancellation.

9.20 pm

B Section, 50th Machine Gun Company, opened indirect fire on the German trenches, Switch Trench and Tea Lane. Then they fired on the Flers Road.

9.55 pm

In response to the communiqué from Fourth Army at 5.20 pm, the orders issued at 5.00 pm were cancelled. XIII Corps would now attack Guillemont on the 8 August. the XV Corps would provide support by firing a bombardment from 5.30 pm to 6.30 pm on 7 August and again from 4.00 am to 6.00 am on 8 August.

10.30 pm

A shaken and depressed Lieutenant-Colonel Cardew sat down in his tent to write his letters and diary. The meeting with Lieutenant Carver had really upset him and caused him to question his own ability to cope with the war. Cardew hoped that he would not lose his nerve as badly as poor Carver had done, though he wrote that he was sure that his nerve was weaker than Carver's. There may well have been another reason for his despondent mood. He had been informed that although he was to remain in command of the 17th Divisional artillery, Brigadier-General Hussey was to take overall command the 5th and 17th Divisional artillery. Cardew would effectively become Hussey's lieutenant at the 17th Division; it was a demotion. Cardew wrote that he was sorry about this but he liked Hussey all the same; he could not really say anything else. This would also mean that he would not yet be promoted to Brigadier-General; he would remain a Lieutenant-Colonel. There is no doubt that this state of affairs would annoy Cardew immensely.

His mood was not helped by the fact that more casualty reports had come in to him concerning the gunners. He had just learned that

Second Lieutenant Robert Bowman of C battery, 81st Brigade had been killed by shellfire the previous evening and that Captain Benham, of the same battery and brigade, had been badly wounded.[191] Cardew also discovered that an officer of A battery, 80th Brigade, Lieutenant Houghton, was shell-shocked and to make matters even worse there had been no letters from home. Lieutenant-Colonel Cardew concluded his diary by expressing how sick he was of the war.

10.40 pm

B Section, 50th Machine Gun Company, ceased firing.

11.00 pm

The 10th West Yorkshires came under fire from German guns. Montauban Alley and the village of Montauban also came under shell fire. D Company of the 8th South Staffords carried rations forward for the 7th Borders.

11.15 pm

B Section, 50th Machine Gun Company, opened fire again.

Midnight

B Section, 50th Machine Gun Company, ceased fire.

The 17th Signal Company recorded that during the night of 6/7 August the 7th Borders had *discovered* an abandoned radio listening set. The commanding officer of the 7th Borders, Major Irwin, had the set brought into his H.Q and by means of D3 telephones with earths in the front line he was able to listen in and respond to requests and reports from his front line troops, sending forward reserves and stores as required. As will be seen shortly, this set was indeed useful but it most certainly had not been abandoned or discovered. This may have been a cover story.

---

191 Benham was shipped home but he died of his wounds.

The machine gun sections reported in to 50th Brigade Machine Gun Company H.Q. C and D Sections reported that all was correct and they had no casualties. C Section reported that they had observed B Section's indirect fire on the German front line. B Section reported that they had engaged the enemy and that they had expended three thousand five hundred rounds per gun. All emplacements had been strengthened by revetting and sandbags and each gun had an alternative emplacement. They had one man wounded but he remained at duty.

Chapter Seven: 7 August

During the night the 51st Division was relieved by the 33rd Division.

1.00 am

While his men worked on the trenches in Delville Wood, Major Irwin of the 7th Borders found that their task was to change and they were to go on the offensive. They had been given orders to attack the strong German positions on the northern edge of the wood. The operation would begin at 4.30 pm and there would be no artillery preparation so that his men may have the element of surprise.

A message from 51st Brigade arrived at the 10th Notts & Derbys H.Q, informing Captain Gilbert that the 7th Borders were to clear the north western edge of the wood and set up observation posts on the edge of the wood. He was ordered to operate in conjunction with this action. His battalion was required to push an outpost line forward, beyond the edge of the wood, to be manned by night and also to set up observation posts that were to be occupied during the day.

Major Irwin drew up his plans for the attack, two platoons of B Company would attack on the left, 2 platoons of C Company would attack on the right, D Company would provide support for the attack. The telephonists in the front line were ordered to keep sending messages back to battalion H.Q., during the attack, even if the telephone wires were cut. Installed at the 7th Borders H.Q. was a very useful and unexpected piece of kit, a radio listening set. It had been provided by the signal staff from XV Corps H.Q. for other, unspecified, purposes but the decision was taken to use it during the attack. The set had not been simply lost and found.

2.40 am

The 8th South Staffords received orders to give immediate support to the 7th Borders' attack.

3.30 am

A short while later, A and C Companies of the 8th South Staffords were ordered to stand to. A Company was ordered to go into the wood before the attack and provide close support to the 7th Borders.

4.00 am

The German bombardment of the Montauban area that had started at 11.00 pm ceased. XV corps noted that the 50th Brigade H.Q had come under bombardment during the night and was out of touch because the wires had been cut.

The 80th Brigade R.F.A, ceased firing. Ordinary day firing would begin soon.

A Company of the Pioneers, the 7th Yorks & Lancs left Fricourt to work with the 78th Field Company, R.E. B Company remained behind as the reserve. C Company went to work with a company of the 9th Northumberlands cutting and dressing YL Alley. D Company worked with the 77th Field Company, Royal Engineers, on a trench south of Longueval. Three men of A Company were wounded. The hard labour of digging and salvaging equipment and stores carried on all night and into the day.

During the day the 9th Northumberlands were ordered to provide a working party of one hundred and fifty men to work under the orders of the officer commanding the Pioneers.

The 77th Field Company, R.E., continued their work on the communication trench and the support line. The 78th Field Company, R.E., reported that one section and a company of infantry was deepening and widening the check and support line during the day. Another company of infantry was digging, deepening and widening a communication trench. Another section was preparing a forty yard straight section of trench that would run from Montauban Alley to the top end of the communication trench. It is recorded that this straight was "to be carved by fire."[192] The 51st (Highland)

---

192 TNA: PRO WO95/1993. War Diary 78th Field Company, R. E, August 1916

Division had encountered problems digging trenches nearby at High Wood and they employed a 'Bartlett Forcing Jack'.

> *The Bartlett Jack was designed to drive iron pipes loaded with tin canisters of ammonal (containing two lb. of ammonal per foot run) through the ground at a depth of from four to five feet. When a sufficient length of pipe had been driven into the ground in the required direction, the charge was exploded. The explosion blew a fissure in the ground which served as a trench.*[193]

The 78th Field Company may well have been employing the same tool.

The 93rd Field Company, R. E, reported that the work continued as previously stated, except that number two section was consolidating the old German second line that ran through Longueval. Acting Sergeant, 49850, George Lee was killed as the Engineers worked. A new support line was being dug by a section but that section would have to leave the work for the Pioneers to finish as they were required elsewhere. When finished this trench was to be only three feet six inches deep. One complete section was employed digging a dugout for the 27th Brigade, R.F.A. It was mined under a chalk cliff and the men of the section worked in shifts because no gunners were available to provide the labour. The 50th Brigade H.Q needed some attention as well. Though the dugouts had a good solid iron rail roofs they were inadequately supported and had no protection.

The 17th Signal Company continued to work on the armoured cables that had been laid to the front line on the previous day. One was for additional communication and the other went to a Forward Observation Post.

5.00 am

The 7th East Yorks sent a progress report. Montauban Alley had been cleared up. All refuse had been buried and any useable equipment had been salved. Four Lewis gun emplacements had been made, traverses were being built along the length of the trench and an officers' dugout had been excavated. The south west end of

---

193 Bewsher, *The History Of The Fifty First (Highland) Division,* p. 83

the trench was being dug out to its original depth and the duck boards were being cleaned up and re-laid to help with the drainage. Work had been held up for a while because of a cable laying job.

5.45 am

Complying with the orders given at 2.40 am, a carrying party from the 8th South Staffords were sent up to the 7th Borders with rolls of wire and sandbags.

6.00 am

The 51st Field Ambulance recorded that thirty-six patients had passed through the Divisional Collecting Station since 9.00 pm the previous night.

7.00 am

XV Corps passed a 17th Division report to Fourth Army. It said that contact had been lost with the 50th Brigade because the wires had been cut by the heavy shelling between 11.00 pm and 4.00 am. Contact could not be established even by runners because they could not get through the heavy barrage.

8.40 am

Lieutenant-General Horne contacted Major-General Robertson at 17th Divisional H.Q. Horne tersely informed him that the reason why the enemy had appeared in the wood was because of a lack of observation and reconnaissance by his troops in the line. In effect Major-General Robertson's division was being held responsible for the arrival of the Germans in the wood. Specifically the troops of 51st Brigade, the 7th Borders and the 10th Notts & Derbys. Major-General Robertson had already ordered Brigadier-General Trotter's 51st Brigade to launch another attack.

9.30 am

Feeling much better after having a good sleep, and with his nerves restored, Lieutenant-Colonel Cardew travelled by car from Bellevue

Farm up to Fricourt village. From Fricourt he took a horse and rode on to visit his artillery Brigades and tour the batteries. Despite hostile shelling, Cardew made certain that he lingered as long as he could with each battery. He noted that one battery commander was displaying signs of being 'shell shy' and another, the commander of one of the artillery brigades, had no idea where his howitzer battery was...[194]

11.00 am

The 52nd Field Ambulance recorded that three officers and one hundred and thirteen other ranks passed through the Advanced Dressing Station. Captain Barclay and seven squads of bearers from the 51st Field Ambulance relieved the squads at Bernafay Wood. One rider reported for duty at the Advanced Dressing Station.

During the morning Lieutenant-Colonel Fife took his customary stroll and went to visit Brigadier-General Glasgow. Fife wondered if there was any news; Glasgow had none for him.[195]

Noon

The 52nd Brigade Machine Gun Company reported that there was a heavy German attack on the right flank. Lieutenant-General Morland, the commander of X Corps visited the Machine Gun Company's H.Q. Major Lintott showed him to the top of the redoubt so that he could get a good view of the surrounding countryside.

The 52nd Brigade Machine Gun Company received a special divisional order. Second Lieutenant J.K. Michell, commander of B Section, was awarded the M. C. and 3775 Private H. Cocks the D.C.M. Both men had earned these awards during the fighting around Quadrangle Support Trench.[196]

---

194 IWM: Cardew 86/92/1.

195 Personal diary of Lieutenant-Colonel Fife.

196 Michell received his medal for attempting to save Lieutenant Stanbury and rescuing a Northumberland Fusilier on 7 July. Cocks received his for beating off an attack by German Guardsmen with his Lewis gun on the same day. His

1.30 pm

Lieutenant-General Horne contacted the divisions and the B.G.R.A. He listed the batteries that were firing that day and the points from where their fire could be observed. 17th Division, like 33rd Division, was ordered to send three regimental officers to observe the shoot later in the day, 5.30 pm to 6.30 pm and again in the morning, 4.00 am to 6.00 am. This was done so that infantry officers might see for themselves how and where the artillery shot and to restore confidence, "which infantry lately appears to have lost."[197]

Having been picked up by his car at Mametz, Lieutenant-Colonel Cardew arrived back at his H.Q at Bellevue Farm. He made no mention in his diary of the orders issued by Lieutenant-General Horne.[198]

2.30 pm

Lieutenant-General Horne held a conference for his divisional commanders and staff officers. Major-General Robertson attended. Throughout the day the artillery was active and it was reported that British snipers had met with success.

As ordered at 11.00 am Captain Barclay and thirty men went forward from the Divisional Collecting Station to the Advanced Dressing Station at Bernafay Wood.

2.40 pm

The 8th South Staffords received operation orders from the 7th Borders. A company of the 8th South Staffords were ordered forward under Captain Burnett and was placed under the orders of the Officer commanding Delville Wood. The senior battalion commander in the line was at this time the C.O of the 7th Borders.

---

solitary action also allowed men of the 10th Lancashires get into the safety of the British front line.

197 TNA: PRO WO 95/922. War Diary XV Corps, August 1916

198 IWM: Cardew 86/92/1.

4.00 pm

The British heavy artillery barrage to support operations by XIII Corps and the French began. It also prepared the way for the attack by the 7th Borders and the 10th Notts & Derbys.

4.30 pm

The artillery barrage lifted and then fell just in front of Orchard Trench. Right on time, the 7th Borders attacked on the right flank and the 10th Notts & Derbys on the left. They were to clear the wood of the enemy and reach the Longueval-Flers road. The 10th Notts & Derbys plan was as follows. On the right of the Notts & Derbys attack, alongside the Borders, A Company would set up one post in conjunction with the 7th Borders, both units would hold it together and then A Company would set up another post independently. On the left of the attack, D Company was to set up two posts and C Company one post. The 7th Lincolns had come forward from Montauban Alley to support the 10th Notts & Derbys and the 8th South Staffords were in support of the 7th Borders.

Major Irwin's 7th Borders began their attack as planned. Two platoons from B Company advanced through the splintered wood on the left and two from C Company advanced on the right. D Company provided the support. The distance to the German positions on the northern edge of the wood was 70 yards. The German defensive positions were made up of shell holes and fallen trees and were manned by riflemen and machine gun teams. The assaulting platoons managed to advance thirty-four yards without trouble and then at the thirty-fifth yard they came under heavy and sustained defensive fire. The 7th Borders' attack failed at this point; the platoons took cover and were pinned down. Nine men were killed, thirty-four other ranks were wounded as was Lieutenant Edward Sanger,[199] and Second Lieutenants Harry Douglas Cope[200]

---

[199] The war diary recorded Sanger as a second lieutenant but his MiC states that he was a lieutenant for the entire war. He returned to the battalion on 12 August 1916. Sanger later earned the M.C. and survived the conflict.

[200] Cope had been a corporal in the 8th Middlesex and had originally gone out to the Western Front on 9 March 1915. He was commissioned on 2 November

and F. H. Gascoigne Roy.[201] When the roll was called after the platoons managed to withdraw, five men were missing. They were soon added to the death toll and in the end it transpired that sixteen men had been killed in the attack.

Inevitably, as soon as the attack began, the telephone wires from the front line to battalion H.Q., were cut by artillery fire. Following their orders the telephonists in the 7th Borders' section of the front line continued to send coded messages back and the signallers using the Corps listening set heard everything that was sent. Major Irwin found the set very useful indeed.

The 10th Notts & Derbys had much the same experience. As soon as they advanced over the shell-scarred ground, through the splintered tree trunks, they came under rapid rifle and machine gun fire from the German positions in the wood. The fire was heavy and the right of the Notts & Derbys attack and the whole of the 7th Borders attack was halted. The men took cover and could go no further forward. On the left C and D Companies of the 10th Notts & Derbys braved the fire and pushed forward, successfully setting up and manning their posts as ordered. Even so, twelve men of the Notts & Derbys had been killed in the operation. Despite this partial success the 17th Division staff recorded the attack as a failure. A new attack was ordered for midnight and this time there would be an artillery bombardment beginning at 11.40 pm and ceasing at zero hour, midnight.

5.00 pm

Meanwhile, in Pont Street Trench, Captain Mozley received his orders. A Company of the 6th Dorsets were to push a strong patrol out to capture a German strong point at the junction of the trenches Wood Lane and Orchard Trench. The patrol had to go out at 6.30 pm. With only one and a half hours to go, Captain Mozley and his men made their preparations. He decided to send out a line of

---

1915 and after service with the 7th Borders he was promoted to lieutenant and joined the R.A.F in 1918.

201 Gascoigne Roy had been a sergeant in the Royal Fusiliers at the outbreak of war. He was later promoted to Captain, survived the war and moved to New South Wales, Australia.

skirmishers under the command of a sergeant and they would be closely followed by two bombing squads. The main patrol would then go out. One of his Lewis Gun teams under the command of his C.S.M, J. A. W. MacMullen was to stand by to follow the patrol if the operation was successful. Captain Mozley wanted his other Lewis Gun Team to give the patrol covering fire but the nature of the terrain and the trenches made this difficult. Instead, it was decided that Sergeant Jackman would go out into no-man's-land and give covering fire from a shell hole. They were *not* ordered to take the position at all costs and D Company received similar orders.[202]

5.30 pm

XV Corps noted that the 17th Division took advantage of the artillery bombardment in support of XIII Corps and the French Army and attacked Orchard Trench. The 78th Brigade, R.F.A, began to shell the enemy front line; each gun was ordered to fire ninety rounds. The 79th Brigade, R.F.A began to bombard Orchard trench, between Delville Wood and Wood Lane. The 80th Brigade, R.F.A, joined the barrage and as they fired, three German phosphorous shells arched over the batteries. The 81st Brigade, R.F.A, began to bombard Orchard Trench, to give cover and support to the 6th Dorsets. A Section of the 50th Brigade Machine Gun Company also joined in firing in support of the artillery barrage. During this period of hectic activity, Second Lieutenants James George Sproule and Francis Norman Stickland arrived at the 81st Brigade, R.F.A., H.Q and reported for duty. Second Lieutenant A.L.G. Alder was posted away to the 17th D.A.C.

5.50 pm

The 8th South Staffords ordered B Company to take over C Company's position as they were to take over A Company's position when they moved forwards to Delville Wood.

---

202 IWM: Mozley 0148/1.

6.00 pm

The 8th South Staffords reported that during their support for the 7th Borders they had two men killed, Privates 12285, Thomas Edwards and 15601, George Henry Myatt. Nine more men had been wounded and two had gone missing. A Section, 50th Machine Gun Company, ceased fire. B Company prepared to open fire.

Captain Gorman and his bearers returned from the Advanced Dressing Station to the Divisional Collecting Station

6.20 pm

The 79th Brigade, R.F.A, lifted its barrage from Orchard Trench and established it on a rear area. The guns carried out a slow rate of fire.

6.25 pm

B Section, 50th Brigade Machine Gun Company, now opened fire on an area three hundred yards behind the corner of Wood Lane and Orchard Trench. This was to support the 6th Dorsets' operation and they were to fire for twenty minutes.

6.30 pm

17th Division recorded that the 6th Dorsets launched a small attack from the east end of Pear Street on the north-east corner of the small orchard. Their main objective was to establish a post in Orchard Trench itself.

Captain Mozley wrote later that the operation was spoiled by the British Artillery. The eighteen-pounder barrage burst very short and sprayed shrapnel balls directly over the heads of the patrol. The barrage pinned his men down and they were unable to leave Pont Street.[203] Then, at 6.30 pm, to the relief of Captain Mozely and his men, the British artillery barrage ceased. Now the two patrols from A and D Companies could get moving. A Company had orders to reconnoitre the junction of Wood Lane and Orchard Trench. If it

---

203 IWM: Mozley 01/48/1.

was unoccupied then the patrol was to occupy it and set up post there.

As the lead elements of the A Company patrol approached the objective, the men were met by heavy machine gun fire from three sides and from rifle fire from Orchard Trench. They had managed to get forward one hundred yards. The men were ordered to lie flat and take cover. A reconnaissance party crawled forward to see how well the strongpoint was held. They returned with the news that the position was strongly held. Having accomplished the primary orders the patrol kept their heads down and wormed their way back to Pont Street. Four men were wounded in the process of the withdrawal. In Pont Street Trench Private Joe Hepworth of number two platoon watched the men get hit. Realising that one of them was his friend he dashed out of the trench and, under fire, dragged the helpless man out of the shell hole where he had fallen and then pulled him back to the British line. Hepworth managed to get the wounded soldier to the parapet but as they arrived, Hepworth was shot through the chest; the former Hussar was killed instantly. The other three wounded men managed to crawl back to Pont Street.[204]

The second battle patrol, from D Company, had orders to join the southern end of Pear Street with a trench that was shown on the map as running through the orchard. The patrol was very successful and the two trenches were connected. Second Lieutenant Ronald D'Albertanson, a Portuguese man attached from the 3rd East Surreys, was mortally wounded during the operation. Captain Mozley said that an eighteen-pounder shell burst short and D'Albertanson was hit in the neck by shrapnel.[205] Three other men, Privates, 16878 A. G. Alner, 17127 J. Blandamer and 10806 E. J. White were all killed. Young Second Lieutenant D'Albertanson was taken to a Field Ambulance at Dernancourt but he died of his wounds the following day.

Captain Mozley recalled that there had been a number of incidents of the British artillery shooting short. There was obviously a debate on the subject because the gunners pointed out that Delville Wood formed a salient in the German line that allowed the German guns to

---

204 IWM: Mozley 01/48/1.

205 IWM. Mozley 01/48/1.

shell some British trenches in the rear. Mozley went on to say that relations between the infantry and the artillery were generally very good and such "complaints were not made without very solid reason."[206] In other words, the explanation offered was not accepted.

During a lull in the British artillery bombardment Lieutenant-Colonel Fife went out for an evening walk to inspect the captured German trenches near Maricourt. He said that while he was out a bombardment was directed at the German line between High Wood and Flers. It was, he later noted, very loud.[207]

Major E. L. Gowlland arrived at the 17th Divisional Collecting Station to take command of the 51st Field Ambulance.[208]

7.08 pm

Because the 4.30 pm attack had failed, 51st Brigade contacted Divisional H.Q by carrier pigeon and suggested that a second attack be made by the Borders and the Notts & Derbys on the same objective at midnight. The assault would be preceded by a bombardment by the divisional artillery. Major-General Robertson agreed and his staff telephoned the orders through to the artillery. Apparently the gunners were unable to make the necessary arrangements within the specified time and the second attack was postponed. It was re-arranged for 7.40 am the following morning. The 7th Borders received orders informing them that the attack was postponed. The 10th Notts & Derbys did not; they actually received orders from 51st Brigade to attack at midnight. It was arranged with 17th Division that the heavy artillery would not bombard further east than North Street on the following morning.

In 1934, when Brigadier-General Edmonds was editing the part of the Official History that dealt with August 1916, the draft version stated that this attack had failed due to lack of co-operation between the infantry and artillery. When Major-General Robertson read this

---

206 IWM. Mozley 01/48/1.

207 Personal diary of Lieutenant-Colonel Fife.

208 Major, soon to be Lieutenant-Colonel Gowlland had commanded the unit before.

he demanded that the statement be investigated for the sake of the good name of the Division. Though he did concede that the operation was "badly planned" he pointed out that it was also "difficult" to mount the attack because of the nature of the terrain and the disjointed state of the lines. Evidence does suggest that the artillery was having trouble hitting their targets but later in his letter Robertson defended them, saying that "the ill defined [sic] position held by the enemy rendered it extremely difficult for the supporting artillery to bring accurate fire on it." [209] It does seem that Major-General Robertson did not blame Cardew and his gunners at all.

7.30 pm

The XV Corps intelligence summary noted that the enemy was continuing work on their trenches. Orchard Trench had been continued and linked up with existing trenches in Delville Wood.

The 50th Brigade staff recorded that the British heavy guns fired on Orchard Trench again. After the bombardment a patrol was sent out from the east end of Pear Street with orders to occupy a disused trench one hundred and fifty yards further east. The patrol reported no sign of the enemy and that the ground was dry and suitable for digging. A previous report had stated that the ground was swampy. Brigadier-General Glasgow and his staff were forced to move their H.Q back to Pommiers Redoubt because of the intense shelling.

The translation of a captured order, from the German 35th Division, was passed on to XV Corps H.Q. Its content would be heartening for the British; the Germans had been damaged by the British offensive on the Somme so far. They had been trying to come up with ways to counter the British tactics, particularly the British use of artillery. The order, dated 5 July, read

> *So far as events can be judged, the enemy owes his success against the 121st Division to the fact that our infantry was unnecessarily dense in the front line, and consequently suffered very heavy losses during the bombardment. The troops which were then brought up in support were too far back,*

---

209 Letter from Sir Philip Robertson to Brigadier General Edmonds, 15 April 1934. CAB 45/137.

consequently, they also suffered very heavy losses on the way up and could not be employed with sufficient rapidity and vigour.

The infantry must, therefore, be distributed in such a way that, on one hand, the enemy is compelled to disperse the fire of his heavy artillery over the widest possible area, and on the other, that the troops kept in reserve may be immediately ready to hand at the decisive moment.

The art of command lies in the skilful combination of these two conflicting principles. Full use must be made of every inch of the trench system with this object in view. Several cases have apparently occurred of detachments retiring as soon as they were outflanked. This procedure is almost always wrong in trench warfare, because the enveloping enemy is forced to expose his flank to other portions of the front.

(Signed) von Hahn[210]

More translated letters arrived at XV Corps H.Q and they contained more news of sorrow and depravation on the German home front. Food was scarce, hunger was rife and margarine had replaced butter. People were wondering how long the situation, the war, could carry on but according to the letters no one dared speak such thoughts aloud. All of this news displayed the weakening of enemy resolve that General Haig wanted and expected to see.

8.00 pm

The 8th South Staffords reported heavy shelling around Bernafay Wood.

8.30 pm

The 50th Brigade Machine Gun Company reported that all of the Section reliefs were complete. Reports from the Sections came into H.Q. C Section had three men wounded; two of them remained at duty. A Section reported one man wounded and at duty, all correct. B Section reported all was correct and it had no casualties. Pommiers Redoubt and Montauban Alley were shelled that night.

---

210 TNA: PRO WO157/469. Intelligence Summaries XV Corps, August 1916

8.55 pm

Captain S. Clarke's D Company, of the 7th Lincolns, were ordered to go into close support of the 10th Notts & Derbys in Longueval. The company was based around the churchyard. Private H. Taylor, of the 7th Lincolns, remembered that he and a small number of comrades took up positions in what remained of Longueval churchyard.[211]

9.00 pm

The 52nd Brigade Machine Gun Company reported a heavy German barrage.

10.12 pm

The 7th Borders sent a situation report and in it they explained that their attack had been held up by machine guns.

11.00 pm

A heavy bombardment of Delville Wood began and Pommiers Redoubt was heavily shelled again. According to the war diary of the 9th Northumberlands, they lost twelve men killed and seventeen wounded. In fact, five men were recorded as killed on 8 August; none are recorded as killed on 7 August.

11.30 pm

In his tent, Lieutenant-Colonel Cardew settled down to write his diary. Once again, there had been no letters from home but he wrote one himself. He noted that the weather had been hot all day. He was not, it seemed, particularly pleased with the infantry. Perhaps some of their criticism of his brigade's gunnery had reached his ears. The 50th Brigade had attacked but had failed, though their failure, he wrote, was not as bad as that of the 52nd Brigade. He was of course referring to the small operations mounted by the 6th

---

[211] Imperial War Museum. (IWM): Unpublished Papers, Private H. Taylor 84/22/1.

Dorsets and latterly to the operation mounted by the 9th Northumberlands and the 12th Manchesters. He wrote briefly that he had sent Lieutenant Carver off today.[212]

11.40 pm

The 79th Brigade, R.F.A, carried out a bombardment of Orchard Trench. The 80th Brigade, R.F.A, recorded that the batteries and H.Q were heavily shelled. Five men were killed, 133591, Gunner Hannah, 28376, Driver Pound, 123528, Gunner Wakeman, 74262, Gunner Watson and 19592, Gunner Williams. Nine men were wounded. Three horses were also killed. After the shelling sixteen guns remained in action.

Montauban was heavily bombarded by the German guns during the night. One shell that burst over the village reportedly looked like a firework display. The 9th Duke of Wellingtons sent out labour parties for work on the communication trenches that led to Longueval from Delville Wood.

Midnight

At midnight the British heavy artillery barrage reached its zenith and the German gunners joined in. A number of shells fell around Pommiers Redoubt. At the Redoubt the 7th Yorks H.Q had a number of surprise visitors; a bunch of 9th Northumberlands arrived and took cover in the H.Q dugout. Lieutenant-Colonel Fife was not at all pleased and resolved to do something about it.[213]

The 7th Borders should have attacked at midnight but they did not move. The divisional guns were active shelling Orchard Trench but according to the 7th Borders no barrage was falling upon their objective, the northern edge of Delville Wood. The war diary of the 7th Borders simply recorded "no barrage was laid down and attack did not take place."[214] They made no mention of receiving orders postponing the attack, they watched, saw no barrage and did not

---

212 IWM: Cardew 86/92/1.

213 Personal diary of Lieutenant-Colonel Fife.

214 TNA: PRO. WO 95/2008. War Diary, 7th Borders, August 1916.

attack. Major Irwin knew what awaited his men in the German positions and he probably did not want to repeat the failed attack of earlier in the day. He would have wanted the gunners to bombard those positions before his men attacked.

Chapter Eight: 8 August

After Midnight

There was a certain amount of chaos and confusion. Some of the divisional artillery *did* carry out their bombardments of the German positions. The 81st Brigade, R.F.A, carried out another bombardment of Orchard Trench. They recorded that the barrage was specifically in preparation for an infantry attack by the 7th Borders. They noted that nothing came of the attack. In turn the 81st Brigade came in for heavy counter-battery fire throughout the night. A, B and C batteries of 79th Brigade, R.F.A, lifted their barrage one hundred yards north of the Brigade barrage line. The slow rate of fire on the enemy's rear area ceased but the German guns kept up a heavy barrage on the British gun positions. The 79th suffered no casualties.

The 10th Notts & Derbys attacked again, this time alone and they were, once again partially successful. Although, as before, their right flank made little or no progress the left had better fortune and, possibly because they already had posts on this left flank, they managed to push further on and establish three posts north of the road. It was then that they discovered that the artillery could not provide the preliminary barrage on time; even though two brigades at least had done so. Making no mention of the postponement, 51st Brigade noted the 10th Notts & Derbys partial success. The 7th Lincolns moved up to the 'Check Line' in support of the 7th Borders and the 10th Notts & Derbys.

Orders were sent to the 7th Borders for an attack on the north edge of the wood at 3.30 pm and it was said that a barrage would be laid down before the assault.

The 7th East Yorks reported that Montauban Alley was heavily shelled during the night. Two platoons of A Company were forced to leave their dugouts and take up positions further down the trench. Four men of A Company were buried in the shelling but they got out safely. The 52nd Brigade Machine Gun Company reported that Pommiers Redoubt was shelled. The 9th Northumberlands and 10th Lancashires were forced to vacate their trenches. German guns were probing behind the lines and both battalions reported that the

German guns shelled Albert and the transport lines. The 10th Lancashires who had been in and around Pommiers Redoubt recorded that they were heavily shelled throughout the night but only three men were killed, 21304, Private John Edward Rooney, 5490, Lance Corporal David Thompson and 23790, Private Fred Wood. Three other men were wounded. Lieutenant-Colonel Fife recorded that the 9th Northumberlands had 12 men killed and a good deal more wounded in the shelling. He probably discovered this from the interlopers in his H.Q dugout.[215]

12.25 am

The 8th South Staffords tried to get rations forward to the 7th Borders in Delville Wood but the heavy shelling thwarted their efforts.

12.55 am

B Company of the 7th Lincolns, under the command of Lieutenant C. R. Barnes, went forward to reinforce the 10th Notts & Derbys.

3.00 am

The shelling of Pommiers Redoubt ceased.

3.50 am

The 8th South Staffords reported that their whole battalion front was being heavily shelled.

4.00 am

Abruptly, the German bombardment of Delville Wood ceased.

XV Corps recorded that the proposed midnight attack by the 51st Brigade *did not take place*. According to the XV Corps version of events the divisional artillery did not receive their orders in time to

---

215 Personal diary of Lieutenant-Colonel Fife.

begin the barrage. It was noted at Corps H.Q that the 17th Division had therefore ordered the attack to take place at 7.40 am. The 10th Notts & Derbys *had* attacked and 51st Brigade had, later on, informed 17th Division that though the right flank had been forced to withdraw the left had managed to carry out orders and successfully establish posts.

The 10th West Yorks, working as labour for the Engineers and Pioneers, reported that the British artillery began a barrage.

The four guns of A Section, 50th Brigade Machine Gun Company, situated in George Street began indirect fire in support of the British barrage. Their fire searched the Flers Road from the end of Tea Trench and along Tea Lane. They also fired on the road exit from High Wood. Six thousand rounds of ammunition was expended. Second Lieutenant H.R. Malden was admitted to hospital with an inflamed eye.

4.30 am

The pioneers carried on their work. A Company of the 7th Yorks & Lancs remained at Fricourt as the reserve, B Company worked on a trench that came off Yorks and Lancs Alley and C Company worked on connecting a trench to the old German second line. They had elements of the 12th Manchesters working with them widening Yorks and Lancs Alley. D Company had been put to work on a trench behind Longueval Village and this work carried on well into the night. D Company had three men wounded as they worked.

5.30 am

Lieutenant Barnes' B Company of the 7th Lincolns returned to their positions as they had not been required by the 10th Notts & Derbys. The 78th Brigade, R.F.A, bombarded Orchard Trench from the junction with Delville Wood and on to Wood Lane.

6.00 am

The 10th West Yorks recorded that the British artillery bombardment ceased. The battalion continued to work much as it had done the day before. Parties of men worked as labourers for the Royal

Engineers improving the trenches. A new communication trench was dug to a site known as Green Dump and a cable trench for the Signal Company was cut.

A Section, 50th Brigade Machine Gun Company, situated in George Street, ceased indirect fire on the Flers Road.

6.20 am

The 8th South Staffords finally managed to get the rations up to the 7th Borders.

6.30 am

The 78th Brigade, R.F.A, reported that they ceased firing on Orchard Trench.

7.20 am

Orchard Trench from the junction with Delville Wood and on to Wood Lane was re-bombarded by the 78th Brigade, R.F.A. The 80th Brigade, R.F.A, began a bombardment and the 81st Brigade, R.F.A, put down a heavy bombardment on the area to the rear of Orchard Trench. The latter in preparation for an armed reconnaissance of the northern portion of Delville Wood, the 7.40 am attack.

Brigadier-General Hussey toured the artillery brigades on this day so Lieutenant-Colonel Cardew remained in his H.Q at Bellevue Farm and caught up with the mail that had just arrived from Britain.[216]

Captain Mozley remembered that the British artillery heavily bombarded the Guillemont sector.[217]

7.27 am

Lieutenant-General Horne reported to General Rawlinson at Fourth Army H.Q. He said that Delville Wood and Montauban Alley had

---

216 IWM: Cardew 86/92/1.

217 IWM: Mozley 01/48/1.

been heavily shelled. An attempt had been made yesterday afternoon to clear the German troops out of the trench in Delville Wood but the attempt had been unsuccessful. Horne told Rawlinson that another attempt would be made this morning; this would be the 7.40 am attack. Patrols had attempted to reach the enemy trench, Horne told Rawlinson, but they were halted by machine guns. This was a reference to the midnight attack by the Notts & Derbys.

7.40 am

The divisional artillery all noted in their diaries that they were in action at this time. The 78th Brigade, R.F.A, lifted the barrage some four hundred yards beyond Orchard Trench. The 79th Brigade, R.F.A, bombarded Orchard Trench. The 80th Brigade, R.F.A, ceased the bombardment and began another one. The 81st Brigade, R.F.A ceased firing on the rear area of Orchard Trench. Down came the barrage but the attack did not take place, the infantry did not move.

8.30 am

The 17th Division received a situation report from 51st Brigade. It stated that the 10th Notts & Derbys had attacked the junction of Flers Road and Orchard Trench at midnight but they had been held up by machine gun fire. The right company had been forced to withdraw to the original line but the left company had done well and had been able to set up posts. Nothing was said about the activity, or lack of activity by the 7th Borders.

9.00 am

The sections of the 52nd Brigade Machine Gun Company paraded under their officers prior to moving back to the old British front line near Fricourt. Once there they practiced map reading, rifle firing, and exercised. The old trenches and machine gun emplacements were inspected.

Confusingly, the 17th Division noted that the 7.40 am attack had apparently been delivered after a twenty-minute divisional artillery barrage. The 10th Notts & Derbys made no mention of an attack at this time, it is certain that they did not make an attack and, as has been pointed out before, the 7th Borders' diary for this time has not survived. The 51st Brigade's war diary makes no mention of an attack even being ordered for 7.40 am. The XV Corps war diary does shed some light on the matter. There was no attack at 7.40 am because of a "misunderstanding".[218] The attack was rescheduled for 3.30 pm. This was another example of the certain amount of confusion that surrounded events at Delville Wood in August 1916.

10.00 am

The Germans began a heavy shrapnel and H.E bombardment of Longueval.

10.30 am

D battery, 79th Brigade, R.F.A, was ordered to shell Orchard trench, firing twenty rounds an hour. A, B and C batteries established a barrage on Tea Trench firing thirty rounds per hour.

11.00 am

The 52nd Field Ambulance recorded that twelve officers and two hundred and fifty-four other ranks passed through the Advanced Dressing Station. Lieutenant A.L. McCreery joined the unit for duty.

The German shrapnel and H.E barrage of Longueval ceased.

Lieutenant-Colonel Fife wandered over to Brigadier-Glasgow's H.Q for a chat. He learned that a carrier pigeon had delivered the news that Guillemont on the right had fallen during the night and a German trench running between Delville Wood and Guillemont had also been taken.[219] It was wishful thinking; Guillemont had not fallen.

12.30 pm

The sections of 52nd Brigade Machine Gun Company returned to Pommiers Redoubt from Fricourt. Brigadier-General Clarke visited

---

218 TNA: PRO WO 95/922. War Diary, XV Corps Headquarters, August 1916.

219 Personal diary of Lieutenant-Colonel Fife.

their H.Q and was taken to see the officers of the Company. He congratulated Second Lieutenant Clarke on his M.C and was introduced to Second Lieutenants Moon and McInnes whom he had not previously met. The Brigadier-General was not particularly happy that all of the officers of the Company were billeted in the same dugout so he ordered that another be constructed. A wise precaution, in view of the German shelling. A and B Sections were put onto the job.

1.30 pm

Major Ferguson, the commanding officer of the 51st Field Ambulance, received orders to hand over command of the unit to Major E. L. Gowlland.

1.47 pm

A carrier pigeon message, timed at 1.30 pm, was received by XV Corps H.Q from the 7th Borders. The message stated that the artillery barrage had been nearly an hour late and the 7th Borders wanted a re-bombardment later in the day. The message went on to say that the men were much shaken by the shellfire and it questioned the advisability of a third attack. XV Corps H.Q noted that the attack had not gone in because of a misunderstanding. It would appear that the artillery had not been one hour late if the 7.40 am entries by the artillery are to be believed.

1.50 pm

The carrier pigeon message from the 7th Borders was repeated to the 17th Division. Major-General Robertson consulted with Brigadier-General Trotter of 51st Brigade and between them they arranged to mount an attack at 3.30 pm.

Orders arrived at the 10th Notts & Derbys' H.Q stating that the 7th Borders would attack at 3.30 pm and they should push companies forward if the attack was successful. The 17th Division recorded that later in the day these orders were cancelled and the artillery was instructed to carefully register Orchard Trench from Delville Wood to Wood Lane and Wood Lane to High Wood. An artillery brigade of the 5th Division was ordered to attempt to register the German trench in the northern part of Delville Wood. Division then ordered that the 10th Notts & Derbys and 7th Borders would come out of the line. The 51st Brigade noted that the 8th South Staffords and the 7th Lincolnshires would relieve the them.

The 50th Brigade recorded that it had been a quiet day and that work was progressing. YL Alley was through to the support battalion but was very narrow. The support trenches had been improved by a sandbag revetment and Pear Street had been joined to Piccadilly. Only a little work was apparently needed to connect with the Brigade on the right. A communication trench from the support line to the front line had been dug but it was narrow and only two to three feet deep. Work had begun on a new trench in front of Pear Street (front line) had begun. Despite the shelling Montauban Alley was much improved.

3.00 pm

Major Irwin of the 7th Borders contacted the 8th South Staffords and informed them that his attack was going to recommence. A Company of the 8th South Staffords was sent forward in support as agreed.

Back at Pommiers Redoubt Lieutenant-Colonel Fife had defence on his mind and sometime during the afternoon he had a barbed wire fence put up around his H. Q dugout. The 9th Northumberlands would not make an incursion into his H. Q again. Not after pinching his last loaf…[220]

3.10 pm

D battery of the 79th Brigade, R.F.A, was ordered to bombard the northern edge of Delville Wood. The 81st Brigade, R.F.A, put down another heavy bombardment on the area to the rear of Orchard Trench in support of the next attack.

---

220 Personal diary of Lieutenant-Colonel Fife.

3.20 pm

The 79th Brigade, R.F.A, recorded that the infantry attacked a German Trench north of Delville Wood. A, B and C batteries barraged along Tea Trench.

3.30 pm

The 10th Notts & Derbys watched and waited but the 7th Borders did not emerge to attack as planned. The reason for the 7th Borders failure to attack was plain to the watching men of the 10th Notts & Derbys. The artillery was not doing its job; and Captain Gilbert's battalion war diary recorded why. As before, the barrage was not being laid down nearer than the north west edge of the wood and was not being laid down at all on the right. The gunners were missing the target. Major Irwin's men stayed where they were in their line. The attack did not go ahead and in the opinion of the infantry, the gunners were to blame. Shortly afterwards the 81st Brigade, R.F.A, ceased fire on the rear area of Orchard Trench. New orders were issued to the 7th Borders for an attack at 9.00 pm.

4.00 pm

The hand over of the 51st Field Ambulance was completed. Newly promoted to Lieutenant-Colonel, Gowlland assumed command of the unit.

5.40 pm

The 8th South Staffords reported that Second Lieutenant A.H.B Tyrrell had been wounded but he remained at duty. Three men had been killed and eighteen men had been wounded. They also recorded that 51st Brigade had actually cancelled the proposed attack of that afternoon.

5.55 pm

17th Division reported to XV Corps H.Q that there had been no news of the 51st Brigade attack.

6.15 pm

XV Corps was forced to report to Fourth Army that no news could yet be gained regarding the 'clearing up' situation in Delville Wood, which had been timed for 3.30 pm.

The 10th West Yorks recorded that a communication trench from the corner of C Company's position to Pear Street was begun. It was named West Street in honour of the battalion and they were complimented by Major-General Robertson for their good work.

The 6th Dorsets also provided a large working party with orders to dig a new trench across their front to join up with D Company's Pear Street. Tapes were laid out as a guideline for where they should dig and a party of men was sent out into no mans land to provide cover for the working party. In response, the Germans fired a large number of flares over the digging Tommies.

A Section, 50th Brigade Machine Gun Company, reported that they could not fire because the West Yorks were out digging a new trench. The section had no casualties. D Section, 50th Brigade Machine Gun Company, reported that all was well and they had no casualties.

6.35 pm

The 10th Notts & Derbys were informed that the 7th Lincolns would relieve them and guides were immediately dispatched to bring up the relieving platoons. The relief was anything but swift. In the darkness there was considerable confusion and they spent the rest of the night simply trying to effect the relief. The shelling made the operation even more difficult.

7.00pm

The 9th Northumberlands recorded that parades were held in Pommiers Redoubt under company arrangements. Then the battalion marched back to bivouacs near Fricourt.

Captain Walker of the 51st Field Ambulance left the unit and proceeded to the XV Corps Main Dressing Station at Dernancourt.

He relieved Captain J.S. Levis who rejoined the H.Q staff of the 51st Field Ambulance.

7.30 pm

Orders for the relief of the 7th Borders later that night were sent to the companies of the 8th South Staffords. Second Lieutenant Griffiths was sent to the casualty clearing station because he had fallen ill. This meant that the proposed attack at 9.00 pm by the 7th Borders could not go ahead, they would be too busy going through the relief.

Intelligence was passed from Fourth Army H.Q to XV Corps H.Q relating to the 163rd Regiment, the 17th Division's old adversary from Quadrangle Support Trench. The 163rd Regiment no longer had a specialist Marksman machine gun section, and machine guns were hardly ever brought into the front line now. They were employed in the support lines instead. More information about machine guns was received from the Corps on the right. They had captured a German officer and he had given some useful information. The prisoner, from the 127th Regiment, 27th Division informed his captors that his regiment had three machine gun companies with twenty-eight guns between them. Some of the weapons were French, Russian and British.

The intelligence officers noted that on the 17th Division front it was now unclear as to which German unit was holding the line opposite. The German 23rd Regiment, which had been in the line, had been relieved. Both German and British snipers were extremely active around Delville Wood and four machine guns positions had been identified in the German front line there, despite what Fourth Army had discovered.

The firework-like shell that burst over Montauban during the night was identified as a phosphorous shell, of the type recently reported by the French infantry.

Fourth Army H.Q passed on a note sent by the Kaiser to his troops. It had been found on a captured German officer and read:

> *To the leaders and to the troops of the 1st Army I express from the bottom of my heart my deep appreciation and my imperial gratitude for their splendid achievement in warding off the Anglo-French mass attacks of the 30th July. They have accomplished with German faithfulness what I and their country expected of them.*
>
> *God help them further.*
>
> *(Signed) Wilhelm, I.R.*[221]

The intelligence officers realised that this note from the Kaiser indicated that the German units on the Somme were now grouped into the, re-constituted, German 1st Army.

The intelligence summary recorded that information gleaned from prisoners pointed to the fact that German units in the line to the east of Pozieres belonged to a mixture of formations. The British intelligence officers believed that such was the chaos behind the German lines units were being sent into the line as and when they were needed without any regard to which formation they belonged. This could easily have been construed as a sign that the German Army was under severe pressure.

7.40 pm

One gun of B Section, 50th Brigade Machine Gun Company opened fire searching Flers Road, Tea Lane and behind Switch Trench. The Section also fired on a spot where they could see British shells bursting. They were hoping to catch an enemy relief. The Section reported that all was well.

8.25 pm

The events surrounding the non-existent attack at 3.30 pm were still unclear but the 17th Division reported to XV Corps that the attack had not occurred and the infantry in Delville Wood were going to be relieved that night. It was concluded at XV Corps H.Q that the reasons for the failure of this attack to take place had been cited in the carrier pigeon message received earlier in the day. The men of

221 TNA: PRO. WO 157/469. War diary, Intelligence Reports, XV Corps. August 1916

the 7th Borders had been "much shaken by shellfire" and the advisability of the third attack had been questioned by the battalion.[222]

Lewis guns dispersed a German working party in front of Wood Lane.

The 9th Duke of Wellingtons provided working parties for work on the communication trenches that led to Longueval from Delville Wood.

8.30 pm

A and C Companies of the 7th Lincolns left their positions and went to Longueval to relieve the 10th Notts & Derbys. Captain Clarke's D Company was already in position with the Notts & Derbys. In the last twenty four hours the company had suffered about ninety casualties to the shelling, eleven of them had been killed. B Company was also in support. Throughout the day the 10th Notts & Derbys had had seventeen men killed.

8.55 pm

At some time during the day Private H. Taylor, of the 7th Lincolns, and his comrades had taken cover in Longueval churchyard where they came under heavy machine gun and shell fire. He remembered that within minutes all of the men around him were killed and he himself was wounded in the left leg. In agony he struggled to remove one of his bootlaces and saved his own life by tying the lace around his shattered leg. The bleeding stopped and there he lay until he was found and carried away to a dressing station. [223] Taylor recalled that he was wounded on Bank Holiday Monday morning. The evidence suggests that he and his comrades certainly went forward in support of the 10th Notts & Derbys on the Bank Holiday Monday but that the casualties occurred on the Tuesday, 8 August. Of the 90 casualties that the 7th Lincolns suffered on this day, eleven

---

222 TNA: PRO WO 95/922. War Diary XV Corps, August 1916

223 IWM: Taylor 84/22/1.

men were killed. Taylor was probably in Captain Clarke's D Company.

9.00 pm

A and B Sections of the 52nd Brigade Machine Gun Company completed the new officers' dugout at Pommiers Redoubt. Privates 3779 F. C. Conan, 6160 D. Ives and 3786 A. Downing of the 52nd Brigade Machine Gun Company were returned to the base because they were all too young to serve in the British Army.

11.00 pm

Lieutenant-Colonel Cardew wrote his diary. It had been a terrible day as far as he was concerned and he managed to shed some light on why there had been no attack that day. The 51st Brigade had been supposed to attack after the 3.30 pm barrage but they had failed to do so, he wrote. A Forward Observation Officer had informed him that the men refused to leave their trenches and attack the German line. Cardew even went as far as to name the guilty battalion. It was the 7th Borders. Colonel Collins did not initially believe him when it was discussed over tea in the mess but, wrote Cardew, it had been proved to be true. No mention was made of the concerns that the infantry had about the apparent poor shooting by the British guns. All Cardew knew was that the men of the 51st Brigade had refused orders to attack. He went on to lament the lack of artillery lieutenants available to the artillery brigades. He blamed the army for not making any proper arrangements to replace casualties. The army must have known that there would be casualties in this battle he wrote in his diary. Cardew placed the blame squarely on the shoulders of the Staff.

At Delville Wood the 8th South Staffords began their relief of the 7th Borders. It was a difficult relief because the German gunners were busy shelling the British lines.

During the night

B Section, 50th Brigade Machine Gun Company, continued to work on their gun emplacements, sand bagging, revetting and enlarging. Alternate emplacements were also created should they be required.

The commanding officer of the Company visited the advanced dump and guns at Longueval. Corporal West volunteered to guide the C.O back across the open country for about one hundred and fifty yards; all of the time they were under fire. Corporal West had made this journey twice before during the day. He was recommended for a M.M but the recommendation was turned down because evidence of his gallantry was not considered strong enough...

Chapter Nine: 9 August

The weather today was forecast to be exceptionally fine and hot. The wind blew at first from the east and then shifted to blow from the south. It was to be a blazing hot day but the wind heralded a coming change in the weather.[224]

2.00 am

The 6th Dorsets were forced to cease digging the new trench across their front that connected to Pear Street. The men had completed some five hundred yards of trench and were by now extremely tired.

2.30 am

B Company of the 8th South Staffords reported that a minenwerfer had hit their trench and two whole platoons had been buried. Five men had been killed.

4.00 am

All companies of the 8th South Staffords reported that they had completed the relief of the 7th Borders. A Company was in place north of the wood, C Company was providing support and was in the north eastern corner of the wood. B Company was on the east side of the wood and D Company was in Longueval Alley.

4.30 am

The 7th Yorks & Lancs went to work. C Company remained behind as the reserve but were called out at night to work on a fire trench. A Company took over their work on the trench that connected to the old German second line. B Company worked on the trench leading off YL Alley, D Company wired the trench behind Longueval and one man from A Company was wounded.

---

224 Personal diary of Lieutenant-Colonel Fife.

6.00 am

The 51st Field Ambulance recorded that four officers and one hundred and eighty eight other ranks, sitting cases had passed through the Divisional Collecting Station from 6.00 am on the previous day. The new C.O, Lieutenant-Colonel Gowlland, visited the Advanced Dressing Station on the Mametz - Montauban Road. He also visited the Advanced Dressing Station in the north eastern corner of Bernafay Wood. During the day the D. D. M. S arrived and inspected the Division's medical arrangements. He was accompanied in his tour by a Russian Medical Officer.

The 8th South Staffords finally managed to complete the relief of the 7th Borders in Delville Wood. Major Irwin's 7th Borders went into close support positions in and around Montauban Alley. During the relief and while in close support four men were killed and seventeen wounded. Second Lieutenants C. C. Thompson[225] and R. C. Matthews were both wounded. The former seriously but Matthews was well enough to remain with his unit.

6.20 am

The 81st Brigade, R.F.A, reported that the Germans shelled Delville Wood for a short time. An attack was suspected and waited for but the German infantry showed no signs of leaving their trenches.

6.30 am

XV Corps reported to Fourth Army that the situation was normal and that there was nothing to report.

7.10 am

Captain Manger of the 8th South Staffords visited his men in Delville Wood. In contrast, behind the lines, the men of the 9th

225 Thompson had joined the 7th Borders in January 1916. His wounds were severe enough to have him discharged from the army and he was awarded the Silver War Badge. This lapel badge was sometimes called the Silver *Wound* Badge.

Northumberlands enjoyed the luxury of a bath in the river Ancre near Meaulte.

7.30 am

The 10th Notts & Derbys reported that they had at last been relieved by the 7th Lincolns. The relief had been difficult because the shelling that had begun at daybreak had caused great trouble. The 10th Notts & Derbys took over the positions vacated by the 7th Lincolns. Three companies went into Montauban Alley and one went into a new trench between Longueval and Montauban. The 17th Division H. Q. noted that the difficult relief had been completed. It was also recorded that the enemy were also bombarding British positions with trench mortars. These mortars were reported to be positioned within or adjacent to the northern edge of the wood.

The 7th Lincolns first task was to dig a trench eastwards from Piccadilly to connect to the Flers road. It was far from easy, the artillery was active, the Germans were employing indirect machine gun fire and their snipers were very busy. Lieutenant C. R. Barnes, B Company commander and Second Lieutenants H. Ribton-Cook[226], G. E. Skollick[227] and E. W. Milford were all wounded.

17th Division recorded that, as instructed, the divisional artillery registered all of its guns along Orchard Trench up to the junction with Delville Wood. It was reported that the north western edge of the wood was also registered. In return the Germans registered their guns on Pear Street. The 17th Division issued orders that the 51st Brigade be relieved by the 52nd Brigade on the night of 10/11 August. The 51st Brigade recorded that the 7th Lincolns had begun to dig the new trench through the south west corner of Orchard Trench to Flers road.

Lieutenant-Colonel Cardew was given the unwelcome news that he was no longer the acting 17th Division C.R.A. A Brigadier-General, Archie Stewart Buckle, had been appointed to the post and was on his way. Cardew was to return to the command of his old artillery brigade. Cardew went off to visit the 80th and 81st Brigades R.F.A

---

226 Attached from the 3rd Queens.

227 Attached from the 9th Queens.

and to find a billet for himself in the 80th Brigade area. He was absolutely certain that he did not want to share the deep, unventilated, dugout that his officers were currently using. [228]

9.45 am

Brigadier-General Glasgow sent for his battalion commanders. On arrival he briefed them about a forthcoming attack upon Orchard Trench and Wood Trench. No time had been given for the start of the attack but they were told that the 52nd Brigade would attack on their right and the 33rd Division on their left. Glasgow ordered his battalions to prepare.[229]

10.00 am

The 52nd Brigade Machine Gun Company noted that the 52nd Brigade would relieve the 51st Brigade in Longueval and Delville Wood. The machine gun sections prepared to move in the afternoon.

10.30 am

Major Lintott of the 52nd Brigade Machine Gun Company visited a machine gun position in Delville Wood with Second Lieutenant Fraser of the 51st Brigade Machine Gun Company.

11.00 am

The 52nd Field Ambulance recorded that eight officers and two hundred and seventy seven other ranks passed through the Advanced Dressing Station. A draft of ten privates and one mule arrived at the unit.

---

228 IWM: Cardew 86/92/1.

229 Personal diary of Lieutenant-Colonel Fife.

11.25 am

A report was sent to 51st Brigade H.Q by the 8th South Staffords. A patrol had located the enemy in the northern point of Delville Wood. Second Lieutenant Tyrrell and Lieutenant C. P. Day of the battalion had reported sick and both had been sent to the rear.

12 noon

The 79th Brigade, R.F.A, reported that it was fairly quiet. The batteries had registered on Orchard Trench again, firing gun by gun. 98302 Gunner R. Howick was wounded.

It was not reported to XV Corps until the following day, but units of the 17th Division had ascertained that the Germans had done a considerable amount of work on Orchard Trench. It had been connected to an old German trench on the eastern edge of Delville Wood. A German officer had been spotted in a sap that ran out from Orchard Trench into the north-eastern corner of the wood and two more machine guns had been located in the German line to the north-western side of the wood.

1.15 pm

Lieutenant-Colonel Cardew returned to the 17th Divisional Artillery H.Q after his trip to find a decent billet near Montauban. When he entered H.Q he found that Brigadier-General Buckle had already arrived. Buckle was very pleasant to Cardew and expressed his sorrow at having to turn him out of his H.Q and accommodation. Cardew later noted that it was not Buckle's fault, but despite putting a brave face on things, he was not at all happy. Rather than hang around at H.Q Cardew rode over to the wagon lines to search for a wagon to take his kit up to the front on the following day.[230]

2.00 pm

The sections of the 52nd Machine Gun Company began to move up to the front line via Montauban and Bernafay Wood. A Section

---

230 IWM: Cardew 86/92/1.

under Second Lieutenant McInnes was to place three guns in Delville Wood and one gun with the right hand battalion in the line. C Section under Lieutenant Gowring, was to place four guns in Delville Wood. D Section under Second Lieutenant Mason, was to place two guns in Longueval. Headquarters was to be set up at Pommiers Redoubt with B Section and two guns of D Section as the company reserve.

Afternoon

After a welcome swim in the River Ancre, no doubt a great relief from the heat and dust, thirty-five men per company of the 9th Northumberlands attended a "cinematograph exhibition" at Bellevue Farm. It was not recorded what the men watched.

3.45 pm

An un-named Major-General of the Fourth Army Staff telephoned Lieutenant-General Horne and informed him that because Guillemont had not been captured, there was now no hurry for the XV Corps to attack.

4.00 pm

Major Lintott returned to 52nd Machine Gun Company H.Q after his visit to Delville Wood. A Section, in Longueval Alley, was badly shelled.

5. 00 pm

The 7th Yorks began to move out of Pommiers Redoubt for the front line. The journey forward was awful wrote Lieutenant-Colonel Fife. The sight of two pairs of legs lying by their path stuck in his mind and he wrote about them in his diary later that day.[231]

---

231 Personal diary of Lieutenant-Colonel Fife.

5.05 pm

XV Corps informed 17th Division of the telephone call from Fourth Army and said that the attack planned for 11 August was not now going ahead.

6.00 pm

The 8th South Staffords reported that they had had thirteen men killed, forty seven wounded and five were missing. Records later stated that only five men were killed on this day.

6.20 pm

In response to their report about German positions in the wood and considering the strength of the German defences there, the 51st Brigade sent a wire to the 8th South Staffords. It was essential that the enemy's flank in Delville Wood was located.

6.54 pm

XV Corps passed on a report by 17th Division to Fourth Army H.Q. The situation was normal.

7.00 pm

Rations arrived for the 8th South Staffords and at this point the keeper of their war diary changed.

7.30 pm

Caterpillar Wood came under heavy bombardment.

Among many other pieces of information, the XV Corps intelligence summary for the day recorded that prisoners taken at Guillemont had said that the British artillery was taking a heavy toll on the German troops. Despite this, the morale of the German troops was reported to be high, their food was good and they were amply supplied with soda water. The German 26th Division had now been identified as the formation facing the 17th Division at Delville Wood.

The R.F.C had reported that the German anti-aircraft fire was improving. The guns now had a greater range and could fire more rapidly. The intelligence officers concluded that the German anti-aircraft units had received improved guns. The intelligence summary noted that the enemy was continuing work on a trench on the north-east edge of Delville Wood.

At Divisional H.Q, just before dinner, Lieutenant-Colonel Cardew caught up with Major-General Robertson. Before Cardew could talk about what was on his mind, the loss of his job as C.R.A, Major-General Robertson began a long grumble about the infantry. In his opinion they, the infantry, had done a poor job of getting information back to divisional H.Q from the front line. He was echoing what General Haig thought about the information situation and was possibly responding to a certain amount of downwards pressure from the men above. During the conversation Cardew discovered that in Major-General Robertson's "anxiety" to be rid of Brigadier-General Ouseley, the Major-General had written and officially asked for a Brigadier-General of the Royal Artillery to be appointed to the role of divisional C.R.A. Offended, Cardew took this to mean that the Staff must have thought that he, Cardew, was not up to the job. Major-General Robertson tried to assure him that this was not the case.[232] But then, his gun batteries had been firing short and, in some circumstances, not firing upon given targets.

9.00 pm

West Street communication trench was all but completed by C and D Companies of the 10th West Yorks when they were relieved by the 7th Yorks. D Company was left behind to finish the trench and the rest of the battalion returned to Pommiers Redoubt.

9.09 pm

Second Lieutenants Langton and Hides of the 8th South Staffords were called to Battalion H.Q to see Captain Manger. He explained the situation to the two officers and told them that he wanted two posts set up in a trench. This was probably the trench that B

232 IWM: Cardew 86/92/1.

Company was to begin digging and wiring. The posts were possibly bombing posts manned by men from A, B and C companies.

9.30 pm

The intersection reliefs of the 50th Brigade Machine Gun Company were completed. C Section relieved A Section in support in George Street. A Section relieved B Section and B returned to the reserve at Pommiers Redoubt. A Section reported all was well, the only problem was the smell. C Section reported that all was well. D Section reported that they were shelled at intervals during the night. One man was wounded.

The Commanding Officer of the 41st Brigade Machine Gun Company visited the 50th Brigade Machine Gun Company's H.Q.

9.40 pm

A and C Companies of the 8th South Staffords were ordered to immediately send their bombing squads to the junction between the two companies. The bombers were to assist B Company who were to dig and wire a new trench that was to push out towards the enemy lines.

During the evening more men of the 9th Northumberlands attended the "cinematograph exhibition" at Bellevue Farm.

10.00 pm

The Major-General of General Rawlinson's Fourth Army Staff called Lieutenant-General Horne at XV Corps H.Q again. He said that XIII Corps was going to attack on 15 August and XV Corps was required to mount an attack at the same time.

A unit of the 7th East Yorks relieved Captain Mozley's A Company of the 6th Dorsets but thirty men were left behind to complete the work on Dorset Trench.

10.20 pm

XV Corps warned the 14th (Light) Division that they were to prepare to relieve the 17th Division in the night 12/13 August.

10.30 pm

After a fairly long briefing by Captain Manger, Second Lieutenants Langton and Hides left the 8th South Staffords H.Q to carry out their orders and set up their posts.

10.50 pm

D company of the 8th South Staffords sent forty men to help B company with digging and wiring tasks.

11.00 pm

Cardew wrote his diary for the day. Everyone had been nice to him about his time as the C.R.A and apparently, they said that he had done a very good job. It had even been decided that he should receive a medal for gallantry. An offer of a medal did not seem to mollify him and he wrote ruefully that he did not really *mind* losing the job, but he would miss the pay...[233]

11.15 pm

Lieutenant-Colonel Rowley's 6th Dorsets recorded that they had been relieved in the front line. They returned to 50th Brigade reserve in Montauban Alley. The 7th East Yorks recorded that they relieved the 6th Dorsets in the old German second line. They had put two companies into Pear Street, one in close support in Pont Street and another in support near battalion H.Q.

---

[233] IWM: Cardew 86/92/1.

11.25 pm

The 7th Yorks relieved the 10th West Yorks. The working parties of the outgoing battalions remained behind. All but the working parties of the 6th Dorsets and 10th West Yorks went into reserve. Once the relief of the 6th Dorsets was complete, the 7th East Yorks began work consolidating their positions and making fire steps. The working parties of the 6th Dorsets and the 10th West Yorks continued working on Dorset Trench and West Lane. The 7th East Yorks recorded that their trench strength at this time was thirteen officers, sixteen signallers, thirty-two stretcher bearers, 68 machine gunners, 40 bombers, 406 riflemen. H.Q consisted of four officers and 43 other ranks. The 9th Duke of Wellingtons once again provided working parties for work on the communication trenches that led to Longueval from Delville Wood.

Chapter Ten: 10 August

1.00 am

The 7th Lincolns were relieved by the 9th Northumberlands and left the line for their bivouac.

1.30 am

The working party that had been left behind by the 6th Dorsets rejoined A Company in Montauban Alley.

2.45 am

Captain Manger of the 8th South Staffords received a verbal report from B Company. They reported that they had dug and wired some considerable distance towards the enemy and they had not met any opposition.

3.05 am

Captain Manger called for C Company to provide him with a full report.

3.10 am

Two second lieutenants reported for duty at the 8th South Staffords H.Q. They were immediately assigned to B Company. There was no time to settle in and the two were ordered to take a group of bombers out into no-man's-land and set up a post within sight of the edge of Delville Wood, opposite the new German trench. Whether they were new officers, or men returning from injury or leave was not recorded but it was quite a start for the two men.

4.30 am

C Company sent in the report that had been requested by 8th South Staffords H.Q. The patrol that had gone out crossed the German trench and reported that it was full of dead soldiers. It was impossible for C Company to set up a bombing post.

Early in the morning the Commanding Officer of the 50th Brigade Machine Gun Company took Brigadier-General Glasgow around the front line machine gun emplacements. Two officers of the 41st Brigade Machine Gun Company accompanied them. It was a dull morning and there was a little rain.[234]

The work pattern had now changed for the 7th Yorks & Lancs. Now two companies worked at night and two during the day. A and B Companies worked on YL Alley and the fire trench that led off it. 11352 Private Rodgers was killed; seven other ranks and one Lieutenant were wounded. One of the wounded was 12326, Private Savage.

Today King George V had been visiting Haig at his H.Q and he also visited part of the Somme battlefield.

6.00 am

Second Lieutenant Allen of the 8th South Staffords set out to do a reconnaissance of the German trench east of Delville Wood. When he returned Allen reported that he had advanced out into the open twice and had discovered that the trench was occupied by German troops. This trench ran from the Wood towards Ginchy. It was well wired but not very deep because Allen had noticed that the German soldier on sentry duty had the upper half of his body exposed.

The 51st Field Ambulance recorded that four officers and one hundred and thirty-five other ranks, all 'sitting cases', had passed through the Divisional Collecting Station from 6.00 am the previous day. Later in the day the D. D. M. S called in a new batch of eighteen A.S.C drivers for the unit. Captain Barclay returned from Bernafay Wood with his bearers. He had been relieved by Captain Gorman and the bearers of C Section. The CO of the 43rd Field Ambulance inspected the 17th Divisional Collecting Station to prepare to take over.

---

234 Personal diary of Lieutenant-Colonel Fife.

6.15 am

D Company of the 10th West Yorks rejoined the rest of the battalion at Pommiers Redoubt. For the rest of the day this battalion was put on 'Brigade work' at Beetle Alley under the supervision of the Royal Engineers.

6.30 am

Having just visited his machine gun brigade Brigadier-General Glasgow arrived at Lieutenant-Colonel Fife's H. Q in the support position. Here they were joined by Lieutenant-Colonel Clive, of the 7th East Yorks who were in the front line. Clive and Fife took a tour around their battalions' positions. It was dreadful wrote Fife, there were bodies everywhere. The trenches were not easy to attack from and they were overcrowded. Nor was it easy to get the men in any kind of cover. Fife paid attention to his opposition and thought that the enemy machine guns were situated behind the German front line, which was a salient that thrust out towards the British lines. Later in the morning he received orders that his battalion would attack on 11 August.[235]

6.51 am

XV Corps reported to Fourth Army H.Q that the situation on both left and right divisional fronts was normal.

7.00 am

Major Torrens and the company commanders of the 10th Lancashires arrived at the H.Q of the 8th South Staffords and then proceeded to visit the wood. They were to gather as much information about Delville Wood as they could before they relieved the South Staffords.

---

[235] Personal diary of Lieutenant-Colonel Fife.

7.30 am

Brigadier-General Trotter, 51st Brigade, and Colonel Collins, G.S.O 1 of 17th Division, visited the 8th South Staffords H.Q to discuss the position in the wood. After a short conference they agreed that it was "absolutely essential to establish posts at all costs in (the) German trench."[236]

9.00 am

The 7th East Yorks sent a patrol, under the command of a sergeant, up a disused trench between Point B and Wood Lane – Orchard Trench junction. The patrol reported back that they had discovered that Orchard Trench was unoccupied. It was very good news to the British.

During the rest of the day the battalion was employed digging the trenches deeper, making Lewis gun positions and fire steps. The parapet outside battalion H.Q was built up with sand bags.

Major Lintott of the 52nd Brigade Machine Gun Company conducted Brigadier-General Clarke to the right hand battalion H.Q.

10.30 am

Second Lieutenant Portbury, 8th South Staffords, was sent from B Company to C Company to assist Second Lieutenant Langton who was to lead a party of bombers out to set up a post in the German line north east of the wood.

11.00 am

The 52nd Field Ambulance recorded that five officers and one hundred and sixty-eight other ranks passed through the Advanced Dressing Station.

---

[236] TNA: PRO WO95/2007. War Diary 8th South Staffords, August 1916

12.15 pm

Captain Burnett of the 8th South Staffords reported to his battalion H.Q that he had seen parties of German troops in loose dress arriving and troops with packs leaving their front line trench.

The 51st Brigade reported to 17th Division that the 8th South Staffords had tried to set up stops in the German front line. It was believed that the German line was not held along its entire length. Eventually, a post had been set up within sixty feet of the German front line by Second Lieutenant Langton and his bombers, who had gone out nearly two hours earlier.

The 52nd Brigade began to relieve the 51st Brigade in the right sector and Brigadier-General Clarke's H.Q opened at Pommiers Redoubt. The 10th Lancashires were to occupy the right sub-sector and the 9th Northumberlands the left. The Lancashires would relieve the 8th South Staffords in Delville Wood. They were to put three companies in the line and keep one in reserve near Battalion H.Q in Longueval Alley. The 9th Duke of Wellingtons had already relieved the 7th Borders in Montauban Alley. They reported the situation to be very quiet and the bombardment of Delville Wood had eased off. The 7th Borders had moved back to Pommiers Redoubt, losing six men killed, six wounded and one missing in the process. Working parties from the 6th Dorsets and 10th West Yorks rejoined their units.

The 50th Brigade noted that the work on improvement continued and that the G.O.C of the 41st Brigade toured the front with his Brigade Major with a view to the forthcoming relief.

The 17th Division noted that reconnaissance of a position in Delville Wood showed that the enemy were in possession of a trench running east-south-east through the northern portion of the wood which then ran down the outer edge of the wood. From here the trench ran due east. An attempt had been made to move up an old trench that ran from the British line to the enemy's line. The old trench was found to be full of corpses and all attempts to get into the enemy trench were met with, and stopped by, machine gun fire and rifle fire.

By now, Lieutenant-Colonel Cardew was back in command of the 80th Brigade R.F.A. During the morning, before he left Bellevue Farm, and despite what he had written the night before, Cardew met with and "attacked" Major-General Robertson about losing his job. Not surprisingly, the Major-General gave the Lieutenant-Colonel short shrift. Still sore about the whole episode Cardew spoke his mind about the affair to the H.Q staff and to Brigadier-General Hussey. Despite Cardew's mood and behaviour Brigadier-General Buckle was still being pleasant to Cardew. He rode up to the 80th and 81st Brigades with him that morning. In a display of friendship, probably designed to show that neither man bore any ill will to the other, Buckle walked around the batteries with Cardew. After the tour Cardew took up residence in his new dugout, a deep one that stank and was infested with flies, and Buckle went on with his orderly to Brigade H.Q in Pommiers Redoubt.[237]

In the morning all companies of the 9th Northumberlands took part in physical drill which was followed by an inspection of their smoke (gas) helmets. Then the specialists from the companies were put at the disposal of the specialist officers. Orders arrived for them saying that the 52nd Brigade were to relieve the 51st Brigade that night. They were to be the right brigade in the divisional line and the Northumberlands would relieve the 7th Lincolns.

2.00 pm

Lieutenant-General Horne contacted Major-General Robertson and informed him that the 14th Division would relieve the 17th Division on the night of 12/13 August. His divisional artillery would stay in position and be relieved on the nights 16/17 August and 17/18 August.

Two bombing squads from the 10th Lancashires arrived at the 8th South Staffords line. They were to relieve the 8th South Staffords' posts in the German line but the relief was found to be impossible.

The 7th East Yorks responded to telephone orders from 50th Brigade H.Q and sent a party from A Company, supported by bombers from C Company under the command of Second Lieutenant Major, to try and secure Orchard Trench. The sergeant who had previously reconnoitred the trench at 9.00 am and reported it to be empty of German troops, went forward with the party.

---

237 IWM: Cardew 86/92/1.

Lieutenant-Colonel Fife, 7th Yorks, met with his company commanders and gave them preliminary instructions for the forthcoming attack. He told them that they would be attacking alongside the 7th East Yorks[238] and the 52nd and 33rd Divisions were also going to attack.

3.00 pm

Second Lieutenant W.R. Trownson,[239] of the 50th Brigade Machine Gun Company was wounded in the eye.

4.00 pm

Major Lintott returned to 52nd Brigade Machine Gun Company H.Q after taking Brigadier-General Clarke to the right hand battalion.

4.30 pm

Brigadier-Glasgow's Brigade Major visited the 7th Yorks H.Q and met with Lieutenant-Colonel Fife. The attack, Fife was told, was off.

5.00 pm

A wire from 51st Brigade arrived at the 8th South Staffords H.Q. Lieutenant-General Horne and Major-General Robertson had sent their personal congratulations to all of those men who had gone out on patrol and gathered information during the previous night.

5.30 pm

Number four section of the 93rd Field Company, R.E, left their camp at Mametz and went to work on the battle H.Q at the junction of Pont Street and Black Watch Alley.

---

238 Personal diary of Lieutenant-Colonel Fife.

239 So far, Trownson cannot be traced.

5.40 pm

Fourth Army issued instructions to XV Corps for the clearance of Delville Wood and the capture Orchard Trench, Wood Lane and the east corner of High Wood. The 8th South Staffords received orders from 51st Brigade to re-occupy the northern half of Angle Trench and then hand it over to the 10th Lancashires.

6.05 pm

Second Lieutenant Major returned from the attempt to occupy Orchard Trench and made his report at 7th East Yorks H.Q. It was not the good news that was expected. The sergeant who had gone out on patrol at 9.00 am, and once more with Second Lieutenant Major, now said that he *had not* got to the junction of Orchard Trench as had been reported in the morning.[240] This time he did advance further up the trench and found that, far from being abandoned, a forty-yard straight stretch of the trench was dominated by a German machine gun. Second Lieutenant Major verified the sergeant's report and the operation by A Company to occupy Orchard Trench was cancelled.

Brigadier-General Glasgow at 50th Brigade responded to this news by ordering the 7th East Yorks to set up a bombing post, supported by a Lewis gun, in the disused trench. During the evening B, C and D Companies of the 7th East Yorks continued the work of completing Dorset Trench. A Company was ordered to advance a 'stop' fifty yards towards Wood Lane. This was to be supported by a Lewis gun emplacement. The company was also ordered to complete a trench toward Piccadilly.

Each company of the 6th Dorsets sent 50 men forward to dig a communication trench in front of Longueval and they were placed under the command of Lieutenant A. E. Barton. The working party was shelled. One man from A Company, Private 16052, Down was killed, and another wounded; Second Lieutenant Edwin Lindow, of B Company, suffered a serious leg wound.[241] He died of his wound

---

240 If the sergeant had become confused, which was very possible in this part of the line, or he had been economical with the truth has not been recorded.

241 IWM: Mozley 01/48/1.

the following day. Before the 6th Dorsets left Montauban Alley, Captain Mozley visited his old positions around Wood Trench, Bottom Wood and Quadrangle trench. He found the old battlefield a hive of activity and gun batteries were placed everywhere. A battery of eight-inch guns was in position behind the remains of Bottom Wood and was in the process of firing over it.

6.45 pm

It was reported by 8th South Staffords H.Q that Second Lieutenant Langton, who had taken his bombing party out at around 10.30 am, had advanced one hundred and forty yards and had managed to get within sixty yards of the German line. He had been fired upon from three sides and an attempt to set up a post further to the east had failed. The 8th South Staffords reported that they had lost Private, 12490, Briscoe, killed, and eleven men had been wounded.

During the night, 17th Division recorded that after Major Torrens' 10th Lancashires had relieved the South Staffords he sent out patrols. They made contact with the enemy on a two hundred yard front in the north of Delville Wood. The 10th Lancashires reported that the Germans were holding a string of posts out in front of their own front line. Their reports backed up the intelligence gathered by the 8th South Staffords.

7.07 pm

XV Corps reported to Fourth Army H.Q that the situation on the divisional frontages was unchanged.

7.30 pm

The 78th Brigade, R.F.A, fired a desultory barrage at the northern end of Delville Wood.

8.30 pm

The 10th Notts & Derbys noted in their war diary that they had been relieved by the 12th Manchesters and that Major R.J Milne[242] of the 9th Devonshires had arrived at battalion H.Q to take command of the battalion.

The 78th Brigade, R.F.A, ceased firing on the northern end of Delville Wood.

9.25 pm

The 10th Notts & Derbys moved back and went into positions near Mine Trench.

10.30 pm

The 79th Brigade, R.F.A, was ordered to begin a desultory barrage of the north of Delville Wood. The Brigade was ordered to fire sixty rounds an hour. A, B and C batteries were put onto the job, firing for two hours each.

The 50th Brigade Machine Gun Company completed its reliefs. Half of D Section in reserve at Pommiers Redoubt relieved the half of D in the line. C Section reported that one gun had fired five hundred rounds at High Wood and Switch Trench. They also reported that the 7th East Yorks made a bombing attack.

During the night, Lieutenant-Colonel Fife's 7th Yorks were chiefly employed by digging trenches between their position in support and the front line.[243] Lieutenant-Colonel Cardew had a dreadful night in his deep dugout at the front. Despite the fact that he had a mosquito net something, he did not know what, spent the night biting him.[244]

---

242 Lieutenant-Colonel Milne had been Mentioned in Despatches in June 1916 and involved in the heavy fighting at Mametz Village and Montauban.

243 Personal diary of Lieutenant-Colonel Fife.

244 IWM: Cardew 86/92/1.

Night of 10/11 August

The 12th Manchesters moved into Montauban Alley and relieved the 10th Notts & Derbys as the left hand support battalion. The 9th Northumberlands moved up to the line via the Mametz Road and Montauban Alley. At Green Dump they met their guides who led them to Longueval. The 51st Brigade reported that it had been relieved by the 52nd Brigade. The 51st Brigade went into Divisional reserve.

D Section of the 50th Brigade Machine Gun Company reported to H.Q that all was well. The Germans bombarded along Piccadilly fairly freely during the night. Several shells landed near the entrance of their dugout but they suffered no casualties. A Section reported that all was well and that they had suffered no casualties. Meanwhile C and D Companies of the 7th Yorks and Lancs worked during the night on a new trench from the left of the northern tip of Trones Wood and up near Waterlot Farm. They cut a length of seven hundred and seventy yards.

Chapter Eleven: 11 August

12.30 am

The 7th East Yorks came under heavy machine gun fire and, after a short while, they decided that they required artillery support so they launched their S.O.S rockets.

1.00 am

Seeing the rockets, the 80th Brigade, R.F.A duly responded to the S.O.S. Their fire suppressed the machine guns but the S.O.S was to cause a little trouble later on.

1.10 am

The 7th East Yorks reported that it was now quiet, their work upon the trenches continued. B and C Companies carried on working in Dorset Trench and A Company dug towards Piccadilly. D Company was employed deepening Pear Street. Both B and C Companies were ordered to complete Dorset Trench before dawn. Each Company was to push a sap twenty yards forwards. The saps had to be two feet six inches wide and five feet deep. A Company was ordered to push their sap forwards another twenty yards towards Wood Lane. They also had to complete a trench on the right that would connect with the right flank Brigade. The battalion also sent out two patrols to reconnoitre and assess the state of the German wire.

1.30 am

The 17th Division reported to XV Corps that the enemy put down a half hour barrage on the rear of the 51st and 52nd Brigades who were undergoing a relief. The infantry in the German lines burst into life as well. Every rifle and machine gun opened up forcing the working Tommies to take cover. Lieutenant-Colonel Fife recorded, that in the last twenty-four hours, his battalion had suffered fourteen or fifteen men hit and only five were killed.[245]

2.00 am

The bombardment that was falling upon on the 51st and 52nd Brigades now ceased.

2.40 am

The 8th South Staffords reported that the 10th Lancashires had completed their relief and the battalion was leaving the front line in companies for the bivouac.

4.00 am

By now, the 9th Northumberlands had relieved the 7th Lincolns and Major Westmacott of the 9th Northumberlands was not at all happy. The 7th Lincolns had apparently left the trenches, the reserve line and the battalion H.Q in a "far from clean" state.[246] D Company commander reported this fact to Major Westmacott and he in turn reported this to 52nd Brigade H.Q. To be fair to the 7th Lincolns, nowhere in the front line of this sector was in a clean state.

Two platoons of A Company were in the front line with two platoons in support. B and C Companies followed the same deployment. D Company and the battalion bombers remained in reserve at Longueval. Each of the companies received ten tins of water each. They were coming under shellfire and the battalion had men wounded during the relief. The battalion came under the command of Major Torrens of the 10th Lancashires, who had assumed command of all troops in Delville Wood and Longueval.

The 9th Duke of Wellingtons reported that they had successfully reconnoitred all routes up to the front line. The 10th Lancashires arranged for the Duke of Wellingtons to bring up water from the

---

245 Personal diary of Lieutenant-Colonel Fife.

246 TNA: PRO WO95/2013. War Diary 9th Northumberland Fusiliers, August 1916

dump in Trones Wood. Communications with the 12th Manchesters were cut except for the H.Q runners. It was therefore decided that the S.O.S call of five red rockets would also be the call for reserves from the 9th Northumberlands. This arrangement was later cancelled.

4.30 am

Construction and consolidation carried on day and night. This morning, A and B Companies of the 7th Yorks & Lancs began the day shift and A Company had one man wounded. When daylight came the battlefield was covered in mist and it was obvious that it would be very hot again. Lieutenant-Colonel Fife received orders to send men to dig a connecting trench between the 7th East Yorks and the 33rd Division that night. He tried to do some observation of the German lines but found it rather difficult because the German trenches were not easily seen from his position.[247]

5.15 am

Relief of the 51st Brigade by 52nd Brigade was reported to be complete. 52nd Brigade carried on the work of constructing a front line and support line inside Delville Wood and north of Longueval. The 10th Notts & Derbys were still in position near Mine Trench. The 52nd Brigade reported that its units were in the line as follows; right front line the 10th Lancashires, right support 9th Duke of Wellingtons. Left front line 9th Northumberlands, left support 12th Manchesters. The 50th Brigade recorded another quiet day. Parties of officers from the 41st Brigade toured the positions and trenches during the day, preparing for the forthcoming relief.

5.30 am

All companies of the 8th South Staffords had reached the bivouac that was situated a mile-and-a-half south-west of Fricourt. The men spent the day resting and bathing in the River Ancre, near Meaulte.

---

[247] Personal diary of Lieutenant-Colonel Fife.

6.00 am

The 51st Field Ambulance recorded that only thirty seven other ranks, all sitting cases, passed through the Divisional Collecting Station from 6.00 am on the previous day.

6.57 am

XV Corps noted that the 17th Division's 51st and 52nd Brigades were bombarded during their relief.

10.00 am

Lieutenant-Colonel Cardew hastily wrote his diary for the previous day. Among other things he noted that, because of the lack of water, he could only have *one* bath a day. Eight of his men from the Brigade had been awarded the M. M the previous day. This was more than the other artillery brigades, a fact that he was immensely proud of. He was dubious about the 1.00 am S.O.S and he felt that there had been no real reason for it. After writing his diary, he was going to see Brigadier-General Glasgow about it in person. Before he did, Cardew put in for ten days leave believing that he had earned it but knowing that he would not get it.[248]

11.00 am

The 52nd Field Ambulance recorded that five officers and 98 other ranks passed through the Advanced Dressing Station. One R.A.M.C private was evacuated because he had fallen ill. The A.D.M.S and the commanding officer of the 44th Field Ambulance visited the aid posts in preparation for taking over from the 17th Division.

2.15 pm

Major-General Robertson instructed 52nd Brigade to verify the report that the Germans were holding the entire trench that ran through the northern point of Delville Wood. The 52nd Brigade was to push out

---

248 IWM: Cardew 86/92/1.

patrols with orders to get a view of the enemy position and to establish posts from where the enemy line could be observed. Arrangements were to be made to get a footing in the German trench in the eastern portion of Delville Wood. From here, a bombing attack was to be made west, up the trench. A post was also to be established at the east end of the enemy trench where it entered the wood.

Divisional Operation Order No.74 was issued. It ordered that the 17th Division would be relieved by the 14th Division on the night of the 12/13 August. Command of the line was to pass to the G.O.C of 14th Division at 10.00 am on 13 August. The 17th Divisional artillery was to remain in the line and cover the 14th Division until relieved on the 16/17 and 17/18 August.

During the afternoon, the 7th Yorks watched a heavy bombardment fall on the German lines. Lieutenant-Colonel Fife later wrote that the bombardment was carried out by 9.2-inch howitzers. Fife saw that a part of the German parapet was being badly damaged and, as he watched, a party of about fifty German soldiers broke cover to get away from the shelling. Seeing where they had gone, Fife hurried to the nearest forward observation post and telephoned their co-ordinates through to the field gun batteries. There was no record of what happened next.[249]

5.00 pm

The 8th South Staffords noted that a Court of Enquiry was convened at 51st Brigade H.Q at Rose Cottage in Fricourt. The task of the enquiry was to discover why posts were not established in the German line inside Delville Wood.

The 52nd Brigade Machine Gun Company reported that the day was quiet. The reserve section spent the day cleaning up their trenches and constructing better dugouts. The 50th Brigade's reserve battalions were relieved. The 6th Dorsets and the 10th West Yorkshires, who had finished their excavation work in Beetle Alley, were relieved by the 7th Kings Royal Rifle Corps. The two battalions then marched to Bellevue Farm.

---

249 Personal diary of Lieutenant-Colonel Fife.

6.50 pm

General Rawlinson visited XV Corps H.Q to discuss future operations with Lieutenant-General Horne.

6.54 pm

XV Corps H.Q reported to Fourth Army H.Q that the situation remained unchanged.

7.30 pm

Both the 78th and 81st Brigades, R.F.A, began a desultory barrage of an area three hundred yards north of Delville Wood.

Observers in the front line reported to XV Corps H.Q that they had seen lines of German wounded being continually carried from Delville Wood. The observers went on to report that German troops had strengthened their trench behind the wood and men had been seen carrying coils of wire towards the wood. Despite the casualties, it did not appear that the German Army was ready to give up on Delville Wood just yet and, according to the German press, the nation was not ready to give up on the war either.

The XV Corps intelligence summary recorded a few more instalments of life on the German home front, this time from very recent newspaper articles. The newspapers gave an interesting counter-point to the sentiments of the captured private letters. More than aware of the problems that the ordinary working people of Germany were facing, the papers were doing their best to raise public morale and justify the continuation of the war. They tried to justify a war that they believed was for their very survival. The *Kolnische Zeitung* said

> *Victory in short is our watchword. We do not preach the hatred of nations (Velkerhass): we do not desire overlordship of the world (Weltherrschaft); we do not wish to be the lord of the world market. But every remaining day of this world war we must think of and repeat from morning to night; no peace, no understanding, no slackening of attack or of defence, no pause on the way to victory until this admission is sealed and guaranteed by the*

other side; "We recognise that you have equal right and are fully justified: we give up wishing to annihilate you: we give in."[250]

The German press blamed Britain for the war; what else could they do? Britain's aim was to crush Germany, they said. Georg Dernhard the editor of the *Vossische Zeitung* wrote "England's aim has always been the crippling of German competition. The fact of her striving after this has alone been responsible for the whole war."[251]

The British, Dominion and French press carried on in much the same vein; they blamed Germany for the conflict. The truth of the matter was that, on both sides, many ordinary men, women and children were suffering. Soldiers were fighting, and dying. Civilians were hungry, desperate and depressed and in Germany, some had already starved to death. The ordinary people may have been suffering and wondering how long the war could last but the war had to go on. Peace talks, when they were mooted by the Germans later in the year, were rejected and in the British press, anyone who supported them was labelled as cowardly and unpatriotic. Victory was all that mattered. War, raged a Vicar writing in the *The Beeston and West Notts Gazette & Echo* in December 1916, ennobled the British people, it strengthened the character. There would be no premature peace![252]

This edition of the *The Beeston and West Notts Gazette & Echo* also carried unsympathetic stories about children as young as nine and ten being sent through the adult criminal system for stealing food. Little was said about their hunger or about their father already killed in the war. Another article railed at local miners for staying down the pit and not fighting in the trenches, as if the pit was any safer than the front line or any easier a task. The hack who wrote this piece made no reference or remark about the number of miners who had joined up in 1914/15. Nor did the he mention that a good number of them were 'combed' out of the army against their will to be sent back to the pits to dig coal for the industry of war. In Beeston as in all villages, towns and cities across the United

---

250 TNA: PRO WO 157/469. XV Corps Intelligence Summaries, August 1916

251 TNA: PRO WO 157/469. XV Corps Intelligence Summaries, August 1916

252 Beeston Library, Nottingham. *The Beeston and West Notts Gazette & Echo,* December 1916.

Kingdom, France and in Germany, the casualty lists were lengthening.

7.40 pm

Fourth Army asked G.H.Q if the 17th Divisional artillery could march from the line on the 21 August. The 17th Divisional artillery brigades were therefore asked to be ready to march on the 21 August . Their relief would be on the 18/19 and 19/20 August.

8.15 pm

The 9th Northumberlands reported that the enemy shelled Longueval around their H.Q and the church but there were no casualties.

8.30 pm

The barrage on Longueval ceased. The 78th Brigade, R.F.A, ceased firing.

The 7th King's Royal Rifle Corps continued the relief of the 10th West Yorks. The 10th West Yorks began to march to Bellevue Farm.

9. 00 pm

The Germans opened another heavy barrage on the 9th Northumberlands in the left front line but there were no casualties.

10.00 pm

The heavy barrage on the 9th Northumberlands sector ceased. B Company requested water and carrying parties from D Company took it to them. After darkness had fallen a party of 300 men from the 7th Yorks, along with two Lewis Gun sections as cover, went forward to dig the connecting trench between the 7th East Yorks and the 33rd Division. Localised attacks were being put in on both flanks and Lieutenant-Colonel Fife was worried that his working party would take heavy casualties.[253]

10.30 pm

Deep in his fly-infested dugout, Lieutenant-Colonel Cardew wrote his letters and then turned to his diary. He had visited Brigadier-General Glasgow that morning and had found that Glasgow was also unhappy about the S.O.S signal. In the Brigadier-General's opinion the S.O.S was needless. Cardew agreed and went on to visit Lieutenant-Colonel Fife of the 7th Yorks and Lieutenant-Colonel Clive of the 7th East Yorks to try and find out who was to blame. It had turned out that Clive's men had been responsible for the S.O.S. It must be assumed that Clive and his men received some kind of reprimand but no one recorded any punishment; perhaps the matter was quietly dropped.

During his trip around the batteries Cardew saw a good many dead horses and the bodies of long dead German soldiers. It was "beastly" he wrote. Cardew then returned to his new billet with two live German whizz-bangs, 77 mm shells, as souvenirs. He had been informed that the division was being pulled out of the line and he noted that, though he was sorry to leave the fight, he was looking forward to getting back to comfortable accommodation again. He noted, happily, that he had played cards that evening and had won five pounds and ten shillings.[254]

11.40pm

Relief of the 10th West Yorks was completed by the 7th King's Royal Rifle Corps.

Night of 11th/12th

The 12th Manchesters were relieved in Montauban Alley by the 6th Somerset Light Infantry. The 12th Manchesters marched to a bivouac three miles west of Albert and became XV Corps reserve.

---

253 Personal diary of Lieutenant-Colonel Fife.

254 IWM: Cardew 86/92/1.

The sections of the 50th Brigade Machine Gun Company, reported to their H.Q. A Section had had a rough night; the front line had been shelled for a number of hours and the German guns had bombarded the British rear areas. The new communication trench was now complete so reliefs could take place during the day. Dorset Trench, in front of Pear Street, had also been completed. The extreme left gun of the company had been placed in an emplacement in Dorset Trench. C Section reported that they had fired as per instructions during an artillery bombardment. D section reported that all was well and that they had no casualties.

C and D Companies of the 7th Yorks and Lancs relieved the A and B Companies and worked through the night.

Chapter Twelve: 12 August

1.30 am

Lieutenant-Colonel Fife's working party returned from their labours in the front line. To his pleasant surprise there had only been four casualties.[255]

1.40 am

Orders arrived for the 10th Notts & Derbys stationed near Mine Trench. The battalion was to be relieved at 9.00 am that morning. They would proceed to bivouacs near Buire. At some time between 1.40 am and 12.30 pm fifteen men of the 10th Notts & Derbys were killed by shellfire. Private, 24469, G. H. Clarke of Beeston, Nottingham could have been one of these men.[256]

2.00 am

Orders arrived for the 7th Yorks; they were going to be relieved. Parties of the 7th Rifle Brigade were coming forward at 7.00 am to begin the process.[257]

3.45 am

Second Lieutenant Solly of the 7th East Yorks led another patrol up Piccadilly Trench in an attempt to seek out enemy positions.

---

255 Personal diary of Lieutenant-Colonel Fife.

256 Although his gravestone has the date 8 August 1916 carved on it, the *Soldiers Died* database and his Medal Index Card both record that Private George Henry Clarke of Beeston, Nottingham died on 12 August 1916. A member of a draft to the 10th Battalion Clarke had previously been a 9th Battalion soldier and had joined in 1914; he had already seen action at Gallipoli. He was 16 when he died meaning that he was very young when he volunteered.

257 Personal diary of Lieutenant-Colonel Fife.

5.00 am

The 79th Brigade, R.F.A., ceased firing in support of minor infantry operations on the north of Delville Wood. 107968 Gunner C. Hewer of A battery and 36918 Gunner N. A. Froggatt of D battery were both wounded. The Brigade recorded that the rest of the day was quiet. The usual day/night firing was due to carry on and hostile batteries were engaged throughout the day.

6.00 am

The 7th Yorks were relieved at Pommiers Redoubt by the 7th King's Royal Rifle Corps and the battalion returned to Bellevue Farm. Casualties for this tour of duty were six men killed and eleven wounded. Also stationed at the Redoubt were the 7th Borders and they were relieved during the morning by the 10th Durham Light Infantry. Major Irwin's 7th Borders went back to bivouacs in the rear.

6.10 am

XV Corps reported to Fourth Army H.Q that the situation was normal and that there was nothing to report.

6.52 am

XV Corps reported to Fourth Army that the enemy artillery had been active through the night.

8.00 am

Information was received by the 17th Division saying that, as per instructions, the 52nd Brigade had set up three posts during the night. They covered a front of about two hundred yards in front of the British line in Delville Wood; the enemy's trench could now be seen. The German post at the junction of their trench in the eastern edge of Delville Wood and the German trench covering the east flank had been captured and consolidated.

8.30 am to 9.00 am

Lieutenant-Colonel Fife reported that the relief was complete. The 50th Brigade recorded this and the 7th Yorks marched back towards Bellevue Farm in blazing heat.[258] The 50th Brigade now had the 7th East Yorkshires in the front line, the 7th Rifle Brigade in support and the 7th King's Royal Rifle Corps in reserve. At Bellevue Farm the men of the 6th Dorsets went for a swim and wash in the river Ancre.[259]

9.00 am

The 7th Lincolns left their bivouac and marched to a new one near Dernancourt. C and D Companies of the 7th Yorks & Lancs ceased their work and headed back to Fricourt.

Two staff officers, one from Army H.Q and one from Corps H.Q arrived at the 9th Northumberlands headquarters dugout in Longueval. They had orders to learn the current dispositions and positions of the British trenches.

9.30 am

The 8th South Staffords reported that they were relieved by the 42nd Infantry Brigade. The battalion marched via Becordel north of Meaulte. They crossed a pontoon bridge south of 'Vivies Mill' and headed for their old bivouac area north-east of Buire.

11.30 am

The 51st Field Ambulance packed up their equipment and the 43rd Field Ambulance arrived at the Divisional Collecting Station to relieve them.

---

258 Personal diary of Lieutenant-Colonel Fife.

259 IWM: Mozley 01/48/1.

11.15 am

An R.F.C aircrew spotted vehicles moving behind the German lines and reported this fact back to XV Corps H.Q.

11.45 am

In the front line at Longueval the 9th Northumberlands came under sniper fire. One man of the battalion, Private 21160 Hart, was killed on this day but it was not recorded how he was killed. Irritated by the sniper fire a lieutenant of the 9th Northumberlands took a Lewis gun out into no man's land to try and get the sniper.[260] It was possibly the most important action of the 17th Division's tour in the line at Delville Wood.

Noon

The G.O.C of 41st Brigade, Brigadier-General P.C.B Skinner, arrived at the 50th Brigade H.Q prior to taking command of the sector.

The 78th Brigade, R.F.A, came under an intense barrage by the German guns. The men there estimated that they were shelled by about two hundred guns of mixed calibre, ranging from 4.2 and 5.9 to 8.2-inches.

12.30 pm

The 10th Notts & Derbys reported that the relief was complete. The battalion was now on its way to Buire. During the afternoon, the men of the 6th Dorsets attended a cinema show at 17th Division headquarters. Sadly, no-one made a note of what they saw there.

12.40 pm

The companies of the 8th South Staffords arrived at their bivouacs north east of Buire. Lieutenant-Colonel Barker returned to the battalion and resumed command.

---

260 Unfortunately, it has not been possible to decipher the man's name in the 9th Northumberlands' war diary.

12.45 pm

The 17th Division recorded that the relief of the 51st Brigade by the 42nd Brigade was completed.

1.15 pm

Orders arrived from 17th Division H.Q stating that the 52nd Brigade would be relieved by the 43rd Brigade that night. The 10th Durham Light Infantry would relieve the 9th Northumberlands.

The lieutenant who went hunting a sniper returned to his position. He reported that he had observed six German soldiers in a shell hole and opened fired on them, killing them all. The sniping ceased but a greater prize had been won. Their position turned out to be very useful, it not only had a good view of the British lines but of the German ones as well. It was soon occupied by artillery observers. From here, fire could be directed onto the German trenches of Orchard Street and Wood Lane. The 81st Brigade, R.F.A carried out the usual day and night firing. They noted that the new observation post gave an excellent enfilade view of Orchard Trench and Wood Lane. Indeed, it was the first time, in the Delville Wood sector, that the British guns could be directed with any degree of accuracy and effect.

2.00 pm

The 10th Durham Light Infantry began the relief of the 9th Northumberlands. This was possible in daylight because of the position of some of the platoons. The hand over of all collection duties and aid posts from the 52nd Field Ambulance to the 44th Field Ambulance was completed. The 52nd Field Ambulance travelled via Meaulte and Dernacourt to their bivouac. The 7th Yorks and Lancs left Fricourt for their former camp near Dernancourt and the 78th Brigade, R.F.A, reported that the heavy enemy barrage had ceased.

3.00 pm

All work on their trenches was completed by the 7th East Yorks and the 7th Rifle Brigade moved forward to relieve them.

4.00 pm

The 51st Field Ambulance handed the Divisional Collecting Station to the 43rd Field Ambulance. The 51st moved to Dernancourt. The CO reported to the Assistant Director of Medical Services at Bellevue Farm.

4.45 pm

The 7th Yorks & Lancs arrived at their old bivouacs at Dernancourt. Here they received the following message from Major-General Robertson: "Divisional Commander is very pleased to hear of the work done last night and this morning on [the] communication trench from York [and Lancs] trench to Delville Wood."[261] The battalion rested at Dernancourt for two days before moving on.

5.00 pm

The 10th Notts & Derbys arrived at Buire-sur-Ancre. Captain Partridge, the affectionately nicknamed 'George Jimmy',[262] adjutant of the battalion, recorded the cost to the battalion during the period 4 to 9 August. Second Lieutenant Arthur G. Dent had been wounded on 6 August. Major W. A. McClelland and Second Lieutenant W. Bradbury had been shell shocked on 7 August. Second Lieutenants R.A. Barker, R. Gustard, and A.W. James had all been wounded on 7 August. Lieutenant R. G. Milward had also been wounded on 7 August but he was still at duty. Thirty-eight other ranks had been killed and five had died of their wounds. One hundred and fifty-four had been wounded, six of which were still at duty. Twenty-three men were missing, although five had been reported as found but wounded. The official record states that forty-

---

261 TNA: PRO WO95/1995. War Diary 7th Yorks and Lancs (Pioneers), August 1916

262 'George Jimmy' was known to be a kind soul and very helpful to newly arrived Second Lieutenants. Lieutenant Hoyte wrote that when the telephone rang in the early hours of the morning, it was always 'George Jimmy's' gentle voice at the other end. 'George Jimmy' was known to be an efficient adjutant and was soon taken away for a staff job. He, like his friend and colleague, Lieutenant 'Willie' Pearsall, the battalion Quartermaster, helped Lieutenant-Colonel Banbury, from the early days of formation, make the battalion an efficient unit.

eight men had died during this period, five of whom died of their wounds.

6.00 pm

D Company of the 9th Northumberlands had been relieved by elements of 10th Durham Light Infantry and by this time were well on their way to the rear. Guides from the 7th East Yorks were sent to 50th Brigade H.Q to bring forward the 7th Rifle Brigade to Pommiers Redoubt.

6.45 pm

The 52nd Field Ambulance arrived at their allotted bivouac area. The 6th Dorsets left Bellevue Farm and marched to Dernancourt where they were to bivouac for 48 hours.

7.30 pm

It was noted at XV Corps H.Q that the R.F.C had reported a good deal of traffic moving behind the German lines during the day. The Germans had continued to work on their trenches and they had extended the trench called Cocoa Lane to Delville Wood. The British front line had now been named Devil Trench.

8.00 pm

The 10th West Yorks arrived at Dernancourt from Bellevue Farm. On the gun line, B Battery of 80th Brigade, R.F.A, was heavily shelled by eight inch guns. Lieutenant-Colonel Cardew withdrew the gunners from the gun pits during the barrage and got them under cover. Consequently, there were no casualties.[263]

8.15 pm

The 93rd Field Company, R. E, left the front for billets in Dernancourt. Lieutenant E.C. Harris joined for duty.

---

263 IWM: Cardew 86/92/1.

9.00 pm

The 7th Rifle Brigade took over the front line from the 7th East Yorkshires and the last company of the 7th East Yorkshires began to move back into the support line.

10.00 pm

The Germans began to shell Longueval once again and this barrage continued, intermittently, throughout the relief of the 9th Northumberlands. Casualties were light. The 78th Field Company, R.E arrived at Dernancourt.

10.30 pm

Writing in his diary, Lieutenant-Colonel Cardew recorded that he had gone around his batteries again during the day and then he paid his customary visit to Brigadier-General Glasgow's H.Q. There he met Brigadier-General Skinner of the 41st Brigade, a man that Cardew dismissed as "an ass". Later in the day Cardew heard that Brigadier-General Alexander was very much impressed by his visits to his batteries, particularly when they were under shell fire. After tea he had watched a British observation balloon break free of its moorings and drift over the German lines. The German gunners fired on it and Cardew thought that they had probably brought it down.[264]

11.30 pm

The 9th Duke of Wellingtons were relieved by the 5th Somerset Light Infantry and moved back to their bivouacs.

Midnight

The 7th King's Royal Rifle Corps had relieved the 7th East Yorkshires in support and the 7th East Yorkshires went into Pommiers Redoubt. The 7th Rifle Brigade held the line and they now had the 7th King's

---

264 IWM: Cardew 86/92/1.

Royal Rifle Corps in support. The 41st Brigade Machine Gun Company began the relief of the 50th Machine Gun Company.

At about midnight four German soldiers approached the 17th Division's right flank battalion. One was shot and the other three surrendered. Later another group approached the same company and were fired on by British machine guns. Two were wounded and a party of men were sent out to get them in. Two more of the Germans fought back and they were silenced with bayonets. One of the German soldiers killed was an officer. All of the men from the two groups came from the 119th Grenadier Regiment. It was not made clear if these two groups of German soldiers were patrols or deliberate attempts to desert.

Chapter Thirteen: 13 August

1.30 am

The relief of the 7th East Yorks was completed and the battalion moved to Pommiers Redoubt. They were to have been relieved at the Redoubt by the 8th Rifle Brigade but these orders were cancelled. Still, the 7th East Yorks left Pommiers Redoubt by platoons via Mametz Shrine and Fricourt Cemetery. They halted on the Fricourt to Meaulte road to have breakfast.

2.00 am

The 10th Durham Light Infantry relieved the 9th Northumberlands and the latter moved by platoons to Pommiers Redoubt. Battalion H.Q. staff travelled last.

4.00 am

The 9th Northumberlands' battalion H.Q arrived at Pommiers Redoubt.

6.00 am

The 7th Yorks arrived at Dernancourt, having marched in through light rain from bivouacs at Bellevue Farm.[265]

7.00 am

The 8th Rifle Brigade marched to Montauban Alley and the 7th East Yorks of the 50th Brigade marched back to Buire.

---

265 Personal diary of Lieutenant-Colonel Fife.

8.00 am

Taking over from Brigadier-General Glasgow, the G.O.C of the 41st Brigade assumed command of the sector and 50th Brigade H.Q closed down and moved back to Buire. During the day, relieved by the 41st Brigade Machine Gun Company the 50th Brigade Machine Gun Company marched to Dernancourt along with the 50th Trench Mortar battery, who had also been relieved.

Similarly, the 52nd Brigade was relieved by the 43rd Brigade and command of the sector passed from Brigadier-General Clarke to G.O.C 43rd Brigade. The 10th Lancashires moved from their bivouacs near Fricourt to bivouacs near Dernancourt.

10.00 am

XV Corps recorded that 17th Division had been relieved by 14th Division. Lieutenant-General Horne asked Major-General Robertson to send him a report from the divisional battalion commanders stating exactly the line that they took over from the 2nd Division. Because of the controversy about the German troops getting back into Delville Wood he wanted to know what the exact situation was when they relieved the 2nd Division on 1/2 August. They also had to say if they took over any posts on the edge of the wood and if so, where they were located. In addition, Lieutenant-General Horne wanted to know if the line taken over from the 2nd Division had actually been held.

10.30 am

Fourth Army recorded that the relief of the 17th Division by the 14th Division was complete.

11.15 am

On the side of the Fricourt – Meaulte road, the 7th East Yorks completed their breakfast and marched to Dernancourt.

Afternoon

The 81st Brigade, R.F.A, reported that all batteries were shelled by German 15 cm guns. The bombardment carried on all afternoon and evening. This did not prevent all of the batteries in the brigade re-registering on Orchard Trench and the wire in front of it. They were ably assisted by the Forward Observation Officers now stationed in the new Observation Post at Longueval that had been captured by the lieutenant of the 9th Northumberlands. The registration of Switch Trench, directed by No.4 Section Kite Balloon, was also completed. Lieutenant B.M. Hallward returned from hospital and rejoined A Battery.

Lieutenant-Colonel Fife and Captain Cotton walked over to Quadrangle Support Trench and had a good look around, realising what a truly difficult objective it had been. They visited Lieutenant Macintyre's grave and Fife later wrote that a good cross had been placed there.[266]

2.30 pm

The 7th East Yorks arrived at the camp near Dernancourt. They recorded that during this tour of duty they had lost five men killed, eighteen were wounded and three men were missing. No officers were among the casualties. Official records show that ten men had died in the period between 1 to 12 August 1916; six had been killed in action and four had died of their wounds. The battalions spent their time, before going to rest, cleaning up their equipment and re-organising their platoons and companies.

7.00 pm

The rest of the day passed without incident for the 9th Northumberlands and at this time the battalion began the move back from Pommiers Redoubt to a camp on the Albert – Amiens road near Dernancourt. They left the line by platoons with fifty yard intervals between them. The companies then had a three hundred yard interval between them. When further away from the line the

---

266 Personal diary of Lieutenant-Colonel Fife.

platoons formed up and the battalion moved by companies. At Dernancourt, during the evening, the men of the 50th Machine Gun Company were given a hot meal and then paraded for a bath.

9.15 pm

Orders were sent to the 10th Notts & Derbys informing them that all transport, including bicycles but excluding Lewis gun carts, was to be ready to move off at 6.30 am on the following day.

9.30 pm

The 79th Brigade, R.F.A., reported that all batteries opened fire in a barrage on the German front line and support trenches. The batteries fired for ten minutes and then slowed down to one round a minute. German battery fire slowed and finally ceased. It was reported that the German troops had entered the British held trench in High Wood. This report was incorrect.

10.15 pm

Deep in his unhealthy, stuffy and damp dugout, a tired Lieutenant-Colonel Cardew wrote his diary. He had gone around the batteries as usual then, after tea, he and a couple of his officers had gone to Bazentin-le-Grand to find new gun positions. This area was being heavily shelled when they arrived and they soon concluded that it was a poor spot for artillery. On his return he met Brigadier-General Buckle who greeted him with the unpleasant news that his application for leave had been turned down. It was bad luck Cardew concluded. He closed his diary for the day with the sentiments that his was not a particularly healthy life, what with shells and things.[267] As for Brigadier-General Buckle, life was not particularly healthy for him. His days were numbered; he was about to fall terminally ill.

---

267 IWM: Cardew 86/92/1.

10.30 pm

The 79th Brigade, R.F.A, reported that the enemy 'mistook' British working parties for attacking parties and started to shell them. Even so, it was legitimate for the gunners to shell enemy working parties. Night firing was resumed by the brigade. 40800 Gunner J. Bayers and 21147 Gunner H.V. Harrison were both wounded.

11.00 pm

The 52nd Machine Gun Company reported that they had been relieved by the 43rd Machine Gun Company. The 52nd spent the night at Pommiers Redoubt.

Chapter Fourteen: 14 August

Leaving the line

Transport began to arrive for the battalions and units of the 17th Division and the men began the journey to the rear in the Bernaville area near Doullens.

2.30 am

The 6th Dorsets paraded in the camp above Dernancourt, ready to move to Prouville a village in the countryside near Doullens.

6.00 am

All of the 51st Brigade transport set off towards the new area. Second Lieutenant Allen of the 8th South Staffords was sent with the battalion transport. Lieutenant-Colonel Barker held a marching order inspection and a kit inspection. Captain C.H. Manger, who had been appointed as D. M. A. and Q. M. G of III Corps, left the battalion to take up his new duties. He had done a very good job as temporary battalion commander in Barker's absence; his posting to III Corps was a reward.

6.30 am

The 10th Notts & Derbys' transport moved out of Buire-sur-Ancre and travelled towards Moulliens-au-Bois as instructed. Meanwhile, the 6th Dorsets boarded their rail transport at Mericourt. They travelled by rail to Fienvillers where they detrained and marched the remaining six miles to Prouville on arrival they announced that their billets were fair.

The transport of the 50th Brigade Machine Gun Company left Dernancourt under the command of the 50th Brigade Transport Officer. The rest of the company paraded for inspection. The 50th Brigade transports marched to an area near Moulliens-au-Bois and billeting parties accompanied the transports, as did the 78th Field Company, Royal Engineers, the 7th Yorks and Lancs and the 53rd Field Ambulance.

Some of the 52nd Brigade proceeded by road to the Fienvillers area. The 9th Northumberlands recorded that their transports were brigaded at Dernancourt and began a two day trek to Candas Fienvillers. The battalion remained at Dernancourt and attended a concert that evening. Orders arrived for them to move to Fienvillers by train on the following day. At Dernancourt, Lieutenant-Colonel Wannell's Duke of Wellingtons spent the day bathing, doing PT and company close order drill. The 12th Manchesters recorded that they were still the Corps reserve.

8.00 am

The horse transport of the 52nd Field Ambulance marched from the bivouac area under the command of Captain Bury. All motor transport, cars and motorcycles, and personnel connected to the motor vehicles, were handed over to the 17th Divisional Supply Column. One private soldier of the unit had fallen ill and had to be evacuated.

9.00 am

Leaving Pommiers Redoubt, the 52nd Brigade Machine Gun Company headed for the 52nd Brigade bivouac area on the Albert – Amiens road.

4.30 pm

The 78th Field Company, R.E noted that their cyclists and transports left for Contay under the orders of the C.R.E. The dismounted men remained at Dernancourt and during the afternoon the 10th West Yorks paraded for bathing.

8.45 pm

Orders arrived at the 10th Notts & Derbys H.Q at Buire-sur-Ancre. The battalion was to move to Mericourt where they would entrain at 2.30 pm on the next day. The train would stop at Candas and, from there, they would march to billets at Longuevillette and a another short rest. The tour in the 'Devil Wood' was over.

As was said at the beginning of the book, the 17th Division's tour of duty at Delville Wood in August demonstrated that Horne treated them differently than he had in July. He did not push too hard or demand too much of them. Conversely, knowing the Division was still in a bad way after the Quadrangles operations, he seems to have recognised the shaken nature of the men in the division's ranks and he handled them sensitively. There were no reprisals for the a lack of 'push' in August. There was no stream of orders demanding piecemeal attacks sent to Major-General Robertson, instead he allowed Robertson to make a number of decisions himself, including allowing him to give instructions to the heavy artillery and to make choices about reliefs. About the latter the only order Horne gave was to take no unnecessary risks. His behaviour in August towards the 17th Division was far removed from his behaviour towards the Division in July.

The 17th Division's tour of duty at Delville Wood demonstrates that the Somme Battle was now, indeed, a campaign. It was not one, relentless, offensive; but a series of battles punctuated by lulls. It would appear that Major-General Robertson's 17th Division, under Rawlinson and Horne's direction, had carried out Haig's orders to the letter, despite Haig becoming irritated with Rawlinson and despite confusion on the ground. The men of the 17th Division had improved the line, dug new trenches and consolidated; they had not mounted any major operations but remained stationary and carried out a mainly defensive operation. In fact, with the capture of the snipers' post by one man and a Lewis gun, the 17th Division had very much improved observation of the German line in the centre and had thereby secured a very useful objective. Better observation of the German line was one of III and XV Corps' tasks for the month. They had played a part in the preparation for the battle for the German third line.

Delville Wood and Longueval had been places of confusion; difficult for the men in the line and at the H.Qs. Brigadier-General Clarke agreed, he wrote: "Conditions in Delville Wood were appalling. It was full of gas and corpses; no regular line could be discerned, and the men fought in small groups, mostly in shell holes hastily improvised into fire trenches; communication both lateral and from front to rear was exceedingly difficult, dangerous and barely possible."[268] Major-General Robertson thought that the Division's achievements at Longueval and Delville Wood received scant credit and, while recognising the chaotic state of the line and the weakened composition of his Division, through heavy losses and untried drafts, he said in April 1934, "I think that the holding of Longueval and Delville Wood from 1st to 13th August … As being one of the most noteworthy of the 17th Div's defensive actions."[269]

Now the 17th Division took its leave of Henry Rawlinson and Henry Horne. They would return to this part of the Somme in October, facing Zenith Trench, after a tour of duty at Gommecourt, in the north of the Somme Battlefield.

---

268 J.L. J. Clarke in in Hilliard Atteridge, *A History of the 17th (Northern) Division,* p.161

269 CAB 45/137. Letter from Major-General Sir Philip Robertson to Brigadier-General Edmonds, 15 April 1934.

Appendix 1:
Postscript for Lieutenant-Colonel Cardew

The infantry of the 17th Division had left the line but the divisional artillery was still in it and was due to leave on 20 August. On Tuesday 15 August Cardew went to a meeting with the other divisional artillery colonels and Brigadier-General Buckle. When Buckle came into the meeting Cardew was shocked by the man's appearance. He was definitely ill and had a very high fever. The meeting was not a success, wrote Cardew later, Buckle issued a string of orders to the colonels but they concluded that the orders were impossible to carry out. On the following morning Cardew heard that Buckle had gone sick and it was reported that he was suffering from Ptomaine Poisoning. Any reports of Buckle's illness would naturally interest Cardew as he hoped that he, Cardew, would take over as C.R.A once again. His hopes, ever high, were dashed. Cardew soon learned that he was not to take over the divisional artillery as he had done previously; even for a short time. Brigadier-General Hussey, 5th Division, was to temporarily command both his own artillery and that of the 17th Division.

On 17 August the news came that Buckle had Meningitis. The following day, as Cardew grumbled about the lack of comfort in his dugout, news reached him that Brigadier-General Buckle had died of Spinal Meningitis. In his diary Cardew wrote that he was sorry about Buckle's death and, with a characteristic eye on the main chance, he speculated about the possibility of taking over as C.R.A once again.

On 20 August when the 17th Divisional artillery left the gun line, determined to push his case and with Brigadier-General Alexander's blessing, he chased around the countryside in his car to try and find the 17th Division H.Q. His mission was to get Robertson to promote him to the post of C.R.A.. Two days previously the 17th Division had been ordered to relieve the 56th Division in the line opposite Gommecourt and Cardew found Major-General Robertson's H.Q at Doullens.

When Cardew arrived at H.Q he found Major-General Robertson and his staff waiting for a dinner party to begin. Without any further ado, Cardew managed to get a meeting with Major-General Robertson and G.S.O. 1 Collins in the General's private rooms. Cardew put his case for promotion once again and Major-General

Robertson, in Cardew's own words was "very civil and nice." Nevertheless, it was to no avail, Major-General Robertson informed him that Brigadier-General P. Wheatley, R.H.A, had been appointed C.R.A only the day before. Major-General Robertson observed the niceties of hospitality; he bade Cardew wash his hands in his room and then invited him to dinner. They ate fish and the band played in the background; it was all very pleasant. After the meal Major-General Robertson personally saw Cardew off, promising to recommend him for promotion as soon it was decently possible.

Cardew still had one important task to perform. Three days later, on 23 August, Lieutenant-General Horne came to inspect the 17th Divisional Artillery. Cardew, as the senior artillery colonel, had to officiate. Horne inspected the batteries and gunners and then gave them a speech in which he thanked them for their efforts and told them how good they were. Even though he desperately wanted to be one, generals did not seem to impress Cardew and this occasion was no exception. Perhaps he was feeling sorry for himself but he dropped a social gaffe at the end of the inspection. Cardew decided that Horne was pleasant but nothing special and did not thank the general for his kind words.

Brigadier-General Wheatley arrived on 23 August and Cardew could not resist a dig. Wheatley was shrivelled looking, probably because of the time that he had spent in India, Cardew wrote. Wheatley did not seem too bad but he was rather conceited, Cardew concluded. At 11.00 pm that night Cardew made what was to be the last entry in his diary of 1916 as 80th Brigade, R.F.A., C.O, describing what was a minor debacle as the artillery brigades became mixed up leaving the gun line.[270] The rest of the pages in the Army book that he used as a diary remained blank. Shortly after this date he was transferred to command the 190th Brigade, R.F.A., 41st Division. Perhaps Robertson had kept his word and recommended him for promotion but it does not seem likely. This was a sideways move and not the promotion to Brigadier-General that Cardew coveted. In all probability Cardew's efforts to secure his promotion and not his performance as the temporary C.R.A., had irritated Major-General Robertson to the point where he simply decided to rid himself of this troublesome gunner. Cardew was personally very brave and, by

---

270 IWM. Cardew. 86/92/1

now, not a bad artilleryman but gate-crashing the Major-General's dinner party and not thanking Lieutenant-General Horne for his kind words to the divisional artillery were not particularly good career moves.

Appendix 2: Roll of Honour

1 August

7th East Yorks

Ackroyd, Gerald, 22088, Private. Died of wounds. Born in Halifax, Yorkshire and enlisted in Hull. Buried at Moorend United Reform Chapel yard, UK in grave A. 107.

10th Lancashire Fusiliers

Smith, John, 13034, Lance Corporal. Died of Wounds. Aged 42. Born in Whitfield, Lancashire and enlisted in Bury. The husband of Elizabeth Smith of 3, Riding Street, Radcliffe, Manchester. Buried at La Neuville British Cemetery Corbie in grave I. E. 44.

2 August

79th Brigade, R.F.A

Sorrel, George Herbert, 20995, Gunner. Killed in action by counter-battery fire. Born in Redcar, Yorkshire, enlisted in Middlesbrough. A member of A Battery. Commemorated on Thiepval Memorial, Pier and Face 1A and 8A. The entry in the war diary states that he was killed on 3 August but the Commonwealth War Graves Commission website and *Soldiers Died* record his death as 2 August.

Boden, William Henry, 114770, Gunner. Killed in action by counter-battery fire. Born and enlisted in Birmingham. A member of A Battery. Commemorated on Thiepval Memorial Pier and Face 1A and 8A. The entry in the war diary states that he was killed on 3 August but the Commonwealth War Graves Commission website and *Soldiers Died* records his death as 2 August.

9th Northumberland Fusiliers

Howes, E, Second Lieutenant. Killed in action by British artillery. Buried in Dantzig Alley British Cemetery in grave 1. A. 37.

3 August

7th Borders

Bardy, Mark Stewart, 14582, Lance Corporal. Killed in action. Born in Station Town, Durham and enlisted in Blyth, Durham. Commemorated on Thiepval Memorial Pier and Face 6A and 7C.

Carr, Frederick, 14925, Private. Killed in action, probably on 2 August. Aged 22. The son of Martha and George Carr of South View Cottage, Tantobie, County Durham. Buried in Dantzig Alley Cemetery in grave IX. B. 10.

Stainton, Alfred John, 12845, Private. Killed in action, probably on 2 August. Aged 21. The son of Thomas and Mary Jane Stainton of Ghyll Foot, Gosforth, Cumberland Buried in Dantizig Alley Cemetery in grave IX. B. 9.

9th Northumberland Fusiliers

Atkinson, Mathew, 23790, Private. Killed in action. Born in Newburn-on-Tyne and enlisted in Newcastle-on-Tyne. Commemorated on Thiepval Memorial Pier and Face 10B, 11B and 12 B.

Gowland, Walter Ballantnye, 13788, Private. Killed in action. Born in Newcastle-on-Tyne and enlisted at Blyth, Northumberland. Commemorated on Thiepval Memorial Pier and Face 10B, 11B and 12B.

Hargreaves, Robert, 5211, Private. Killed in action by British artillery. Born and enlisted in Cleakheaton, Yorkshire. Buried in Dantzig Alley British Cemetery in grave 1. A. 38.

Harvey, Vincent, 15881, Private. Killed in action. Born in Sheffield and enlisted in Sheffield. The brother of Mrs. E Barnett of 511

Allen Street, Sheffield. Commemorated on Thiepval Memorial Pier and Face 10B, 11B and 12B.

Ryder, Joseph, 20675, Private. Killed in action by British artillery. Enlisted in Durham. Buried in Dantzig Alley British Cemetery in grave 1. A. 36.

Silverton, Thomas, Septimus, M.M, 12884, Sergeant. Killed in action by British artillery. Born in Chester-le-Street, Durham and enlisted in Blyth, Northumberland. Buried in Dantzig Alley British Cemetery in grave 1. A. 39.

Stevens, George Henry, 13873, Private. Died of wounds. Born in Walker, Northumberland and enlisted in Blyth, Northumberland. Son of Emily Stevens, 30 Co-Operative Terrace, New Delaval, Newsham, Northumberland. Husband of Sarah Lennox Kirkup (formerly Stevens) of 18, Disraeli Street, Cowpen Quay, Blyth, Northumberland. Commemorated on Thiepval Memorial Pier and Face 10B, 11B and 12B.

79th Brigade, R.F.A

Cook, A, 24354, Sergeant. Killed in action by counter-battery fire. Although mentioned in the war diary as being a member of B Battery, 79th Brigade, Cook is recorded as being COOKE and a member of 78th Brigade. He is buried in Flat Iron Copse Cemetery in grave IX. F. 10.

Groom, Frank, 103235, Gunner. Killed in action by counter-battery fire. A member of B Battery. Born in Denford near Thrapston, Northants, he enlisted in Wellingborough. Buried in Flat Iron Copse Cemetery in grave X. C. 8.

Parker, C. H., 12811, Gunner. Killed in action by counter-battery fire. A member of D Battery. Aged 25. Born in Derby. The son of Charles Henry Parker and E. E. Parker, he lived at 5, Buxtons Cottages, Back Parker Street, Derby. He enlisted in Birmingham. Buried in Flat Iron Copse Cemetery in grave V. E. 6.

Ware, William Kent, 35078, Bombardier. Killed in action by counter-battery fire. A member of D Battery. Born in Gravesend, Kent and enlisted in Camberwell, London. Buried in Flat Iron Copse Cemetery in grave VI. C. 3.

10th West Yorks

Dobson, Harry, 23838, Private. Died of wounds. Aged 19, born in Scorton, Yorkshire and enlisted in Ripon, Yorkshire. Son of Mary Thorpe, Carthorpe, Bedale, Yorkshire. Buried at St. Pierre Cemetery, Amiens in grave II. E. 7.

4 August

7th Borders

Higginson, Walter, 18385, Lance Corporal. Killed in action. Born and enlisted in Bolton Lancashire. Commemorated on Thiepval Memorial Pier and Face 6 A and 7 C.

Jackson, George Robert, 14612, Acting Corporal. Killed in action. Born in Middlesborough, enlisted in Bishop-Auckland, Durham and a resident of Old Shildon, Durham. Commemorated on Thiepval Memorial Pier and Face 6 A and 7 C.

Johnston, Charles, 12801, Private. Killed in action. Born in and a resident of Lowca, Cumberland and enlisted in Whitehaven, Cumberland. Commemorated on Thiepval Memorial Pier and Face 6 A and 7 C.

9th Northumberland Fusiliers

Holms, James, 14441, Sergeant. Died of wounds. Born and enlisted in Gateshead-on-Tyne. Buried at Heilly Station Cemetery, Mericourt-L'Abbe in grave III. B. 15.

Morton, William Daglish, 13042, Private. Killed in action. Enlisted in Newcastle-on-Tyne. Commemorated on Thiepval Memorial Pier and Face 10B, 11B and 12B.

Stewart, Lewis James, 14815, Private. Killed in action. Born in Leith, Edinburgh and enlisted at Wool, Dorset. Commemorated on Thiepval Memorial Pier and Face 10B, 11B, and 12B.

12th Manchesters

Blythe, Norman Harry, Second Lieutenant. Killed in action. Son of Mr A.J and Mrs E.A Blythe of Swinton Schools, Manchester. He had joined the Manchesters on 26 June 1916 and died in the botched attack upon Orchard Trench. Commemorated on Thiepval Memorial Pier and Face 13A and 14C.

Moulton, William Ralph Osborne, Second Lieutenant. Killed in action in the botched attack upon Orchard Trench. Buried in Bernafay Wood British Cemetery, Montauban in grave C. 1.

Andrews, William, 5837, Lance Corporal. Killed in action. Born in Hulme and enlisted in Manchester. Commemorated on Thiepval Memorial Pier and Face 13A and 14C.

Atkins, John, 24361, Private. Killed in action. Born in Tamworth and enlisted in Manchester. Commemorated on Thiepval Memorial Pier and Face 13A and 14C.

Barnard, Herbert Ellson, 31212, Private. Killed in action. Born in London, enlisted in Manchester and lived in Pendleton. Commemorated on Thiepval Memorial Pier and Face 13A and 14C.

Black, Joseph, 31202, Private. C Company. Killed in action. Aged 23, born and enlisted in Manchester. Only son of Joseph and Elizabeth Black of 64 Barmouth Street, Bradford, Manchester. Commemorated on Thiepval Memorial Pier and Face 13A and 14C.

Briggs, Joseph, 32089, Private. Killed in action. Aged 31, born in Keighley, Yorkshire. Enlisted in Oldham. The son of Charles Briggs and the husband of Lily J. Smith (formerly Briggs) of 3, Copwer Street, Middleton Junction, Manchester. Commemorated on Thiepval Memorial Pier and Face 13A and 14C.

Brown, John Henry, 31173, Private. Killed in action. Aged 16, born and enlisted in Manchester. The son of James Brown, 10, Chapman Grove, Hulme, Manchester. Commemorated on Thiepval Memorial Pier and Face 13A and 14C.

Cullen, George William, 2840, Lance Corporal. Killed in action. Born in St. George Manchester, enlisted in Manchester. Commemorated on Thiepval Memorial Pier and Face 13A and 14C.

Hall, Herbert, 5567, Private. Killed in action. Born in Penzance, Cornwall and enlisted in Manchester. Commemorated on Thiepval Memorial Pier and Face 13A and 14C.

Harvey, Thomas, 4968, Sergeant. Killed in action. Born in Hulme, Lancashire and enlisted in Manchester. Buried in Delville Wood Cemetery Longueval in grave XXXIX. B. 10

Jones, James, 4666, Lance Corporal. Killed in action. Aged 22, born in Middlesbrough, Yorkshire, enlisted in Ashton-Under-Lyne and lived in Dukinfield, Cheshire. Son of James and Sarah Anne Jones of 5 Atin Street, Dukinfield. Commemorated on Thiepval Memorial Pier and Face 13A and 14C.

Lodge, John Joseph, 6401, Private. Killed in action. Aged 25, born in Birkdale, Southport and enlisted in Manchester. Son of Phillip and Matilda Lodge of 24, Dorset Street, West Gorton, Manchester. He enlisted in 1914. Commemorated on Thiepval Memorial Pier and Face 13A and 14C.

McConville, James, 423, Private. Killed in action. Born in Belfast and enlisted in Ashton-Under-Lyne. Commemorated on Thiepval Memorial Pier and Face 13A and 14C.

Miller, Arthur, 18333, Private. Killed in action. Born in Otley, Yorkshire and enlisted in Manchester. A resident of Chorlton-on-Medlock, Manchester. Commemorated on Thiepval Memorial Pier and Face 13A and 14C.

Parr, Thomas, 13880, Private. Killed in action. Born and enlisted in Leigh, Lancashire. Commemorated on Thiepval Memorial Pier and Face 13A and 14C.

Perks, Charles, 13796, Private. Killed in action. Born in Marbury Lancashire and enlisted in Manchester. A resident of Withington Lancashire. Commemorated on Thiepval Memorial Pier and Face 13A and 14C.

Shawcross, Stanley, 13713, Corporal. Killed in action. Aged 23, born in Worsley, Lancashire and enlisted in Manchester. The son of Daniel and Miriam Shawcross of 8, Hayes Road, Cadishead, Manchester. He is buried in Cerisy-Gailly Military Cemetery ten kilometres south west of Albert in grave II. C. 9. This cemetery opened in February 1917 and was extended after the Armistice when bodies were brought in from the battlefield and other smaller cemeteries.

Valentine, John, 5205, Corporal. Killed in action. Born in Ardwick, Manchester and enlisted in Manchester. A resident of Gorton, Lancashire. Commemorated on Thiepval Memorial Pier and Face 13A and 14C.

Woolley, James Slater, 8928, Sergeant. Killed in action. Born in Leesfield, Saddleworth, Yorkshire. He enlisted in Fleetwood, Lancashire and was a resident of Oldham, Lancashire. Commemorated on Thiepval Memorial Pier and Face 13A and 14C.

9th Northumberlands Fusiliers

Holmes, James, 14441, Sergeant. Died of wounds. Born and enlisted in Gateshead-on-Tyne. Buried at Heilly Station Cemetery, Mericourt-L'Abbe, in grave III. B. 15.

78th Brigade R.F.A

Brakes, Harold, 82576, Gunner. Killed in action. A member of 78th Brigade R.F.A., H.Q. A resident of and enlisted in Chesterfield, Derbyshire. Buried in Quarry Cemetery in grave VI. A. 12. He was possibly killed when acting as a signaller in Lloyd's Forward Observation Post.

Lloyd, Alan Scrivener, Lieutenant of C Battery. Died of Wounds. Aged 27, the son of John Henry and G.E Lloyd of Edgbaston Grove. The husband of Dorothy Margaret Marshall (formerly Lloyd) of Edgbaston Grove, Birmingham. Buried at Dartmoor Cemetery, Becordel-Becourt in grave I. C. 67. He died twenty minutes after his Forward Observation Post was heavily shelled.

5 August

7th Borders

Hutchinson, Matthew, 13132, Lance Corporal. Killed in action. Born in Bishop-Auckland, Durham and enlisted in Newburn-on-

Tyne, Northumberland. Commemorated on Thiepval Memorial Pier and Face 6 A and 7 C.

Inman, Samuel Arthur, 22491, Private. Killed in action. Born in Dronfield, Derbyshire, enlisted in Sheffield and a resident of Hillsborough, Sheffield. Commemorated on Thiepval Memorial Pier and Face 6 A and 7 C.

Jackson, George, 18364, Private. Killed in action. Born in Sutton, Lancashire, enlisted in Wigan Lancashire and a resident of Upholland, Lancashire. Commemorated on Thiepval Memorial Pier and Face 6 A and 7 C.

Jones, Thomas, 17309, Private. Killed in action. Born in and a resident of Birkenhead and enlisted in Liverpool. Commemorated on Thiepval Memorial Pier and Face 6 A and 7 C.

Pearson, George, 23120, Private. Killed in action. Born in North Heigham, Norfolk, enlisted in Norwich and a resident of Stiffkey, Norfolk. Formerly 16213 Pearson of the Norfolk Regiment. Commemorated on Thiepval Memorial Pier and Face 6 A and 7 C.

7th Yorks & Lancs (Pioneers)

Power, Phillip, 12391, Private. Killed in action by shellfire. Lived in Sheffield. Commemorated on Thiepval Memorial Pier and Face 14A and 14B. He had been buried alongside the communication trench that he had been working on but his grave and body were lost.

Townend, Luke, 12744, Private. Killed in action by shellfire. Aged 29, he was the son of George Richard and Phoebe Townend. Husband to Alice of 76 Castle Street Barnsley. Commemorated on Thiepval Memorial Pier and Face 14A and 14B. Like his comrade Phillip Power, Townend was buried alongside the communication trench where he was working but his grave and body were lost.

78th Field Company, R. E

Le Maitre, Alfred Henry, 59162, Sapper. Killed in action. Killed by shelling. Aged 30, he was born in Islington, Middlesex and enlisted at Southend-on-Sea in Essex. The son of George Frederick and Gertrude Emily Le Maitre of 140, North Road, Southend-on-Sea. He is buried in Quarry Cemetery, Montauban in grave V. C. 12.

10th Notts & Derbys

French, Edmund, 41390, Private. Killed in action. Born and enlisted in Nottingham. Commemorated on Pier and Face 10 C, 10 D and 11 A on the Thiepval Memorial.

Lammin, Sidney H., 38360, Private. C Company. Killed in action. Age 30. Born and enlisted in Grimsby, Lincolnshire. The son of Susannah M. and Haman Lammin of 75, Patrick Street, Grimsby. Buried in grave VI. J. 4. in Quarry Cemetery, Montauban

Smith, Henry H., 42330, Private. Died of wounds. Age 22. Born in and a resident of Bulwell, Nottinghamshire. Enlisted in Nottingham. The son of James and Hannah Smith of 34, Austin Street, Bulwell. Buried in grave VI. J. 3. in Quarry Cemetery, Montauban.

81st Brigade, R.F.A

Bowman, Robert Moore, Second Lieutenant. Killed in action. He was killed when his dugout was hit during German counter-battery fire. Aged 22, the son of Thomas Kynaston Bowman of 50, Hanover Gate Mansions, Regents Park, London. Buried in Carnoy Military Cemetery in grave N. 34.

12th Manchesters

Marsden, Thomas, 4334, Private. Died of wounds. Born and enlisted in Manchester. The son of Anthony and Alice Marsden. Husband of Annie Marsden, of 7, Upper Mount Street, Harpurhey, Manchester. Buried at Manchester General Cemetery, UK.

9th Duke of Wellingtons

Hopkinson, William, 17797, Private. Died of wounds. Aged 21, born and enlisted in Halifax. The son of John Hopkinson of 8, Studleigh Terrace, Hove Edge, Hipperholme, Halifax. Buried in Dernancourt Communal Cemetery in grave J. 26.

6 August

7th Borders

Ashmore, Henry, 12187, Private. Killed in action. Born in and a resident of Bicester, Oxford and enlisted in Kirkby Lonsdale, Westmoreland. Commemorated on Thiepval Memorial Pier and Face 6 A and 7 C.

Heenan, James, 18422, Lance Corporal. Killed in action. Born in Winlaton, Durham and enlisted in Newcastle-upon-Tyne. Buried in Delville Wood Cemetery in grave XII. A. 5.

Morris, George, 14933, Private. Killed in action. Born in Waldridge, Durham, enlisted in Chester-le-Street and a resident of Hartlepool, Durham. Commemorated on Thiepval Memorial Pier and Face 6 A and 7 C.

Rance, Frank, 23251, Private. Killed in action. Born in and a resident of Berkhampstead and enlisted in Bedford. Formerly 12144 of the Norfolk Regiment. Commemorated on Thiepval Memorial Pier and Face 6 A and 7 C.

52nd Field Ambulance

The following four men were buried when a shell hit their deep dugout. One man was rescued but these men were not. They have no official grave so it must be assumed that their bodies were later buried as unidentified or that they are still down in their dugout.

Askew, W., 41504, Private. Killed in action. Age 22, born and enlisted in Preston Lancashire. Son of John and Clara Askew of 26 Kenmore Place, Preston. Commemorated on Thiepval Memorial Pier and Face 4C. This man is recorded on the Commonwealth War Graves website as Askey even though his parents are named as

Askew. Askey is the name given to him by the war diary and the *Soldiers Died* database.

Dunkerley, James, 76938, Private. Killed in action. Age 20 born and lived in Reddish, Stockport. Enlisted in Manchester. Son of James Dunkerley of 553, Gorton Street, Reddish, Stockport. Commemorated on Thiepval Memorial Pier and Face 4C.

Gluckstein C. S., M.M, 41542, Private. Killed in action. Born in Edgbaston and enlisted in Birmingham. Commemorated on Thiepval Memorial Pier and Face 4C. He won his Military Medal for bravery during the action against Quadrangle Support Trench.

James, Harry Edward, 72851, Private. Killed in action. Born in Marylebone, London. Enlisted in Kilburn and a resident of North Kensington. Commemorated on Thiepval Memorial Pier and Face 4C.

7th East Yorks

Leigh, Thomas, 12100, Private. Killed in action. Aged 36, born and enlisted in Sheffield. Son of Mr and Mrs George Henry Leigh late of 1, Court 7 House, Greystock Street, Sheffield. Buried in Dantzig Alley British Cemetery, Mametz in grave IV. D. 5.

Wells, William, 11/125, Private. Killed in action. Aged 18, born and enlisted in Hull. Son of Mr. A and Lavina Sophia Wells of 15, Albert Avenue, Wellsted Street, Hull. Buried in Dantzig Alley British Cemetery, Mametz in grave IV. D. 6.

10th Notts & Derbys

Burgin, Lawrence, 14762, Private. Killed in action. Born in Anston, Yorkshire and enlisted at Kiveton Park, Yorkshire. One of the original 10th Battalion volunteers, he entered France and Flanders on 14 July 1915. Commemorated on Pier and Face 10 C, 10 D and 11 A on the Thiepval Memorial.

Gilbank, John, 15036, Private. (His MIC records his number as 15056). Killed in action. Age 22. Born in Workington, Yorkshire and enlisted in Retford, Nottinghamshire. A resident of Beverley, Yorkshire. The son of Matthew and Mary Jane Gilbank of Belby,

Howden, Yorkshire. He entered France and Flanders on 23 March 1915 and is recorded on his MIC as being a member of the 1st Battalion[271] When he joined the 10th Battalion is not recorded. Buried in grave XXII. Q. 5. in Delville Wood Cemetery, Longueval.

Hardy, William Edward, 16865, Private. Killed in action. Age 26. Born and a resident in Huthwaite, Nottinghamshire and enlisted in Sutton-in-Ashfield, Nottinghamshire. The husband of Mary Jane Hardy of 34, King Street, Huthwaite. Originally a 12th Battalion man, he entered France and Flanders on 28 August 1915. It was not recorded when he joined the 10th Battalion. Buried in grave XXII. Q. 9. in Delville Wood Cemetery, Longueval.

Harris, Enoch, 9034, Private. Killed in action. Age 30. Born and enlisted in Leicester. A resident of Ontario, Canada. The son of Enoch and Ellen Harris. A regular solider from the 2nd Battalion who entered France and Flanders on 10 October 1914. His original service number changed from 9234 to 9034 at some point. The date of his transfer to the 10th Battalion was not recorded. Commemorated on Pier and Face 10 C, 10 D and 11 A on the Thiepval Memorial.

Hepworth, Fred, 24628, Private. Died of wounds. Age 26. Born at Whittington Moor, Derbyshire and enlisted in Chesterfield, Derbyshire. A resident of Brampton, Derbyshire. The husband of Mrs. H. E. Bowler (formerly Hepworth), of 45, Catherine Street, Brampton, Chesterfield. His MIC records that he was a member of the 9th Battalion and then the 10th Battalion. He entered France and Flanders on 25 October 1915 and therefore did not go to war with the 9th Battalion.[272] Buried in grave VI. J. 1. Quarry Cemetery, Montauban.

Housley, Arthur, 23854, Private. Killed in action. Born and enlisted in Sutton-in-Ashfield, Nottinghamshire. Buried in grave XXII. Q. 6. in Delville Wood Cemetery, Longueval.

Palmer, Albert, 23199, Private. Killed in action. Born in Hanley, Staffordshire and enlisted in Longton, Staffordshire. A resident of

---

271 The 1st Battalion was not on the Somme front in August 1916, it was in the Bethune Sector. It returned to the Somme in October 1916.

272 The 9th Battalion had gone to Gallipoli in August 1915.

Fenton, Staffordshire. His MIC records that he was originally a member of the 2nd Battalion who entered France and Flanders on 17 August 1915. Buried in grave XXII. Q. 8. in Delville Wood Cemetery, Longueval.

Parnham, Thomas, 15816, Private. Killed in action. Born in Colston Bassett, Nottinghamshire and enlisted in Nottingham. A resident of Carlton, Nottingham. Buried in grave XXII. Q. 10. in Delville Wood Cemetery, Longueval.

Ponsford, Albert, 37931, Private. Killed in action. Age 29. Born and enlisted in Leicester. The husband of Annie Ponsford of 323, Olphin Street, Belgrave Road, Leicester. Commemorated on Pier and Face 10 C, 10 D and 11 A on the Thiepval Memorial.

Reeves, Jesse, 15571, Private. Killed in action. Born in Huthwaite, Nottinghamshire and enlisted in Sutton-in-Ashfield, Nottinghamshire. He joined the 10th Battalion on 29 July 1915. Commemorated on Pier and Face 10 C, 10 D and 11 A on the Thiepval Memorial.

Rose, George, 40085, Private. Killed in action. Born in Thorneywood, Nottinghamshire and enlisted in Nottingham. Buried in grave XXII. Q. 3. in Delville Wood Cemetery, Longueval.

Toplis, Leonard, 30832, Private. Killed in action. Born in Long Eaton, Derbyshire and enlisted in Castle Donnington. A resident of Ilkeston, Derbyshire. Buried in grave II. E. 5. in Peronne Road Cemetery.

6th Dorsets

Alner, Albert George, 16878, Private. Killed in action. Born in and a resident of Farnham, Dorset. Enlisted in Blandford. Buried in Quarry Cemetery, Montauban in grave VI. J. 6.

Blandamer, James, 17127, Private. Killed in action. Born and enlisted in Dorchester, Dorset. Commemorated on Thiepval Memorial Pier and Face 7B.

White, Ernest John, 10806, Private. Killed in action. Born and enlisted in Weymouth, Dorset. Commemorated on Thiepval Memorial Pier and Face 7B.

50th Brigade Machine Gun Company

Crawford, Henry Allen, 36452, Private. Killed in action by shellfire. Born in Catshill, Worcestershire. Enlisted in Bromsgrove. Formerly 27299, Crawford of the Worcesters. Commemorated on Thiepval Memorial Pier and Face 5C and 12C.

9th Duke of Wellingtons

Bailey, George, 12878, Private. Died of wounds. Born in and a resident of Addingham, Yorkshire. Enlisted in Ilkley, Yorkshire. Buried in Quarry Cemetery, Montauban in grave VI. J. 2.

Boyd, Duncan, 14119, Private. Died of wounds. Born in Islington and enlisted in Halifax. A resident of Kirriemuir, Forfarshire. Buried in Heilly Station Cemetery, Mericourt-L'Abbe in grave III. B. 23.

Muff, Tom, 17448, Private. Died of wounds. Aged 39, born in and a resident of Bradford, Yorkshire. Enlisted in Burton-on-Trent. The son of Benjamin and Ann Muff of Moss-Side, North Bierley, Barnsley. Buried in Heilly Station, Mericourt-L'Abbe in grave III. B. 21.

78th Brigade, R.F.A

Masterson, Patrick, 70807, Gunner. Killed in action. Aged 21, born in St. Thomas, Dublin. Enlisted in Dublin. A member of A Battery. Buried in Dartmoor Cemetery in grave I. F. 72.

80th Brigade, R.F.A

Pleavin, William, 108909, Gunner. Killed in action. Aged 22, born and enlisted in Wrexham. Son of Thomas William and Sarah Jane Pleavin of 25, King's Mills Road, Wrexham, Denbighshire. Buried in Dartmoor Cemetery in grave I. E. 69.

93rd Field Company, R. E

Lee, George, 49850, Acting Sergeant. Killed in action. Aged 38 lived in Braston Yorkshire and enlisted in Darlington, County Durham. Husband of Sarah Hunter (formerly Lee) of 26, Surtees Street, Hopetown, Darlington, County Durham. Commemorated on Thiepval Memorial Pier and Face 8A and 8D.

10th Lancashire Fusiliers

Rooney, John Edward, 21304, Private. Killed in action. Aged 27, born in Salford Lancashire and enlisted in Manchester. Husband of Mrs. M.A. Rooney of 106, St. Simon Street, Springfield Lane, Salford. Buried in Dantzig Alley British Cemetery in grave IV. C. 7.

Thompson, David, 5490, Lance Corporal. Killed in action. Aged 19, born and enlisted in Burnley. Son of Mrs Elizabeth Thompson of 11, Cobden Street, Burnley Lane, Burnley. Buried in Dantzig Alley British Cemetery in grave IV. C. 9.

Wood, Fred, 23790, Private. Killed in action. Aged 35, born and enlisted in Rochdale. Son of Henry Wood and husband of Sarah Elizabeth Wood of 3, Holt Street, Rochdale. Buried in Dantzig Alley British Cemetery in grave IV. C. 8.

7th Borders

Atkinson, Fred, 23436, Private. Killed in action. Aged 26, born in Pen Ruddock, Cumberland. Enlisted in Keswick and a resident of Scales, Cumberland. Son of George Atkinson of Scales, Threlkeld, Penrith, Cumberland. Commemorated on Thiepval memorial Pier and Face 6A and 7C.

Barnes, William, 11520, Private. Killed in action. Born in Pendlebury, Lancashire and enlisted in Pendleton, Lancashire. Commemorated on Thiepval memorial Pier and Face 6A and 7C.

Brown, James, 18398, Private. Died of wounds. Born in Whitley, Northumberland and enlisted in Blyth. A resident of New Hartley,

Northumberland. Buried in La Neuville British Cemetery, Corbie in grave I. E. 75.

Callister, Arthur Sydney, 21438, Private. Killed in action. Aged 27, born in Whitehaven, Cumberland and enlisted in Rhyl, Flint. The son of Elizabeth and William Callister of 6, Sandhills Lane, Whitehaven, Cumberland. Commemorated on Thiepval memorial Pier and Face 6A and 7C.

Edwards, Robert, 13002, Lance Sergeant. Killed in action. Born in Spennymoor, Durham and enlisted in Durham. A resident of Spennymoor. Commemorated on Thiepval memorial Pier and Face 6A and 7C.

Forster, Isaac, 12678, Sergeant. Killed in action. Aged 24, born in Gateshead, Durham and enlisted in Newburn, Northumberland. A resident of Lemington-on-Tyne. The son of John and Anne Forster of 15, Eva Street, Lemington, Scotswood-on-Tyne, Northumberland. Buried in Delville Wood Cemetery, Longueval in grave II. G. 2.

Grey, William Thomas, 23510, Private. Killed in action. Aged 26, born in Arlecdon, Cumberland and enlisted in Frizington, Cumberland. The son of M. A. Sandwith (formerly Grey) and the late William Thomas Grey of 222, Frizington Road, Frimmington, Cumberland. Commemorated on Thiepval memorial Pier and Face 6A and 7C.

Hammond, Robert Henry, 23071, Lance Corporal. Killed in action. Aged 36, born in, and a resident of, Runhall, Norfolk and enlisted in Norwich. The son of Mrs. Matilda Hammond of Little Ellingham, Norfolk. The husband of Laura Amelia Hammond of 69, Low Street, Hardingham, Norwich. He had been 17869 Hammond of the Norfolk Regiment. It is a distinct possibility that he had only just arrived at the 7th Borders in a draft to replace the losses from the Quadrangles episode. Commemorated on Thiepval memorial Pier and Face 6A and 7C.

Hully, Allan, 14875, Private. Killed in action. Aged 24, born and enlisted in Kendal, Westmorland. A resident of Lancaster. The son of Henrietta Hully, of 20, Finkle Street, Kendal. Buried in Delville Wood Cemetery, Longueval in grave II. G. 9.

Hutton, Robert Compston, 12791, Lance Corporal. Killed in action. Born and enlisted in Kendal, Westmorland. Buried in Delville Wood Cemetery, Longueval in grave VI. E. 6.

King, William, 23124, Private. Killed in action. Aged 35, born in Stoke Holycross, Norfolk and enlisted in Norwich. A resident of Horning, Norfolk. The son of the late Mr and Mrs. George King. The husband of Annie E. King of 3, Row, 11, North Quay, Great Yarmouth. He had been 18734 King of the Norfolk Regiment and, like Hammond, may have been a part of a draft that had recently arrived to replace losses after Quadrangle Support. Commemorated on Thiepval Memorial Pier and Face 6A and 7C.

Litherland James, D.C.M., 11281, Sergeant. Killed in action. Born in Ince, Lancashire and enlisted in Wigan, Lancashire. Buried in Delville Wood Cemetery, Longueval in grave II. G. 8.

Middlebrough, Thomas, 23407, Private. Died of wounds. Aged 19, born at Cartnell Fell, Lancashire and enlisted in Kendal. A member of C Company. The son of Thomas William and Esther Middlebrough of Yew Tree, Crosthwaite, Kendal, Westmorland. Buried in Meaulte Military Cemetery in grave E. 34.

Patterson, William Isaac, 16004, Lance Corporal. Killed in action. Aged 26, born in Frizington, Cumberland and enlisted in Egremont, Cumberland. The son of Andrew and Sarah Patterson of 2, Park View, Bigrigg, Cumberland. Buried in Delville Wood Cemetery, Longueval in grave II. G. 7.

Proom, Alfred, 17730, Corporal. Killed in action. Aged 20, born in Seaton Delaval, Northumberland and enlisted in Blyth, Northumberland. A resident of New Hartley, Northumberland. The son of James William and Lucy Anne Proom of 1, The Crescent, Seaton Sluice, Seaton Delaval, Northumberland. Buried in Delville Wood Cemetery, Longueval in grave VIII. P. 4.

Simpson, Robert Irving, 11613, Lance Corporal. Killed in action. Aged 26, born in Caldewgate, Cumberland and enlisted in Carlisle. The son of Thomas and M. A. Simpson of 28, Port Road, Carlisle. Commemorated on Thiepval Memorial Pier and Face 6A and 7C.

Waddell, Gavin, 14950, Private. Killed in action. Born and enlisted in Carlisle. Commemorated on Thiepval memorial Pier and Face 6A and 7C.

Wardle, Robert, 16570, Private. Killed in action. Born in, and a resident of, New Hartley, Northumberland and enlisted in Blyth. Commemorated on Thiepval Memorial Pier and Face 6A and 7C.

10th Notts & Derbys

Bee, Herbert, 20871, Lance Corporal. Killed in action. Born and enlisted in Nottingham. An early member of the 10th Battalion, he joined it on 26 August 1915. Commemorated on Pier and Face 10 C, 10 D and 11 A on the Thiepval Memorial.

Bourne, William, 12321, Private. Killed in action. Age 21. Born in Dodderhall, Worcestershire and enlisted in Derby. A Resident of Crewton, Derbyshire. The son of Mr. and Mrs. H. Bourne of 58, Allestree Street, Crewton. He was a regular from the 2nd Battalion and had entered France and Flanders on 11 November 1914. When he joined the 10th Battalion was not recorded but the Commonwealth War Graves Commission website states that he was a 10th Battalion man at the time of his death. Commemorated on Pier and Face 10 C, 10 D and 11 A on the Thiepval Memorial.

Brewer B., D.C.M., 14582, Sergeant, Killed in action. Born in Cosall, Nottinghamshire and enlisted in Nottingham. A resident of Beeston, Nottinghamshire. He was awarded his D.C.M. while a Corporal on 30 March 1916. Commemorated on Pier and Face 10 C, 10 D and 11 A on the Thiepval Memorial.

Jepson, Edgar, 25506, Private. Killed in action. Born in Brindley, Nottinghamshire and enlisted in Nottingham. A resident of Eastwood, Nottinghamshire. He had been in the 9th Battalion and seen action at Gallipoli before joining the 10th Battalion. Buried in grave XI. A. 9. in Delville Wood Cemetery, Longueval.

Jones, Enock, 20060, Lance Corporal. Age 26. Killed in action. Born and enlisted in Derby. The son of Enoch and Mary Ellen Jones of 168, Harrington Street, Pear Tree, Derby. He joined the 10th Battalion on 26 August 1915. Commemorated on Pier and Face 10 C, 10 D and 11 A on the Thiepval Memorial.

Marriott, Albert, 21305, Died of wounds. Born in and a resident of Sutton-in-Ashfield, Nottinghamshire. Enlisted in Mansfield, Nottinghamshire. Buried in grave III. A. 11. in Heilly Station Cemetery, Mericourt-L'Abbe.

Marvill, Arthur, 10530, Private. Killed in action. Born in Uttoxeter, Staffordshire and enlisted in Derby. A regular soldier he had been in the 1st Battalion before joining the 10th Battalion. He entered France and Flanders on 4 November 1914. Buried in grave IV. A. 6. in Delville Wood Cemetery, Longueval.

McLacklan, Robert Malcolm, (The Commonwealth War Graves Commission website records his name as McLachlan) 14935, Private. Killed in action. Age 20. Born in and a resident of Mansfield, Nottingham. Enlisted in Chesterfield. The son of Robert and Fanny McLachlan. An original 10th Battalion volunteer, he entered France and Flanders on 14 July 1915. Commemorated on Pier and Face 10 C, 10 D and 11 A on the Thiepval Memorial.

Pierce, Robert, 15824, Private. Killed in action. Born in Liverpool and enlisted in Nottingham. His original unit was not recorded but he joined a Notts & Derbys battalion on the Western Front on 16 February 1915. When he joined the 10th Battalion was not recorded. Commemorated on Pier and Face 10 C, 10 D and 11 A on the Thiepval Memorial.

Rhoades, Frank (his MIC records his name as Francis), 40747, Private. Killed in action. Age 30. Born in Croft, Lincolnshire and enlisted in Spilsby, Lincolnshire. A resident of Skegness. The son of Mrs. E. Jarvis of 154, Drummond Road, Skegness. Commemorated on Pier and Face 10 C, 10 D and 11 A on the Thiepval Memorial.

Stokes, William Henry, 13540, Private. Killed in action. Born and enlisted in Worksop. Commemorated on Pier and Face 10 C, 10 D and 11 A on the Thiepval Memorial.

Wright, Wilfred Ernest, 43025, Private. Killed in action. Age 37. Born and enlisted in Chesterfield, Derbyshire. A resident of Brampton, Derbyshire. The son of the late Mrs. Hannah Wright. Commemorated on Pier and Face 10 C, 10 D and 11 A on the Thiepval Memorial.

8th South Staffords

Edwards, Thomas, 12285, Private. Killed in action. Born in, and a resident of, Pelsall, Staffordshire and enlisted in Walsall, Staffordshire. Commemorated on Thiepval Memorial Pier and Face 7B.

Myatt, George Henry, 15601, Private. Killed in action. Aged 19, born and enlisted in Darlaston, Staffordshire. Son of Moses James and Sarah Myatt of 18 Cope Street, Darlaston, Staffordshire. Commemorated on Thiepval Memorial Pier and Face 7 B.

6th Dorsets

Wells, Harold Eric, 17300, Private. Died of wounds. Aged 20, born in Ledbury, Hereford and enlisted in Blandford, Dorset. The son of James and Harriett C. Wells of Tarrant Keynston, Blandford, Dorset. Buried at Chocques Military Cemetery in grave I. J. 33.

80th Brigade, R.F.A.

Hannah, Joseph Hamilton, 133591, Gunner. Killed in action. A member of D Battery. Aged 26, born and enlisted in Glasgow. The son of Andrew Hannah. Buried in Dartmoor Cemetery, Becordel-Becourt in grave I. C. 70.

Pound, Richard Ernest, 28376, Driver. Killed in action. A member of C Battery. Aged 29, born and enlisted in Merthyr, Glamorgan. Son of William and Rhoda Pound of Merthyr Tydfil. Buried in Carnoy Military Cemetery in grave D. 31.

Wakeman, Timothy Albert, 123528, Gunner. Killed in action. A member of D Battery. Aged 21, Born in Lee, Kent. Enlisted in Lewisham, Kent. The son of Mr and Mrs. M. Wakeman of 28, Boones Road, London. Buried in Carnoy Military Cemetery in grave G. 49.

Watson, James, 74262, Gunner. Killed in action. A member of C Battery. Enlisted in Preston, Lancashire and a resident of Leyland, Lancashire. Commemorated on Thiepval Memorial Pier and Face 1A and 8A.

Williams, Austin, 19592, Gunner. Killed in action. A member of C Battery. Born in Cardiff and enlisted in Newport. Commemorated on Thiepval memorial Pier and Face 1A and 8A.

9th Northumberland Fusiliers

Gallagher, James, 18/1714, Private. Killed in action. Born in Gateshead and enlisted in Cramlington, Northumberland. Buried in Dantzig Alley British Cemetery in grave I. C. 44.

Graham, John, 15447, Private. Killed in action. Born and enlisted in Whitehaven, Cumberland. Buried in Dantzig Alley British Cemetery in grave I. C. 45.

7th East Yorks

Woodward, William, 15285, Sergeant. Died of wounds. Born in East Hetton, Bishop Auckland and enlisted in Bishop Auckland. A resident of Wheatley Hill. Recorded by the Commonwealth War Graves Commission website as 15385 Woodward of the 3rd East Yorks. Buried at Dantzig Alley British Cemetery in grave I. C. 34.

8 August

9th Northumberland Fusiliers

Barnes, John Thompson, 11895, Lance Corporal. Killed in action. Born in Heaton, Northumberland and enlisted in Newcastle-on-Tyne. Buried in Dantzig Alley British Cemetery in grave I. C. 37.

Dove, James, 15707, Private. Killed in action. Aged 22, born in Addingham, Yorkshire and enlisted in Keighley, Yorkshire. The son of Thomas and Frances Dove of 49, High Street, Steeton, Yorks. Buried in Dantzig Alley Cemetery in grave I. C. 39.

Hardy, Thomas, 28388, Private. Died of wounds. Born and enlisted in Bradford, Yorkshire. Buried at Dantzig Alley British Cemetery, Mametz in grave I. C. 33.

Richardson, John, 11374, Private. Died of wounds. Born in Newcastle-on-Tyne and enlisted in Wool, Dorset. Recorded by the Commonwealth War Graves Commission website as R/374 Richardson. Buried at Heilly Station, Mericourt-L'Abbe, in grave III. B. 17.

Smith, William, 23762, Private. Killed in action. Born and enlisted in North Shields. Buried in Dantzig Alley British Cemetery in grave I. C. 41.

78th Brigade, R.F.A

Sharples, Thomas, L/23906, Gunner. Killed in action. A member of D Battery. Aged 22 enlisted in Wigan and a resident of Hindley. The son of William and Esther Sharples of 33a, Ladies Lane, Wigan. Buried in Péronne Road Cemetery, Maricourt in grave II. F. 30.

6th Dorsets

Hepworth, Joe, 13534, Private. Killed in action. Formerly 14384 Hepworth of the Hussars of the Line. Commemorated on Thiepval Memorial Pier and Face 7B.

D'Albertanson, Ronald, Second Lieutenant. Died of wounds. Attached from the 3rd East Surreys. Aged 22, the son of Canon D'Albertanson and Mrs. D'Albertanson of Rua da Cerca 338, Foz do Douro, Oporto, Portugal. Buried in Dernancourt Communal Cemetery in grave J. 16.

7th Lincolns

Some of the following men were possibly killed during the episode in the Church yard mentioned by Private H. Taylor.

Dales, Arthur, 11921, Private. Killed in action. Born and enlisted in Louth, Lincolnshire. A resident of Milton, Hants. Buried in Delville Wood Cemetery, in grave III. E. 10.

Draper, Bertie, 12631, Private. Killed in action. Aged 21, born in Sproxton, Leicestershire and enlisted in Grantham. A resident of Sedgebrook, Lincolnshire. Son of John Henry and Emma E. Draper. Commemorated on Thiepval Memorial Pier and Face 1C.

Grantham, Walter Henry, 12294, Lance Corporal. Killed in action. Aged 28, born in Navenby, Lincolnshire and enlisted in Misterton, Lincolnshire. A resident of Friesthorpe, Lincolnshire. The son of John Henry and Elizabeth Grantham of The Terrace, Claxby, Lincolnshire and the husband of Kate Blanford (formerly Grantham) of Station Road, Wickenby, Lincolnshire. Commemorated on Thiepval Memorial Pier and Face 1C.

Hardy, William, 21657, Private. Killed in action. Aged 27, born and enlisted in Grantham. The son of John Hardy, 18, Portland Place, Grantham, Lincolnshire. Buried in Serre Road Cemetery Number 2 in grave XVII. H. 16.

Hepton, Benjamin, 9420, Lance Corporal. Killed in action. Aged 22, born in Radbourne, Lincolnshire and enlisted in Lincoln. A resident of Gainsborough, Lincolnshire. The son of David and Anne Hepton, 24 Lincoln Square, Grantham, Lincolnshire. Commemorated on Thiepval Memorial Pier and Face 1C.

Perkins, John, 19055, Private. Killed in action. Aged 19, born in and a resident of Grassmoor, Derbyshire. Enlisted in Chesterfield, Derbyshire. The son of Mrs. H. Fleeman of 4, New Street, Grassmoor, Chesterfield, Derbyshire. Commemorated on Thiepval Memorial Pier and Face 1C.

Prike, John, 12091, Lance Corporal. Killed in action. Born and enlisted in Grimsby, Lincolnshire. Commemorated on Thiepval Memorial Pier and Face 1C.

Smith, Alfred Henry, 21658, Private. Killed in action. Aged 20, born in Little Hale, Lincolnshire and enlisted in Lincoln. A resident of Folkingham, Lincolnshire. The son of Frederick William and Mary Smith of Hungerton, Lincolnshire. Buried in London Road Cemetery and extension, Longueval in grave 7. A. 5.

Till, James, 12203, Private. Killed in action. Aged 24, born in Homerton, Middlesex. Enlisted in Shoreditch, Middlesex. The son of James and Emma Till. Commemorated on Thiepval Memorial Pier and Face 1C.

Walker, Charles, 12953, Private. Killed in action. Born in Sibsey, Lincolnshire and enlisted in Boston, Lincolnshire. A resident of Swineshead, Lincolnshire. Commemorated on Thiepval Memorial Pier and Face 1C.

Walters, John, 12776, Sergeant. Killed in action. Born in Wainfleet-All-Saints, Lincolnshire and enlisted in Skegness, Lincolnshire. A resident of Lower Walmer, Kent. Commemorated on Thiepval Memorial Pier and Face 1C.

10th Notts & Derbys

Alvey, Tom, 6885, Private. Killed in action. Born in Pleasley Hill, Nottinghamshire and enlisted in Mansfield, Nottinghamshire. A resident of Sutton-on-Ashfield, Nottinghamshire. He had originally been in the 9th Battalion and had seen action at Gallipoli before joining the 10th Battalion. Commemorated on Pier and Face 10 C, 10 D and 11 A on the Thiepval Memorial.

Bradshaw, Charles, 20081, Private. Killed in action. Born and enlisted in Chesterfield. Commemorated on Pier and Face 10 C, 10 D and 11 A on the Thiepval Memorial.

Brentnall, Edward M., 12325, Private. Killed in action. Born in Hucknall Torkard, Nottinghamshire and enlisted in Nottingham. He was a regular soldier, probably from the 1st Battalion and had entered France and Flanders on 28 November 1914. A resident of Arnold, Nottingham. Commemorated on Pier and Face 10 C, 10 D and 11 A on the Thiepval Memorial.

Brusell, James, 21665, Private. Killed in action. Born in and a resident of Dronfield, Derbyshire. Enlisted in Sheffield. Commemorated on Pier and Face 10 C, 10 D and 11 A on the Thiepval Memorial.

Coverley, William, 14844, Private. Killed in action. Born in Stockport, Cheshire and enlisted in Derby. A resident of Whaley Bridge, Derbyshire. An original 10th Battalion volunteer, he entered France and Flanders on 14 July 1915. Commemorated on Pier and Face 10 C, 10 D and 11 A on the Thiepval Memorial.

Eldridge, Walter J., 6265, Private. Killed in action. Age 38. Born in Cirencester, Gloucestershire and enlisted in Derby. A resident of Clowne, Derbyshire. The husband of Frances Selina Eldridge of 7, Garden Avenue, Shirebrook, Mansfield. He was a 9th Battalion man and had seen action at Gallipoli before joining the 10th Battalion. His low service number suggests that he had been a regular soldier and his MIC records that he joined the 9th Battalion as a Sergeant. The Commonwealth War Graves Commission website records that he was a Private when he was killed. Commemorated on Pier and Face 10 C, 10 D and 11 A on the Thiepval Memorial.

Fox, Percy William, 19333, Private. Killed in action. Age 28. Born and enlisted in Derby. The son of Mrs. Matilda Lizzie Dean of

Dalbury Lees, Derbyshire. A member of B Company. He had been in the 9th Battalion and seen action at Gallipoli before joining the 10th Battalion. Commemorated on Pier and Face 10 C, 10 D and 11 A on the Thiepval Memorial.

Lang, C. H., 17518, Private. Killed in action. Born in Chard, Somerset and enlisted in Nottingham. He was a member of the 11th Battalion before joining the 10th Battalion. He entered France and Flanders on 27 August 1915. Commemorated on Pier and Face 10 C, 10 D and 11 A on the Thiepval Memorial.

Lee, Harold, 23091, Private. Killed in action. Age 25. Born in and a resident of Beeston, Nottinghamshire. Enlisted in Nottingham. The son of Mrs. Emma Lee of 28, Imperial Road, Beeston. He had originally been in the 9th Battalion and had seen action at Gallipoli before joining the 10th Battalion. Commemorated on Pier and Face 10 C, 10 D and 11 A on the Thiepval Memorial.

Mosley, John, 31941, Private. Killed in action. Born and enlisted in Derby. Commemorated on Pier and Face 10 C, 10 D and 11 A on the Thiepval Memorial.

Short, John, 14963, Private. Killed in action. Born in and a resident of Newbold, Derbyshire. Enlisted in Chesterfield, Derbyshire. An original 10th Battalion volunteer, he entered France and Flanders on 14 July 1915. Commemorated on Pier and Face 10 C, 10 D and 11 A on the Thiepval Memorial.

Spencer, George Jackson, 14842, Private. Killed in action. Age 24. Born in Nottingham and enlisted in Derby. A resident of Ilkeston, Derbyshire. The son of Sarah E. (formerly Spencer) and G. Orchard of 17, Randolph Street, Carlton Road, Nottingham. An original 10th Battalion volunteer, he entered France and Flanders on 14 July 1915. Commemorated on Pier and Face 10 C, 10 D and 11 A on the Thiepval Memorial.

Spendlove, Edwin, 19697, Private. Killed in action. Born in and a resident of Shottle, Derbyshire. Enlisted in Derby. He joined the 10th Battalion on 28 July 1915. Commemorated on Pier and Face 10 C, 10 D and 11 A on the Thiepval Memorial.

Trott, James Julian, 33951, Private. Killed in action. Age 21. Born and enlisted in Boston, Lincolnshire. The son of John William and Fanny Trott of Boston. The husband of Annie Trott of Boston. Buried in grave XXII. Q. 7. in Delville Wood Cemetery, Longueval.

Tucker Isaac A., M.M, 14314, Private, Killed in action. Age 20. Born in and a resident of Stapleford, Nottinghamshire. Enlisted in Derby. The son of Mary Ann and John Hallam Tucker of 35, Anthill Street, Stapleford. An original 10th Battalion volunteer, he entered France and Flanders on 14 July 1915. Commemorated on Pier and Face 10 C, 10 D and 11 A on the Thiepval Memorial.

Varley, Isaiah, 21737, Private. Killed in action. Born and enlisted in Hucknall, Nottinghamshire. He joined the 10th Battalion on 11 August 1915. Commemorated on Pier and Face 10 C, 10 D and 11 A on the Thiepval Memorial.

Walton, Thomas W., 21133, Private. Killed in action. Born in Rugby, Warwickshire and enlisted in Mansfield. He joined the 10th Battalion on 23 December 1915. Commemorated on Pier and Face 10 C, 10 D and 11 A on the Thiepval Memorial.

7th East Yorks

Gittins, Reece, 14138, Private. Died of wounds. Aged 18, born in Woodside, Yorkshire and enlisted at Ferryhill, County Durham. The son of Abraham and Maria Gittins of 1 Rowlandson Terrace, Broom, Ferryhill, County Durham. Buried at Heilly Station, Mericourt-L' Abbe, in grave III. A. 4.

10th Lancashire Fusiliers

Wilson, William Oliver, 28098, Private. Died of wounds. Born and enlisted in Bury, Lancashire. Buried at Dernacourt Communal Cemetery in grave J. 15.

8th South Staffords

Rodgers, Herbert Harold, 20519, Private. Died of wounds. Enlisted in Rugeley, Staffordshire and a resident of Walsall, Staffordshire. Buried in Dive Copse British Cemetery, Sailly-Le-Sec in grave II. E. 35.

7th Borders

Proctor, Thomas, 18405. Private. Died of wounds. Aged 28, born in and a resident of Gateshead-on-Tyne, Durham. Enlisted in Newcastle, Northumberland. The son of Robert and Susannah Proctor of Gateshead-on-Tyne. The husband of Lillian Allen (formerly Proctor) of 4, Back, Edward Street, Newcastle-on-Tyne. Buried in Heilly Station Cemetery, Mericourt-L'Abbe in grave III. B. 35.

9th Duke of Wellingtons

Flint, James, 15059, Private. Died of wounds. Born in Heckmondwike, Yorkshire and enlisted in Cleckheaton, Yorkshire. A resident of Bradford, Yorkshire. Buried in Heilly Station Cemetery, Mericourt-L'Abbe in grave III. B. 38.

Herson, George, 11428, Private. Died of wounds. Born and enlisted in Bradford, Yorkshire. Buried in Heilly Station Cemetery, Mericourt-L'Abbe in grave III. B. 22.

Newboult, Benjamin, 18892, Private. Died of wounds. Aged 19, born in Shipley, Yorkshire and enlisted in Guisely, Yorkshire. The son of Albert and Ann Newboult of 10, Oxford Street, Guisely, Yorkshire. Buried in Heilly Station, Mericourt-L'Abbe in grave III. B. 16.

9 August

8th South Staffords

Brown, Frederick Joseph, 11837, Private. Killed in action. Born and enlisted in Wolverhampton. Commemorated on Thiepval Memorial Pier and Face 7B.

Brown, George, 10074, Lance Corporal. Killed in action. Aged 49, born and enlisted in Birmingham. The husband of Fanny Brown of 4, Chapelhouse Street, Deritend, Birmingham. Commemorated on Thiepval Memorial Pier and Face 7B.

Crabtree, John Archibald, 13288, Private. Killed in action. Aged 27, born in and a resident of Oldbury, Worcestershire. Enlisted in

West Bromwich, Staffordshire. Brother of Mrs. M. E. Wilkins of 52, Cyprus Street, Oldbury, Worcestershire. Commemorated on Thiepval Memorial Pier and Face 7B.

Langston, Samuel William, 15532, Private. Killed in action. Born in Dudley, Worcestershire and enlisted in Wednesbury, Staffordshire. A resident of Tipton, Staffordshire. Commemorated on Thiepval Memorial Pier and Face 7B.

Tunnicliffe, Timothy, 11017, Private. Killed in action. Born in and a resident of Willenhall, Staffordshire. Enlisted in Wolverhampton. Commemorated on Thiepval Memorial Pier and Face 7B.

7th Lincolns

Hitchcock, George, 8470, Sergeant. Died of wounds. Aged 26, born in Warming ton, Northants and enlisted in Stamford, Lincolnshire. Son of Mrs. H. Hitchcock, 44, Conduit Road, Stamford, Lincolnshire. Buried in Heilly Station Cemetery, Mericourt-L'Abbe in grave III. A. 7.

7th Yorkshires

Moore, Harry, 14795, Lance Corporal. Died of wounds. Born in Battersea, London and enlisted in Bury. A resident of Bolton, Lancashire. Commemorated on Thiepval Memorial Pier and Face 3A and 3D.

10th Notts & Derbys

Guest, Harold James, 33670, Private. Died of wounds. Born and enlisted in Derby. Buried in grave III. B. 37 in Heilly Station Cemetery, Mericourt-L'Abbe.

Hall, Charles William, 41209, Private. Killed in action. Born and enlisted in Grimsby, Lincolnshire. Buried in grave III. F. 8. in Delville Wood Cemetery, Longueval.

Needham, William, 14928, Private. Killed in action. Born in New Whittington, Derbyshire and enlisted in Chesterfield, Derbyshire. A resident of Creswell, Nottinghamshire. Commemorated on Pier and Face 10 C, 10 D and 11 A on the Thiepval Memorial.

Pearson, Samuel George, 14873, Private. Died of wounds. Age 22. Born in and a resident of Cromford, Derbyshire. Enlisted in Derby. The son of George and Hannah Pearson of 24, North Street, Cromford. Buried in grave III. A. 18. in Heilly Station Cemetery, Mericourt-L'Abbe.

7th Borders

Selby, John James, 16564, Private. Died of wounds. Aged 33, born in and a resident of Byers Green, Durham. Enlisted in Bishop Auckland, Durham. The son of James and Elizabeth Selby of 5, High Street, Byers Green, Spennymoor, County Durham. Buried in Heilly Station Cemetery, Mericourt-L'Abbe in grave III. D. 1.

Witcut, Thomas, 16691, Corporal. Died of wounds. Born in Haydock, Lancashire and enlisted in Atherton, Lancashire. A resident of Tyldesley, Lancashire. Buried in Dernancourt Communal Cemetery Extension in grave I. C. 5.

9th Duke of Wellingtons

Mitchell, Frank, 12181, Private. Died of wounds. Born in Sowerby and enlisted in Halifax. A resident of Greenland, Yorkshire. Buried in Heilly Station Cemetery, Mericourt-L'Abbe in grave III. A. 15.

10 August

7th Yorks and Lancs (Pioneers)

Rodgers, George, 11352, Private. Killed in action. The brother of Mr. F. Rodgers 13, Sheldon Street Sheffield. Commemorated on Thiepval Memorial Pier and Face 14A and 14B.

8th South Staffords

Briscoe, Alfred Herbert. 12490. Private. Killed in action. Born and enlisted in West Bromwich, Staffordshire. Commemorated on Thiepval Memorial Pier and Face 7B. Killed when the South Staffs were attempting to set up a post.

6th Dorsets

Down, Percy Harold, 16052, Private. Killed in action. Killed by shellfire whilst on a working party. Born in Mere, Wiltshire. Enlisted in Gillingham, Dorset. A resident of Burton Wiltshire. Commemorated on Thiepval Memorial Pier and Face 7B.

7th Lincolns

Castledine, David, 12923, Private. Died of wounds. Born in and a resident of Tattershall, Lincolnshire. Enlisted in Spilsby, Lincolnshire. Son of Mr. and Mrs. W. Castledine of School Lane, Tattershall, Lincolnshire. Buried at Heilly Station Cemetery, Mericourt-L'Abbe in grave III. D. 3.

Dodd, John, 21594, Private. Died of wounds. Born in and a resident of Great Gonerby, Lincolnshire. Enlisted in Grantham. Buried at Heilly Station Cemetery, Mericourt-L'Abbe in grave III. D. 1.

9th Northumberland Fusiliers

Ridding, Richard, 13383, Corporal. Died of wounds. A member of B Company. Aged 26, born in Ulverston, Lancashire and enlisted in Alnwick, Northumberland. The son of Thomas and Elizabeth Ridding of Finsthwaite, Newby Bridge, Lancashire. Buried at Dernancourt Communal Cemetery Extension in grave I. C. 7.

11 August

93rd Field Company , R. E

Austin, Arthur Ernest Clifford, 63424, Sapper. Killed in action. Born and enlisted in Swansea, Glamorgan. Commemorated on Thiepval Memorial Pier and Face 8A and 8D.

7th Yorks and Lancs (Pioneers)

Savage, Walter, 12326, Private. Died of wounds. Aged 22 the son of Walter and Elizabeth Savage, 123 Warbrick Road, Blackpool and a native of Sheffield. Wounded on 10 August and transported to the main dressing station at Dive Copse, Sailly-le-Sec near Amiens. Buried in grave II. E. 41 in Dive Copse British Cemetery Sailly-le-Sec.

10th Notts & Derbys

Priestley, Harold Arthur, 40508, Private. Died of wounds. Born in Derby and enlisted in Nottingham. A resident of Littleover, Derbyshire. Buried in grave III. C. 1. in Heilly Station Cemetery, Mericourt-L'Abbe.

7th Borders

Bignell, Herbert Henry, 10796, Private. Died of wounds. Aged 22, born in and a resident of Chelsea. Enlisted in Brackenber Moor, Westmorland. The son of Amelia Best (formerly Bignell) of 21, Bywater Street, Kings Road, Chelsea, London. Buried in grave I. C. 4. Dernancourt Communal Cemetery Extension.

6th Dorsets

Lindow, Edwin, Second Lieutenant. Died of a leg wound. Buried in in grave I. C. 29. Dantzig Alley Cemetery.

12 August

10th Lancashire Fusiliers

Maddox, John Mortimer, Second Lieutenant. On attachment from the 3rd Lancashire Fusiliers. Killed in action. Son of The Reverend John Mortimer and Hannah Maddox of St. Mark's Vicarage, Bury, Lancashire. Former Captain of Bury Grammar School and a Bishop Lee Scholar at Trinity College Cambridge. Commemorated on Thiepval Memorial Pier and Face 3C and 3D.

9th Northumberland Fusiliers

Hart, William, 2160, Private. Killed in action. Aged 38, born and enlisted in Middlesbrough. The son of Cornelius and Mary Hart.

Formerly 8554 Hart of the Durham Light Infantry. Commemorated on Thiepval Memorial Pier and Face 10D, 11B and 12B.

10th Notts & Derbys

The following casualties (apart from those who died of wounds) occurred when the 10th Notts & Derbys were out of the front line in the reserve position of Montauban Trench on the south side of Caterpillar Valley. 52nd Field Ambulance had an Advanced Collecting Station in the valley at the eastern tip of Caterpillar Wood that runs through the valley. There were also artillery batteries in this area. This area was regularly shelled and gassed.

Broome, Robert, 6835, Sergeant. Killed in action. Born and enlisted in Bradford, Yorkshire. Commemorated on Pier and Face 10 C, 10 D and 11 A on the Thiepval Memorial. No one claimed his medals and authority was sought to dispose of them in April 1922.

Clarke, George Henry, 24469, Private. Killed in action (The Commonwealth War Graves Commission website records his date of death as 8 August 1916 but his medal index card states the date as 12 August 1916.) Age 16. Born and enlisted in Nottingham. A resident of Beeston, Nottingham. The son of Arthur and Annie A. Gimson of 198, Queen's Road, Beeston. He had been in the 9th Battalion[273] and served at Gallipoli (qualifying for the 1915 Star) before joining the 10th Battalion. Therefore, if he was 16 when he died he must have been 14 when he joined up. Buried in grave XXXI. M. 8. in Delville Wood Cemetery, Longueval.

Gillings, James William, 43017, Private. Killed in action. Born in and a resident of Norwich, Norfolk. Enlisted in Staveley, Derbyshire. Commemorated on Pier and Face 10 C, 10 D and 11 A on the Thiepval Memorial.

---

273 The 9th Battalion had arrived at Gallipoli as part of the 11th (Northern) Division in August 1915 and remained there until December 1915. From there the 11th Division went to Egypt and then in July 1916 it was on the Somme. Clarke, like so many other 9th Battalion men could well have been wounded and sent home from Gallipoli to recover. It would explain why so many of the 9th Battalion men found themselves in the 10th Battalion, even though their own battalion was on the Somme.

Harrison, Charles 'Chas', A., 38154, Private. Killed in action. Age 25. Born and enlisted in Market Deeping, Lincolnshire. The son of Samuel John and Helen Eliza Hardy of High Street, Market Deeping. Commemorated on Pier and Face 10 C, 10 D and 11 A on the Thiepval Memorial.

Hoare, E., A., 11066, Private. Killed in action. Born in Basford, Nottinghamshire and enlisted in Nottingham. A resident of Old Radford, Nottinghamshire. Commemorated on Pier and Face 10 C, 10 D and 11 A on the Thiepval Memorial.

Johnson, Ernest William, 14887, Private. Killed in action. Born in and a resident of Buxton, Derbyshire. Enlisted in Derby. An original 10th Battalion volunteer, he entered France and Flanders on 14 July 1915. Commemorated on Pier and Face 10 C, 10 D and 11 A on the Thiepval Memorial.

Keeling, John W., 19330, Private. Killed in action. Age 24. Born in Old Whittington, Derbyshire and enlisted in Chesterfield, Derbyshire. A resident of Brimington, Derbyshire. The son of Arthur and Emily Keeling of 39, Cotterhill, Brimington. He joined the 10th Battalion on 29 August 1915. Buried in grave 4. F. 18. in London Cemetery and Extension, Longueval.

Kinnerley, Frank, 25658, Private. Killed in action. Born in Manton, Derbyshire and enlisted in Nottingham. A resident of Arnold, Nottingham. Commemorated on Pier and Face 10 C, 10 D and 11 A on the Thiepval Memorial.

Kirk, William, 12981, Private. Killed in action. Age 22. Born and enlisted in Nottingham. The son of Mrs. Kirk of 20, Pipe Street, Sneinton, Nottingham. He had been in the 9th Battalion and seen action at Gallipoli before joining the 10th Battalion. Commemorated on Pier and Face 10 C, 10 D and 11 A on the Thiepval Memorial.

Marsh, Harold, 14867, Private. Killed in action. Born in and a resident of Matlock, Derbyshire. Enlisted in Derby. Commemorated on Pier and Face 10 C, 10 D and 11 A on the Thiepval Memorial.

Matthews, J., 6013, Private. Killed in action. Born in and a resident of Ilkeston, Derbyshire. Enlisted in Nottingham. Buried in grave III. D. 9. in Delville Wood Cemetery, Longueval.

Parker, Edgar, 25618, Lance Corporal. Killed in action. Born in Eckington, Yorkshire and enlisted in Sheffield. A resident of Beighton, Yorkshire. His MIC records that he entered France and Flanders on 14 May 1915 indicating that he belonged to another Notts & Derbys battalion before joining the 10th Battalion. It does not record which. Commemorated on Pier and Face 10 C, 10 D and 11 A on the Thiepval Memorial.

Parkin, James, 23189, Private. Died of wounds. Age 19. Born in and a resident of Ollerton, Nottinghamshire. Enlisted in Worksop, Nottinghamshire. The son of Frank and Sarah Parkin of Perlethorpe, Newark. His MIC records that he was originally in the 2nd Battalion and joined it on 17 August 1915. Buried in grave VI. E. 3. in Quarry Cemetery, Montauban.

Phethean, Thomas, 17384, Corporal. Killed in action. Born in Manchester and enlisted in Nottingham. An original 10th Battalion volunteer, he entered France and Flanders on 14 July 1915. His name was (predictably) misspelled as 'Phetbean' on his MIC. The son of Herbert and Sarah Phethean of 11, Park Avenue, Mapperley Road, Nottingham. Buried in grave 4. A. 20. in London Cemetery and Extension, Longueval.

Roddie, James, 17645, Private. Died of wounds at home. Age 33. Born in Manchester and enlisted in Mansfield, Nottinghamshire. The son of Mrs. Roddie of Withington, Manchester and the husband of Eliza Hardy (formerly Roddie) of 26, Simpsondale Terrace, Shirebrook. An original 10th Battalion volunteer, he entered France and Flanders on 14 July 1915. Buried in grave B. N. C. 5819 in Shirebrook Cemetery.

Shaw, John W., 14514, Corporal. Killed in action. Age 22. Born in and a resident of Shardlow, Derbyshire. Enlisted in Derby. The son of Thomas and Hannah Shaw of London Road, Shardlow. An original 10th Battalion volunteer, he entered France and Flanders on 14 July 1915. Buried in grave IV. E. 9. in Delville Wood Cemetery, Longueval.

Smedley, Henry, 21090, Private. Killed in action. Born in and a resident of South Normanton, Derbyshire. Enlisted in Sutton-in-Ashfield, Nottinghamshire. He had been in the 9th Battalion and seen action at Gallipoli before joining the 10th Battalion.

Commemorated on Pier and Face 10 C, 10 D and 11 A on the Thiepval Memorial.

Stocks, William, 20983, Private. Killed in action. Born in South Normanton, Derbyshire and enlisted in Sutton-in-Ashfield. Buried in grave VI. I. 15. in Quarry Cemetery, Montauban.

7th East Yorks

Fox, Harbour, 11624, Private. Died of wounds. Born in Hull and enlisted in Sheffield. Buried at Heilly Station Cemetery, Mericourt-L'Abbe, in grave III. D. 6.

7th Borders

Weir, Samuel Robert, 16978, Lance Corporal. Died of wounds. Aged 22, born in Whitehaven, Cumberland and enlisted in Workington, Cumberland. The son of Samuel Robert and Esther Weir of 52, Bolton Street, Workington, Cumberland. Buried in Corbie Communal Cemetery Extension in plot 2, row A, grave 96.

14 August

7th Lincolns

Edmonds, Edgar Charles, 13634, Private. Died of wounds. Aged 26, born in Yarmouth, Norfolk and enlisted in Grimsby, Lincolnshire. The son of Walter Smith and Maria Elizabeth Edmonds. Buried in Heilly Station Cemetery, Mericourt-L'Abbe in grave III. D. 12.

9th Northumberland Fusiliers

Croft, George, 2631, Acting Sergeant. Died of wounds. Aged 25, born and enlisted in Leeds. The son of Miriam Croft, of 5, Jupper Grove, Hunslet, Leeds. Buried in Heilly Station Cemetery, Mericourt-L'Abbe, in grave III. C. 8.

12th Manchesters

Franklin, Harold, 35562, Private. Died of wounds. A member of B Company. Aged 26, born and enlisted in Manchester. A resident of Moston. The son of Charles and Francis Franklin of Manchester. Husband of Florence Ellen Franklin of 11, Penn Street, Moston, Manchester. Buried at Lebucquiere Communal Cemetery Extension in grave II. H. 21. Franklin was buried here after the Armistice when graves were brought in from the surrounding battlefield.

10th Notts & Derbys

Stevenson, William Henry, 41930, Private. Died of wounds. Born and enlisted in Nottingham. Buried in grave VIII. B. 140. in Boulogne Eastern Cemetery.

Other casualties

23 July

7th Yorks

Hamilton, James, 12321, Lance Corporal. Died (drowned in the River Somme). Born in Gilesgate, Durham. Enlisted in and a resident of Houghton-le-Spring, Durham. The son of David Hamilton of 51, Sunderland Street, Houghton-le-Street. Buried in grave III. A. 3 in Pont-Remy British Cemetery.

1 August

Summer William Assheton, M.C., Captain. 22 Squadron, R.F.C. Formerly of the 18th Hussars. Age 20. Killed in action. The son of Frank and Constance Summer of Froyle Place, Hants. Commemorated on the Arras Flying Services Memorial at Fauberg-d'Amiens Cemetery.

17 August

12th Manchesters

Benton, William Manstead, Captain, the Reverend. Died of his wounds at Heilly Casualty Clearing Station. He had been badly wounded in the attack on 4 August and left lying in a shell hole for thirty hours. Brought in by a patrol that had been sent out to bring the wounded in he was taken down the line to the Casualty Clearing Station. He is buried in Heilly Station Cemetery, Mericourt-L'Abbe in grave II. F. 12.

18 August 16

17th (Northern) Division Artillery

Buckle, Archie Stewart, Brigadier-General. Died of Spinal Meningitis. Age 47. Son of Captain Archibald Lewis Buckle R.E. and husband to Mildred Louisa Buckle. Buried in Heilly Station Cemetery, Mericourt-L'Abbe in grave II. F. 23.

23 August 16

81st Brigade, R.F.A.

Benham, Frank B, Captain. Died of wounds sustained when his dugout was hit by counter-battery fire on 6 August 16. Aged 30, the son of Mrs. Emily A. Benham of Deans Hill Stafford is buried in the northeast part of Castle Church (St. Mary) Church Yard, Stafford, UK.

Appendix 3:
The attack on the German Second Line. Cavalry Action, 14 July 1916.

At 3.35 am on 14 July the infantry attacked a portion of the German second line between Trones Wood and Contalmaison. Standing by to exploit any breakthrough of this major push were three cavalry divisions, the leading one of which was the 2nd Indian Cavalry Division. Initially the attack was successful; the two Bazentins, their woods, Contalmaison Villa and the right hand portion of Trones Wood were taken. It looked possible that High and Delville Woods might be outflanked and the supply routes to their garrisons cut. Momentum slowed as German resistance increased and the infantry dug in to wait for the cavalry to come forward.

The cavalry had been ordered forward from Morlancourt at 7.40 am but movement over the battlefield was painfully slow. The leading element of the division, Brigadier-General C. L. Gregory's 9th Secunderabad Brigade was not in position to attack until 7.00 pm. Two cavalry regiments, the 7th Dragoon Guards and the 20th Deccan Horse, went forward ahead of two infantry battalions, towards the high ground between Longueval and High Wood. Above them flew aircraft of 3 Squadron, R.F.C.

This squadron flew artillery observation, photography and contact missions and operated two flights of Morane Parasol aircraft and one flight of biplanes. In the air at the time, in a Morane, were Second Lieutenant Cecil Lewis and his observer Pip. They saw the cavalry massing below them, where the British infantry were dug in. Captain Miller and Lieutenant Short, another Morane crew, flew over and observed German infantry in position, over the crest of the ridge, in a field of crops and in shell scrapes. They were watching the approach from Longueval and were in the path of the cavalry. Miller flew his aircraft low over the German infantry and attracted a great deal of ground fire, alerting the cavalry to the German presence. Miller and Short made a number of strafing runs and when a German machine gun opened fire from Delville Wood they silenced it with Short's Lewis Gun. Short then drew a rough sketch of the German positions in relation to High Wood and they dropped it on the cavalry. Lieutenant Stallibrass, an observer in another Morane aircraft flying nearby, watched most of the cavalry dismount and take cover while mounted squadrons, one from the 7th Dragoon Guards and one from the 20th Deccan Horse went ahead to the ridge. Cavalry regiments consisted of three squadrons each with six officers, 149 other ranks, an H.Q staff and machine gun section.

Captain Seton Hutchison of the 33rd Brigade Machine Gun Company remembered the squadron of the 20th Deccan horse riding through his position. He was struck by the dark faces of the troopers below their glistening helmets and he admired the way that they skilfully handled their horses, riding round and over shell holes. Then they went at the gallop across the valley, brandishing swords and lances, riding through small arms fire and shellfire. They galloped up the far side of the valley and, still under fire, disappeared over the ridge.

The 7th Dragoon Guards' objective was the infantry in the crops, the 20th Deccan Horse had orders to engage the infantry in the shell scrapes. In the event the fight was a small affair. Some of the infantry were killed by the cavalry's lances and a number surrendered to the troopers; the cavalry won the engagement. Their losses were, 7th Dragoon Guards, twenty-four casualties (three of which were killed) and fourteen horses killed. The 20th Deccan Horse had 78 casualties (records do not appear to exist for the number killed) and 116 horses killed. German casualties were reported to be 100. By now it was considered too dark for any more mounted action and at 9.30 pm the cavalry dug in to await events of the next day. Their appearance in the fighting line gave the German Corps and Army commanders a moment of anxiety and fuelled rumours of a major British breakthrough. There was no cavalry breakthrough and the following day they were withdrawn, but the fight on the high ground between Longueval and High Wood was a moment of pride for the cavalry, particularly these two regiments. Although, without aerial reconnaissance and support it may well have been a different story.[274]

---

[274] Compiled using: C. Lewis, *Sagittarius Rising*. D. S. V. Fosten, R. J. Marrion & G. A. Embleton, *The British Army 1914 – 18*. J. Ellis & M. Cox, *The World War One Databook*. A. H. Farrar-Hockley, *The Somme*. S. Hutchison in *I was There In The Great War, Part 18*. P. H. Liddle, *The 1916 Battle of The Somme A Reappraisal*. L. MacDonald, *Somme*. C. McCarthy, *The Somme*. W. Miles, *The Official History, 1916, Volume II*.

Bibliography and Documents

The war diary of the 12th Manchesters for the month of August 1916 is incomplete and only contains one sheet with little information. The war diary of the 10th Lancashires is poorly kept. It contains no times and the entries are very short, unlike the diary kept in July 1916. The diary of the 77th Field Coy, R.E is short and contains no times. Any entries for this battalion come from other unit diaries.

TNA: PRO WO 157/469. War Diary of XV Corps Intelligence Summaries

TNA: PRO WO 95/1981. War Diary of 17th Division Headquarters

TNA: PRO WO 95/1998. War Diary of 50th Brigade Headquarters

TNA: PRO WO 95/2005. War Diary of 51st Brigade Headquarters

TNA: PRO WO 95/2007. War Diary of 8th South Staffords

TNA: PRO WO 95/2008. War Diary of 10th Notts & Derbys

TNA: PRO WO 95/2008. War Diary of 7th Borders

TNA: PRO WO 95/2009. War Diary of 52nd Brigade Headquarters

TNA: PRO WO 95/2012. War Diary of 10th Lancashire Fusiliers

TNA: PRO WO 95/2012. War Diary of 12th Manchesters

TNA: PRO WO 95/2013. War Diary of 9th Northumberland Fusiliers

TNA: PRO WO 95/2014. War Diary of 9th Duke of Wellingtons

TNA: PRO WO 95/431. War Diary Fourth Army Headquarters

TNA: PRO WO 95/922. War Diary of XV Corps Headquarters

TNA: PRO WO95/1991. War Diary of 78th Brigade, R.F.A

TNA: PRO WO95/1991. War Diary of 80th Brigade, R.F.A

TNA: PRO WO95/1991. War Diary of 81st Brigade, R.F.A

TNA: PRO WO95/1991War Diary of 79th Brigade, R.F.A

TNA: PRO WO95/1993. War Diary of 77th Field Company, R.E

TNA: PRO WO95/1993. War Diary of 78th Field Company, R. E

TNA: PRO WO95/1993. War Diary of 93rd Field Company, R. E

TNA: PRO WO95/1994. War Diary of 17th Signal Company, R. E

TNA: PRO WO95/1995. War Diary of 7th Yorks and Lancs

TNA: PRO WO95/1996. War Diary of 51st Field Ambulance

TNA: PRO WO95/1996. War Diary of 52nd Field Ambulance

TNA: PRO WO95/2000. War Diary of 6th Dorsets

TNA: PRO WO95/2002. War Diary of 7th East Yorks

TNA: PRO WO95/2004. War Diary of 10th West Yorks

TNA: PRO WO95/2004. War Diary of 50th Machine Gun Company

TNA: PRO WO95/2004. War Diary of 7th Yorks

TNA: PRO WO95/2007. War Diary of 7th Lincolns

TNA: PRO WO95/2014. War Diary of 52nd Machine Gun Company

CAB 45/137. Letter from Sir Philip Robertson to Brigadier General Edmonds, 15 April 1934

Documents held by The Imperial War Museum

Imperial War Museum (IWM): Unpublished papers, Captain B.C. Mozley, D.S.O. 01/48/1.

Imperial War Museum. (IWM) Unpublished Papers, Colonel Cardew, C.M.G., D.S.O. 86/92/1

Imperial War Museum. (IWM) Unpublished papers, Lance Corporal E. H. Harlow 03/15/1.

Imperial War Museum. (IWM) Unpublished papers, Private H. Taylor 84/22/1.

Other un-published sources

The personal diary of Lieutenant-Colonel Fife. Held at the Green Howards Museum, Richmond. Courtesy of the National Trust.

Publications

Assher, B. — *A Nomad Under Arms*, (H. F. & G. Witherby, 1931)

Atteridge, A. H. — *The History of the 17th (Northern) Division.* (First published, Robert Maclehose & Co Ltd, 1929. Re-printed, Naval & Military Press, 2003)

Bewsher, F. W. *The History Of The Fifty First (Highland) Division 1914 – 1918* (First printed, 1920. Re-printed, Naval & Military Press)

Bond, B. & Cave, N. *Haig A Reappraisal 70 Years On.* (Leo Cooper, 1999)

Brown, M. *The Imperial War Museum Book of The Somme* (Pan Books, 1997)

Bull, S. *Brassey's History of Uniforms World War One German Army* (Brassey's, 2000)

Chapman, G. *A Passionate Prodigality* (First published, Ivor Nicholson & Watson Ltd, 1933. Re-printed, Ashford, Buchan and Enright, 1993)

Clayton, A. (Ed), *1914 – 1918 Essays on Leadership & War by John Terraine,* (Trustees of The Western Front Association, 1998)

Coppard, G. *With a Machine Gun to Cambrai,* (First published, H.M.S.O, 1968. Re-printed, Cassell Military Paperbacks, 1999)

Edmonds, J. E. *History of The Great War, France and Belgium 1916 Volume I* (First published, 1932. Re-printed, The Imperial War Museum Department of Printed Books and The Battery Press, 1993)

Ellis, J. & Cox, M. *The World War One Databook.* (Aurum Press Ltd, 1993. Re-printed, 2001)

Farrar-Hockley, A. H. *The Somme.* (First published, B. T. Batsford Ltd, 1964. Re-printed, Pan Books Ltd, 1983)

Gilvary, M. *History Of The 7th Service Battalion The York and Lancaster Regiment (Pioneers) 1914 – 1919* (The Talbot Press Ltd, 1921)

Griffin, P. D. *Encyclopedia of Modern British Army Regiments.* (Sutton Publishing, 2006)

Hall, N. S. *The Balloon Buster,* (First published, Liberty Weekly, Inc., 1928. Re-printed, Corgi, 1967)

Hammerton, J. (Ed) *I was There In The Great War, Part 18.* (Monthly magazine. The Amalgamated Press Ltd, 31 January 1939)

Hart, P. *Bloody April Slaughter In The Skies Over Arras, 1917,* (Weidenfeld & Nicolson, 2005)

Heraty, A. J. *A Duration Man A Staffordshire Soldier in the Great War* (Churnet Valley Books, 1999)

Hoyte, W.N. & McNeela, M.T.F.J (Ed), *10th (S) Battalion The Sherwood Foresters The History Of The Battalion During The Great War.* (Naval & Military Press, 2003)

Hussey, A. H. & Inman, D.S. *The Fifth Division In The Great War* (First published, Nisbet & Co Ltd, 1921. Re-printed, Naval & Military Press)

Lewis, C. Sagittarius Rising (First published, 1936. Re-printed, Greenhill Books, 2003)

Liddle, P. H. *The 1916 Battle of The Somme A Reappraisal.* (Leo Cooper, 1992)

Martin, B. *Poor Bloody Infantry, A Subaltern on the Western Front 1916 – 1917.* (John Murray, 1987)

McCarthy, C. *The Somme The Day-By-Day Account* (Brockhampton Press, 1998)

McKee, A. *The Friendless Sky,* (First published, Souvenir Press, 1962. Re-printed, Nel Paperback, 1972)

Miles, W. *History of The Great War, France and Belgium 1916 Volume II* (First published, 1938. Re-printed, The Imperial War Museum Department of Printed Books and The Battery Press, 1992)

O'Hanlon, G. *A Plain History of the Sixth (Service) Battalion The Dorsetshire Regiment 1914 – 1919.* In *The History of the Dorsetshire Regiment 1914 – 1919, part three. The Service Battalions.* (Re-printed by The Naval & Military Press)

Osborne, W. *A History of the 10th Battalion the Notts & Derbys Volume I Dorset 1914 to the Ypres Salient 1915.* (Salient Books, 2009)

Osborne, W. *A History of the 10th Battalion the Notts & Derbys Volume II The Bluff The Somme 1916.* (Salient Books, 2011)

Osborne, W. *Quadrangles,* (First published by Exposure Publishing, 2007. Second edition, Salient Books, 2010)

Prior R. & Wilson, T. *Command on the Western Front, The Military Career of Sir Henry Rawlinson 1914 – 1918,* (First published, Blackwell Publishers, 1992. Re-printed, Pen & Sword Military, 2004)

Sandilands, H. R. *The 23rd Division 1914 – 1919,* (William Blackwood & Sons, 1925. Re-printed, Naval & Military Press)

Shakespear, J. *The Thirty Fourth Division 1915 – 1919,* (Re-printed, Naval & Military Press)

Sheffield, G. & Bourne, J.(Eds), *Douglas Haig War Diaries and Letters 1914 – 1918,* (BCA, 2005)

Simkins, P. *Kitchener's Army The Raising Of The New Armies 1914 – 1916.* (First Published Manchester University Press, 1988. Re-printed by Pen & Sword Military, 2007)

Terraine, J. *Douglas Haig The educated soldier.* (Hutchinson & Co. Ltd, 1963)

Terraine, J. *The Smoke and the Fire,* (Sidgwick and Jackson Ltd, 1980)

Westlake, R. *British Battalions on the Somme* (Leo Cooper, 1998)

Electronic Sources

Ancestry.com

Centre for First World War Studies website. J. M. Bourne's *Lions Led by Donkeys* project, University of Birmingham

Commonwealth War Graves Commission website.

Grace's Guide website. The Best of British Engineering. 1750 – 1960s.

holmesacourt.org

Soldiers Died In The Great War CD Rom. (Naval & Military Press, 1999)

Index

BRITISH FORMATIONS

BEF, 17

Fourth Army 23, 27, 30, 33-4, 38, 40, 45, 49, 59, 60-1, 63, 71, 74, 79-80, 85, 89, 90, 99, 101, 103, 115, 121, 127, 130, 132-4, 136, 139, 150, 155, 156-9, 165, 182, 188-9, 196, 200-1, 203, 209, 214-5, 224, 226, 230, 240, 293

CORPS

I Corps, 30

III Corps, 46, 49, 124-5, 134, 245

X Corps, 166

XIII Corps, 33, 43, 70, 71, 83, 90, 118, 130, 132, 154-5, 157, 159, 168, 170, 203

XV Corps, 12, 22, 30-4, 40, 45-7, 49, 59, 70-1, 73-4, 76, 78-80, 90, 92-3, 95-7, 99-100, 110, 113-5, 119-1, 125, 127, 129-32, 135-6, 140, 142, 150-1, 153-9, 162, 165, 167, 170, 174-5, 180, 184-5, 187-91, 196, 199-04, 209, 214-5, 219, 222, 224-5, 227, 230, 232, 235, 240, 247

DIVISIONS

2nd Division, 43, 71, 79, 88, 93, 100, 122, 126, 129, 240

5th Division, 41, 43-4, 48, 53, 57, 58, 63, 69, 70-1, 75, 89, 91, 117, 185, 249

9th Division, 24

14th Division, 212, 223, 240

17th (Northern) Division, 11, 13, 17, 21-7, 32, 37-41, 43-4, 49, 51-2, 55-6, 58, 63-4, 67, 69-73, 75, 77-80, 83-4, 88-91, 93-4, 97, 100, 102, 108-11, 114, 119-22, 124-5, 127, 129-30, 132-3, 139, 142, 147, 150, 154-9, 165, 167, 169, 170-1, 173, 181, 183, 185, 187, 189-90, 197, 199, 201, 204, 208, 210-12, 215, 219, 222-3, 226, 230, 232-3, 237, 240, 245-50, 293

18th (Eastern) Division, 43

33rd Division, 41, 52, 132, 148, 155-7, 162, 167, 198, 213, 221, 226

51st (Highland) Division, 31, 41, 43, 64, 90, 104, 132, 155-6, 162, 164

56th Division, 249

BRIGADES

15th Brigade, 44, 51, 70, 89, 91

43rd Brigade, 233, 240

41st Brigade, 203, 208, 211, 221, 232, 236-7, 240

50th Brigade, 10, 22, 25-6, 40, 43-5, 61-2, 66, 68, 115, 119, 121-3, 129-30, 133-6, 138-40, 143, 148, 150-1, 153, 156-7, 163-5, 174, 176, 186, 204, 211-2, 214, 221, 223, 231-2, 239, 240, 245,

51st Brigade, 10, 44, 47, 55, 57, 59, 62, 75, 92, 100, 118-9, 122-4, 126, 130, 147, 152-3, 155-6, 162, 165, 173, 179-81, 183-7, 192, 197-8

52nd Brigade, 10, 25-6, 38, 43-4, 48-50, 53, 56-7, 59, 61-2, 64, 66-8, 70-2, 75-80, 88, 90, 93-4, 96, 99, 101-4, 110-1, 113-4, 117, 119, 122, 124, 129-31, 134, 136-7, 139, 142, 147, 155-6, 176, 197-8, 211, 217, 219-22, 230, 233, 240, 246

54th Brigade, 43

61st Brigade, 25

95th Brigade, 53, 57, 64

99th Brigade, 79, 93, 100, 126, 129

152nd Brigade, 64, 104

BATTALIONS

1st Berkshires, 118

1st East Surreys, 59, 61

1st Norfolks, 54, 65, 85, 86, 89, 91

1/5th Seaforth Highlanders, 64, 104

2nd King's Own Scottish Borderers, 89

2nd South Staffords, 95, 96

3rd East Surreys, 172, 274

6th Dorsets, 21, 25, 39, 44, 47, 68, 115, 122, 126, 133, 135, 142, 147-8, 157, 169, 170-1, 177, 188, 195, 203-5, 207, 211, 214, 223, 231-2, 235, 245, 265, 272, 274, 282, 283, 294

7th Borders, 24-5, 44, 57, 75, 85, 123, 126, 128, 140, 150, 153, 155, 159, 160, 162-3, 165, 167-9, 171, 173, 176-7,

179-80, 182-3, 185-7, 189, 191-2, 195-6, 211, 230, 254, 256, 259, 262, 267-8, 279, 281, 283, 287, 293

7th East Yorks, 25, 45, 57, 65-6, 68, 72, 90, 92, 94, 115-6, 118, 123, 126, 137, 138-9, 148, 153, 156, 164, 179, 203-5, 209-10, 212-4, 216, 219, 221, 226-7, 229, 231, 233, 235-6, 239-41, 253, 263, 273, 278, 287, 294

7th King's Royal Rifle Corps, 226-7, 230-1, 236

7th Lincolns, 25, 61, 78, 86, 122, 126, 143, 168, 176, 179-81, 186, 188, 191, 197, 207, 212, 220, 231, 274, 280, 282, 287, 294

7th Yorks & Lancs, 57, 61, 66, 86, 111, 129, 149, 217, 228, 233, 234, 245, 281, 282, 293

7th Yorks,the Green Howards, 10, 23, 25, 40, 43, 67-8, 87, 115, 123-4, 140, 148, 151, 153, 177, 200, 205, 213, 216, 223, 226-7, 229-31, 239, 280

8th Rifle Brigade, 239

8th South Staffords, 25, 47, 53, 59, 61, 73, 92-3, 95, 110, 118, 120, 124, 126, 127, 132-4, 138, 140, 147, 149, 153, 158-9, 160, 162-3, 165, 167-8, 170-1, 175, 180, 182, 186-7, 189, 192, 195, 196, 199, 201-4, 207, 208-15, 220-1, 223, 231-2, 245, 271, 278-9, 281, 293

9th Devonshires, 216

9th Duke of Wellingtons, 26, 39, 44, 49, 51, 54, 65, 67, 70, 72, 74, 79, 80, 85, 86, 90-6, 99, 104, 107, 115, 117-8, 120, 124-5, 129, 134, 137, 143, 149, 150, 155, 177, 191, 205, 211, 220-1, 236, 262, 266, 279, 281, 293

9th Northumberland Fusiliers, 25, 64, 104, 107, 109, 112, 220, 254, 256, 273, 282, 283, 287, 293

9th Notts & Derbys, 24

10th Durham Light Infantry, 230, 233, 235, 239

10th Lancashire Fusiliers,, 25, 102, 113, 253, 267, 278, 283, 293

10th Notts & Derbys, 24-5, 44, 55, 59, 61, 77-8, 84, 92-3, 116, 120, 126, 134, 137, 143, 149, 152, 155, 162, 165, 168-9, 173, 176, 179-81, 183, 185, 187-8, 191, 197, 216, 221, 229, 232, 234, 242, 245-6, 261, 263, 270, 276, 280, 283-4, 288, 293

10th West Yorks, 22, 25, 43, 67-8, 89, 91, 96, 116, 121, 130, 138-40, 148, 160, 181, 188, 202, 205, 209, 211, 223, 226-7, 235, 246, 256, 294

12th Manchesters, 26, 94, 96, 99, 100-4, 108-11, 113-5, 118, 121, 125, 131, 138, 177, 181, 216-7, 221, 227, 246, 257, 261, 288, 293

13th Royal Fusiliers, 49, 84

15th Royal Warwicks, 57, 61, 64

22nd Royal Fusiliers, 65, 79, 93, 120

CAVALRY

2nd Indian Cavalry Division, 291

9th Secunderabad Brigade, 291

7th Dragoon Guards, 135, 291-2

20th Deccan Horse, 135, 291, 292

ROYAL ARTILLERY

166th Brigade, R.F.A., 52

190th Brigade, R.F.A., 250

78th Brigade, R.F.A., 76, 79, 86, 98, 100, 108, 144

79th Brigade, R.F.A., 74, 99-100, 103, 108, 111, 127, 230, 242

80th Brigade, R.F.A., 39, 71, 74, 108, 133, 136, 143, 152, 158, 250

81st Brigade, R.F.A., 100, 127, 145, 170

ROYAL ARMY MEDICAL CORPS

14th Field Ambulance, 48

17th Divisional Collecting Station, 51, 52, 56, 120, 127, 158, 173, 208

43rd Field Ambulance, 208, 231, 234

44th Field Ambulance, 222, 233

45th Casualty Clearing Station, 48

51st Field Ambulance, 48, 51, 52, 55-6, 66, 86, 88, 99, 100-1, 111, 116, 119, 120, 127, 134, 136, 152, 165, 166, 173, 185, 187-8, 196, 208, 222, 231, 234, 293

52nd Brigade Machine Gun Company, 44, 48, 50, 51, 55, 62, 64-5, 68, 72-4, 76, 84-5, 91, 99, 101, 104, 107, 113, 117, 126, 134-5, 137, 139, 140, 166, 176, 179, 183-4, 192, 198, 210, 213, 223, 246

52nd Field Ambulance, 5, 47, 48, 51, 53, 56, 79, 88, 100-1, 104, 111, 116, 118, 119, 120, 126, 134, 144, 152-3, 166, 184, 198, 210, 222, 233, 235, 246, 262, 284, 294

53rd Field Ambulance, 120, 245

ROYAL ENGINEERS

17th Signal Company, 43, 71, 83, 130, 160, 164, 293

50th Brigade Signal Company, 140

77th Field Company, R.E., 112, 163

78th Field Company, R.E., 113, 163

93rd Field Company, R.E., 113, 148

ROYAL FLYING CORPS

4th Brigade, R.F.C., 103

3 Squadron, R.F.C., 97

5 Squadron, R.F.C., 153, 154

22 Squadron, R.F.C., 288

43 Squadron, R.F.C., 141

MACHINE GUN COMPANIES AND OTHERS

13th Brigade Machine Gun Company, 51, 68, 84-5, 135

41st Brigade Machine Gun Company, 203, 208, 237, 240

50th Brigade Machine Gun Company, 44, 87, 98, 105, 113, 121, 123, 135, 137, 139-40, 143-5, 148, 161, 170-1, 175, 181-2, 188, 190, 192, 203, 208, 213, 216-17, 228, 240, 245, 266

51st Brigade Machine Gun Company, 113, 135, 198

17th Division Ammunition Column, 170

52nd Trench Mortar Battery, 64

GERMAN FORMATIONS

18th Bavarian (Reserve) Division, 45, 90

12th (Reserve) Division, 90

17th (Reserve) Division, 45

24th (Reserve) Division, 90

26th Division, 201

27th Division, 189

23rd Regiment, 90, 189

31st (Reserve) Infantry Regiment, 45, 130

84th (Reserve) Infantry Regiment, 130

127th Regiment, 189

119th Grenadier Regiment, 237

29th Field Artillery, 46

GENERAL INDEX

Albert, 23, 37, 41, 43-4, 48, 51, 56, 59, 72, 80, 105, 124, 180, 227, 241, 246, 258, 263, 264, 265, 270, 272, 279

Alder, Second Lieutenant, A. L. G., 170

Alexander, Brigadier-General, Ernest Wright, V.C., 40, 50, 58, 72, 119, 154, 236, 249

Allen, Second Lieutenant, 31, 124, 208, 245, 255, 266, 279

Alner, Private, Albert George, 172, 265

Amiens, 22, 24, 44, 48, 241, 246, 256, 283, 288

Ancre, the River, 200, 221

Andrews, Captain, 59,

Andrews, Sergeant, 68

Askew, Private, W., 5, 144, 262

Assher, Ben, 63

Atkins, Gunner, J., 101, 257

Bacon, Gunner, H., 117

Ballen, Captain, M.D., 53

Balloon, observation, 133, 135-6, 139-41, 241

Banbury, Lieutenant-Colonel, also Brigadier-General, 25, 234

Bapaume, 23, 124

Barclay, Captain, M.D., 100, 119, 120, 137, 152, 166, 167, 208

Barker, Lieutenant-Colonel, 25, 232, 245

Barker, Second Lieutenant, R. A., 234

Barnes, Corporal, 51, 180, 181, 197, 267, 273

Barnes, Lieutenant, C. R., 51, 180, 181, 197, 267, 273

Bartlet Forcing Jack, 164

Barton, Lieutenant, A. E., 60, 214

Bayers, Gunner, J., 243

Bazentin-le-Grand, 23, 43, 53, 63, 64, 132, 138, 242

Bazentin-le-Petit, 23

Becordel, 44, 45, 48, 60, 62, 231, 259, 272

Beetle Alley, 209, 223

Bellevue Farm, 41, 43-5, 47, 57-8, 60, 62, 66-9, 72, 80, 88-92, 94, 96, 98, 101, 105, 110, 112-6, 118-9, 121-3, 125, 147, 154, 166-7, 182, 200, 203, 211, 223, 226, 230-1, 234-5, 239

Benham, Captain, F. B., 145, 160, 289

Benton, Captain, William Manstead, 109, 121, 129, 130, 289

Bernafay Wood, 88, 119, 120, 135, 137, 152, 166, 167, 175, 196, 199, 208, 257

Bland, Gunner, W., 101

Blandamer, Private, James, 172, 265

Blane, Brigadier-General, 41, 45

Blashki, Captain, E. P., 134, 152

Bodin, Gunner, W. J., 101

Bolton, Captain, 87, 135, 139, 140, 256, 280, 287

Bowman, Second Lieutenant, Robert Moore, 145, 160, 261

Bradbury, Second Lieutenant, W., 234

Brakes, Gunner, Harold, 112, 259

Briscoe, Private, 215, 281

Brown, Gunner, H. M., 101, 257, 267, 279, 295

Bryan, Lieutenant-Colonel, H., 25

Buckle, Brigadier-General, Archie Stewart 197, 199, 212, 242, 249, 289

Budworth, Major-General, Charles Edward Dutton, 154, 155

Buire sur Ancre, 44, 47, 57, 229, 231, 232, 234, 239, 240, 245-6

Burnett, Captain, 110, 167, 211

Bury, Captain, M.D., 53, 246, 253, 278, 280, 283

Byass, Lieutenant-Colonel, 61

Candas, 246

Cardew, Lieutenant-Colonel, George Ambrose, 7, 39-41, 45, 50, 52-3, 58, 60, 69, 72, 80-1, 88, 95, 98, 107-10, 112, 114, 117, 119, 122, 125, 131-2, 142-4, 147, 154, 157, 159, 160, 165-7, 174, 176-7, 182, 192, 197-9, 202, 204, 211-2, 216, 222, 227, 235-6, 242, 249-50, 294

Carver, Lieutenant, 143, 157, 159, 177

Caterpillar Valley, also Caterpillar Ravine or The Gully, 48, 53, 56, 94, 98-9, 101-2, 116, 118-9, 135-6, 140, 153, 158, 284

Cavillon Area, 22, 24

Chamber, Major, H. A. G., 144

Chapman, Captain, Guy, 49, 84, 257, 295

Church Street, 65

Clarke, Private, George Henry, 229

Clarke, Brigadier-General, J. L. J., 10, 26, 38, 44, 50, 64-5, 72, 74-5, 76, 81, 91, 94, 96, 102, 111, 115, 119, 121, 134, 184, 210, 211, 213, 240, 247

Clarke, Captain, S., 176, 191- 2

Clarke, Second Lieutenant, 185

Clive, Lieutenant-Colonel, M.P., 25, 40, 209, 227

Cocks, Private, H., 166

Cocoa Lane, 235

Collins, Colonel, Robert John, 40, 72, 81, 122, 125, 192, 210, 249

Combles, 73

Conan, Private, F. C., 192

Congreve, Lieutenant-General Sir Walter Norris, 43, 71, 92

Contalmaison, 17, 22, 291

Cook, Sergeant, 101, 137, 255

Cotter, Captain, M.D., 52, 66

Cotteral, Lance Corporal, 73, 74, 81

Crawford, Private, 145, 266

Cumberland, Captain, T. D. M.D., 77, 254, 256, 267-9, 273, 287

Cutting, Captain, 62

D'Albertanson, Second Lieutenant, Ronald, 172

Dallas, Captain, Vivian Leslie, 103

Davies, Private, E. A., 144

Delville Wood, 8, 11, 15, 17, 23-4, 26-7, 34, 37, 40, 44-6, 49, 51, 55, 62, 69-72, 74, 79, 90, 91, 103, 110, 116-9, 122-3, 126, 128, 130, 131, 133, 139-40, 149-50, 151-3, 155-8, 162, 167, 170, 172, 174, 176-7, 180-2, 184, 185-92, 196-202, 205, 207-9, 211, 214-6, 220-4, 230, 232-5, 240, 247, 258, 262, 264-5, 268-71, 274, 278, 280, 284-6, 291

Dent, Second Lieutenant, Arthur, G., 234

Dernancourt, 39, 41, 43-5, 47, 52, 53, 57, 60, 62, 65-9, 172, 188, 231, 233-6, 239-41, 245-6, 262, 274, 281-3

Dodds, Private, T., 56

Dorset Trench, 148, 203, 205, 214, 219, 228

Dougal, Captain, Daniel, M.D., 53, 101, 116

Doullens, 245, 249

Downing, Private, A., 192

Downing, Sergeant, 74

Dunkerley, Private, J., 5, 144, 263

Dutton, Lieutenant, J. D., 144

Dysentry, 26

Eadie, Second Lieutenant, R. A., 143

Eaucourt L'Abbaye, 46, 113

Edmonds, Brigadier-General, J. E., 21, 23, 32, 173-4, 248, 287

Edwards, Private, Thomas, 9, 171, 268, 271

Farwell, Captain, A. W., 25, 47

Fienvillers, 245, 246

Fife, Lieutenant-Colonel, Ronald D'Arcy, 23, 25, 40, 67-9, 75, 87, 110, 114-5, 124, 127, 134, 137, 145, 151, 153, 166, 173, 177, 180, 184, 186, 195, 198, 200, 208-9, 213, 216, 219-21, 223, 227, 229, 231, 239, 241

Flers, 46, 71, 75, 103, 125, 152, 155, 159, 168, 173, 181-3, 190, 197

Forrest, Lieutenant-Colonel, 25

Fraser, Second Lieutenant, 198

French Lamps, 38

Fricourt, 22, 25, 41, 43-5, 48, 50-1, 53, 55, 56-62, 66, 75, 86, 89-90, 96, 111, 113, 121-2, 132, 147, 163, 166, 181, 183-4, 188, 221, 223, 231, 233, 239-40

Froggatt, Gunner, N. A., 230

Gallipoli, 24, 229, 264, 270, 276-7, 284-6

George Street, 51, 99, 107, 117, 137, 140, 143, 181-2, 203

German Air Service, 49

Gibson, Captain, 147

Gilbert, Captain, L., 25, 59, 75, 78, 149, 162, 187

Ginchy, 34, 46, 95, 208

Glasgow, Brigadier-General, W. J. T., 10, 26, 40, 45, 98, 133, 134, 148, 151, 166, 174, 184, 198, 208, 209, 213, 214, 222, 227, 236, 240, 272

Glasgow, Captain, William James Nesbit, 148

Gluckstein, Private, G. S., 5, 144, 263

Gommecourt, 248, 249

Goodwin, Second Lieutenant, 138

Gorman, Alfred David, M.D., 52, 55, 100, 120, 171, 208

Gowlland, Major, E. L., and Lieutenant-Colonel, 173, 185, 187, 196

Gowring, Lieutenant, John Somerville, 51, 200

Greaves, Sergeant, 76

Gregory, Brigadier-General, C. L., 291

Griffiths, Second Lieutenant, 110, 189

Groom, Gunner, F., 101, 255

Gueudecourt, 46, 47, 131

Guillemont, 33-4, 150, 159, 182, 184, 200-1

Gustard, Second Lieutenant, R., 234

Haig, General, Sir Douglas, 10, 22-3, 27-31, 33-4, 40, 76, 92, 156, 175, 202, 208, 247

Hallward, Lieutenant, B. M., 241

Hammer Head, the, 63, 64

Hannah, Gunner, 177, 261, 271, 272, 281, 283, 286

Happy Valley, also Death Valley or the Valley of Death, 49, 66

Hare, Lieutenant, H. K. C., 87, 123

Hargreaves, Private, R., 104, 254

Harlow, Lance Corporal, Eric H., later Corporal, 77, 78

Harper, Major-General, 31

Harriett, Private, 143, 272

Harris, Lieutenant, E. C., 235, 264

Harrison, Brigadier-General, 110, 119,

Harrison, Lieutenant-Colonel, E.G., 26

Harrison, Gunner, H. V., 243

Hart, Gunner, R., 101

Hart, Lieutenant, Charles Crowther, 78

Hart, Private, 232

Healy, Sergeant, 68

Heilly, 39-41, 92, 130, 153
Hepworth, Private, Joe, 172, 264, 274
Heraty, Gunner, A. J., 136, 296
Hewer, Gunner, C., 230
Hides, Second Lieutenant, 202, 204
High Wood, 8, 12, 23, 27, 43-4, 46, 51, 64, 73, 90, 101, 103, 131, 137, 142-3, 145, 148, 157, 164, 173, 181, 185, 214, 216, 242, 291, 292
Horne, Lieutenant-General, Sir Henry Sinclair, 10, 23, 27, 30-2, 37, 59, 61, 71, 73-4, 79, 88-9, 92, 95, 97, 99, 114, 130, 133, 142, 155, 158, 165, 167, 182, 200, 203, 212-3, 224, 240, 247, 248, 250, 251
Houghton, Lieutenant, 143, 160, 288
Howes, Second Lieutenant, E, 254
Hoyte, Lieutenant, William Norman, 55, 77, 150, 155-6, 234
Hussey, Brigadier-General, A. H., 58, 249
Hutchison, Captain, Seton., 292
Ives, Private, D., 192
Jackman, Sergeant, 170
Jackson, Captain, E. M., 22, 103, 126, 128, 256, 260, 277
James, Private, H. E., 144
James, Second Lieutenant, A. W, 234
Jenkinson, Gunner, A., 117
Jones, Lieutenant, D. A., 143
Jone, Private, E., 128
Jones, Sergeant, E., 101
Kay, Captain, 87, 123
Kendall, Lieutenant, 86
Kenyon-Slaney, Major-General, 17, 21
Killick, Lieutenant, A. H., 56, 62, 66
King George V, 208
King, Major, 41, 112, 117, 142, 147, 154
Kitchener, Lord, 21
Kolnische Zeitung, 224
Lammin, Private, S. H., 143, 261
Langton, Second Lieutenant, 92, 202, 204, 210-1, 215
Le Maitre, Sapper, Alfred Henry, 128, 261
Le Transloy, 73, 151
Lee, Corporal, 74, 81
Lee, Private, S., 147
Lee, Sergeant, George, 164
Leigh, Private, 156, 258, 263
Leuze Wood, 46
Levis, Captain, J. S. M.D., 189
Lewis, Second Lieutenant, Cecil, 97, 98
Lindow, Second Lieutenant, Edwin, 214, 283
Lintott, Major, 55, 62, 69, 72-4, 81, 92, 99, 100, 113, 117, 135, 139, 166, 198, 200, 210, 213
Lloyd, Lieutenant, 27, 112, 259
Longueval Alley, 120, 124, 127, 132, 138, 150, 158, 195, 197, 200, 211
Longueval, 34, 44-5, 51, 53-4, 58-61, 63, 66, 70, 72-3, 83, 86, 88-9, 91, 99, 101-2, 113, 117, 122, 126, 128, 132, 137-9, 142-4, 149-51, 156, 158, 163-4, 168, 176-7, 181, 184, 191, 193, 195, 197-8, 200, 205, 214, 217, 220-1, 226, 231-2, 236, 241, 247-8
Longuevillette, 246
MacMullen, Company Sergeant Major, J. A. W., 170
Major, Second Lieutenant, 212, 214
Mametz Wood, 17, 22, 49, 50, 63, 99, 121
Manger, Captain, C. H., 25, 59, 75, 92-3, 96, 118, 127, 153, 196, 202, 204, 207, 245
Martin, Second Lieutenant, Bernard, 133
Martin, Second Lieutenant, T., 101
Mason, Second Lieutenant, 51, 74, 100, 117, 200
Massey, Captain, 110
Mayhew, Sergeant, 51
McClelland, Major, W. A., 234
McGill, Sergeant, J., 101
McInnes, Lance Corporal, 73-4, 81, 91,
McInnes, Second Lieutenant, 51, 117, 185, 200
Meaulte,, 44, 47-8, 51-2, 59, 125, 197, 221, 231, 233, 239-40, 269
Metcalfe, Major, F. E., 25, 61, 75, 86, 122
Michell, Second Lieutenant, John King, 51, 107, 166
Milford, Second Lieutenant, E. W., 197
Miller, Captain, 258, 291

Milne, Major, R. J., and Lieutenant-Colonel, 216
Milward, Second Lieutenant, R. G., 234
Mine Trench, 93, 120, 216, 221, 229
Montauban, 43-5, 48, 51-6, 58, 59, 62, 66, 68, 71, 73, 76, 81, 83, 86, 88, 91, 94, 99, 101-2, 110, 112-3, 119, 121, 122, 124, 126, 128, 130, 131, 132, 134, 135, 137, 138, 139, 140, 143, 144, 148, 150, 156, 160, 163, 164, 168, 175, 177, 179, 182, 186, 189, 196, 197, 199, 204, 207, 211, 215, 216, 217, 227, 239, 257, 261, 264, 265, 266, 284, 286, 287
Moon, Second Lieutenant, 51, 62, 117, 185
Morval, 73
Mozley, Captain, B. C., 21, 39, 47, 60, 68, 115, 122-3, 135-6, 140, 142, 148-9, 169-73, 182, 203, 214-5, 231
Myatt, Private, George Henry, 171, 272
North Street, 69, 86, 88, 93, 115, 117, 122, 125, 138, 173, 281
O'Moore Creagh, General, Garrett, 21
Oldfield, Brigadier-General, 41
Ouseley, Brigadier-General, 39, 202
Parker, Gunner, C. H., 101
Partridge, Captain, George James, 234
Pear Street, 64, 69, 115, 132, 138, 142, 148, 157, 171-2, 174, 186, 188, 195, 197, 204, 219, 228
Pearsall, Lieutenant, S. J., 234
Piccadilly Trench, 51, 65, 69, 72, 88, 93, 102-3, 108, 117, 122, 124, 137, 186, 197, 214, 217, 219, 229
Pickles, Private, J., 56
Pilcher, Major-General, Thomas David, 17, 21-3, 28, 31, 32, 97, 151
Pleavin, Gunner, 143, 266
Pollard, Sergeant, 69
Pommiers Redoubt, 43-4, 53-4, 57, 59, 61-2, 71, 75, 78, 80, 83-6, 92, 113, 115-6, 118-9, 121-4, 126-7, 130, 133, 136-40, 142, 147, 150, 153, 174, 176-7, 179-80, 184, 186, 188, 192, 200, 202-3, 209, 211-2, 216, 230, 235-6, 239, 341, 243, 246
Pommiers Trench, 52, 78, 116, 121, 147
Pont Street, 64-5, 69, 142, 148, 169, 171-2, 204, 213
Portbury, Second Lieutenant, 210
Pound, Driver, 177, 272
Power, Private, Phillip, 129, 260
Pozieres, 73, 123, 131, 190
Preddie, Captain, T. A., 122
Press, Private, A. R., 56
Quadrangle Support Trench, 17, 22-4, 32, 37, 47, 49, 93, 110, 143-4, 147, 153, 166, 189, 215, 241, 263, 269
Querrieu, 127, 136
Quesnoy, 147
R.F.C., the, 103, 151
Ramsbottom, Second Lieutenant, R. E., 81
Ravenscroft, Corporal, Philip, 144
Rawlinson, General, Sir Henry, 10, 27, 30, 31, 33-4, 73-4, 76, 79, 89, 92, 115, 154-5, 158, 182, 203, 224, 247-8
Reid, Gunner, H., 74
Ribemont-sur-Ancre, 39
Ribton-Cook, Second Lieutenant, H., 197
River Ancre, the, 200, 221
Robertson, Major-General, Philip Rynd, 10, 17-8, 23, 26, 28, 32, 37-8, 40, 69-2, 75, 77-8, 81, 94-5, 97, 114-5, 119, 122, 125, 135-6, 142, 144, 152, 155, 158, 165, 167, 173-4, 185, 188, 202, 212-3, 222, 234, 240, 247, 248-50
Rodgers, Private, 208, 278, 281
Rooney, Private, John Edward, 180, 267
Rose Cottage, 223
Rose, Second Lieutenant, A. D., 103
Rowley, Lieutenant-Colonel, 25, 60, 204
Royal Marines, the, 109
Ryder, Private, J., 104, 255
Saunders, Captain, L. D. M.D., 77
Savage, Private, 208, 282
Short, Lieutenant, 277, 291
Silverton, Sergeant, 104, 255
Simner, Major, 67
Skinner, Brigadier-General, P. C. B., 232, 236
Skollick, Second Lieutenant, G. E., 197
Sloane Street, 122

Smyly, Captain, 92
Solly, Second Lieutenant,, 229
Somerset Light Infantry, the, 227, 236
Somerset, Sergeant, 68, 74, 81, 227, 236, 277
Somme River, the, 40, 80
Sorrel, Gunner, G. H., 101, 253
South African Brigade, the, 24
Spicer, Lieutenant, 95
Sproule, Second Lieutenant, James George, 170
Stallibrass, Lieutenant, 291
Stanhope, Gunner, P. J., 101
Stanley, Second Lieutenant, 110, 258
Stephens, Major-General, R. B., 43, 69, 70
Stickland, Second Lieutenant, Francis Norman, 170
Sturgeon, Corporal, 145
Sutton, Major, 58, 260, 264-5, 270, 276, 286-7
Switch Trench, 46, 92, 96, 99, 101, 103, 107, 111, 116, 137, 145, 159, 190, 216, 241
Tanfield, Captain, 110
Taylor, Private, H., 176, 191, 274, 294
Tea Lane, 138, 159, 181, 190
Tea Support, 92, 107
Tea Trench, 92, 107, 117, 181, 184, 187
Thilloy, 151
Thompson, Lance Corporal, David, 180
Thompson, Second Lieutenant, C. C., 196
Torrens, Major, George Leslie, 25, 102, 115, 209, 215, 220
Townsend, Private, Luke, 129
Tradewell, Lance Corporal, Frank, 51
Trones Wood, 24, 133, 134, 217, 221, 291
Trownson, Second Lieutenant, W. R., 213
Turner, Brigadier-General, M. N., 44
Tyrrell, Second Lieutenant, 187, 199
Uniacke, Brigadier-General, H. C. C., 21
Vecquemont, 48
Vernon, Second Lieutenant, 148
Villers-au-Flos, 103, 113
Vivies Mill, 231
Vossische Zeitung, 225
Wade, Lieutenant-Colonel, Thomas Stewart Herschal, later Brigadier-General, 25
Wakeman, Gunner, 177, 272
Walker, Captain, M.D., 28, 52, 66, 152, 188, 255, 275
Ware, Bombardier, 101
Warlencourt, 46, 47, 131
Watson, Gunner, 177
Watson, Lieutenant, J., 56, 134, 152
Wells, Private, 156
West Lane, 205
West Street, 188, 202
West, Corporal, 193
Westmacott, Major, G. P., 25, 51, 64, 76, 80, 102-4, 111, 220
Wheatley, Brigadier-General, P., 250, 273
Wheeley Captain, 84
Whitaker, Lieutenant, L., 84
White, Private, Ernest John, 172, 265
Whiting, Regimental Sergeant Major, 143
Williams, Gunner, 177, 272
Wing Corner, 121
Winter, Karl, 125, 130
Wood Lane, 69, 95, 96, 115, 138, 155, 169, 170, 171, 181, 182, 185, 191, 210, 214, 219, 233
Wood, Private, Fred, 180
Woodward, Sergeant, 157, 273
Yeatman, Second Lieutenant, R. J., 112
Yorks and Lancs Alley, also YL Alley, 148-9, 163, 186, 195, 208
Ypres Salient, 22, 77, 297
Zenith Trench, 248

About Salient Books ....

Salient Books is a small, independent family-run business, set up in 2009, which works closely with a select group of writers.

Our books range from military history, to memoirs and light fiction.

Visit www.salientbooks.co.uk
or e-mail info@salientbooks.co.uk
to find out more.

Lightning Source UK Ltd.
Milton Keynes UK
UKHW010745161118
332405UK00001B/88/P

9 780957 445901